CONTENTS

CHAPTER THREE

Legal Issues Facing
Marriage and Family Therapists   47

CHAPTER FOUR

Working with the
Courts and Attorneys   71

CHAPTER FIVE

Family Law and the
Marriage and Family Therapist   81

CHAPTER SIX

Regulation, Certification, and Licensure   99

CHAPTER SEVEN

Clinical Practice   109

CHAPTER EIGHT

Educational Practice   133

CHAPTER NINE

The Future of
Marriage and Family Therapy   147

APPENDIX A

Ethical Practices in Marriage and Family Therapy:
A Research Study   151

APPENDIX B

Forms for Clinical Practice   161

APPENDIX C

APPENDIX D

PREFACE

*In the ideal society, composed of wholly responsible human
beings, laws, because I should scarcely be conscious of them,
would gradually wither away."*

Sir Isaiah Berlin
"Two Concepts of Liberty"
October 31, 1958

Our society is filled with laws and ethical directives that continue to expand and govern our daily lives. As responsible human beings, we are faced with determining right from wrong, acceptable from unacceptable behavior, and morality from immorality.

The profession of marriage and family therapy helps people grapple with these issues in their personal, social, and professional relationships. As clinicians, researchers, and educators, we commit ourselves to the highest standards of professional conduct. The ethical code for marriage and family therapists is the framework that practitioners, researchers, and educators share in an effort to provide excellence and beneficence to consumers and colleagues.

However, today's marketplace has changed, and with this change, professional practice has become more complex. Marriage and family therapists must be concerned with more than just the welfare of their clients. The legal system and the profession impact one another as a result of new laws involving client issues such as custody, abuse, and duty to warn. Interestingly, the legal system has borrowed from the ethical standards of the profession, incorporating certain issues into law. In fact, some states have incorporated the ethical standards into their licensing laws. Thus, a violation of the ethical code may result in disciplinary action by the state.

Society is more litigious than ever. Consequently, there is a higher threat of malpractice, which unfortunately creates a new level of suspicion in practice and research. This development means that the marriage and family therapist, researcher, and educator cannot take a cavalier attitude toward the rules, laws, and regulations governing the profession and the practice of psychotherapy.

Today, clinicians must know the ethical and legal ramifications of treatment and its impact on the client, the client's family of origin, the public, the profession, and other constituencies. Therapists must be responsible for their own actions and, at times, reporting or predicting the behavior of their clients. Marriage and family therapists interact with third-party payers, managed-health care providers, utilization review teams, and protective service agencies while delivering quality treatment. Such multilevel interaction creates complex treatment dilemmas involving confidentiality, autonomy, exploitation, and professionalism.

Changes in the professional roles and responsibilities of health care providers have created a different atmosphere in which to practice marriage and family therapy. There is no precedent in psychotherapy for some aspects of practice. The confidentiality issues created by the application of systems theory is one example. There is no turning back to old treatment methodologies, unspecified diagnoses, and the lack of a clear relationship between diagnosis and duration of treatment. This lack of rigor is no longer acceptable in the health care marketplace.

If marriage and family therapy is to survive the convulsions now rampant in the health care industry, the profession must endeavor to offer services that are grounded in sound legal and ethical values. Therapists must provide legally and ethically based treatment to clients while being mindful of cost effectiveness.

The authors' objective in this book is to inform marriage and family clinicians, researchers, and educators of the importance of applying professional ethical and legal principles to their work. The topics covered include the practical application of marriage and family therapy in clinical, research, and educational settings. Information is given on the effective utilization of marriage and family theory and testimony in the justice system.

The text is intended as a guide to the ethical, legal, and professional issues that currently face practicing marriage and family therapists. Because ethical codes can be general and unclear, the authors have given practical examples of probable code violations and ways to avoid them. The guidelines listed in many of the chapters are designed to help the reader solve the ethical dilemmas commonly encountered in practice. Because laws regulating marriage and family therapy vary from state to state, the reader is encouraged to confer with an informed family law and/or malpractice attorney on specific legal questions. It is wise to note that laws are timely; thus, they may be revised or overturned, depending on the needs of the state, profession, or public. Therefore, it is necessary to continually update personal knowledge on local and state laws or ordinances regarding marriage and family therapy.

Several appendices provide useful supplementary information. Appendix A reports results of the first nationwide study of marriage and family therapists' practice behavior related to ethics and the American Association for Marriage and Family Therapy (AAMFT) code. Appendix B contains illustrations of a number of forms commonly used by marriage and family therapists. Appendices C and D are reprints of the *AAMFT Code of Ethical Principles* (including advertising guidelines) and *Procedures for Handling Ethical Matters.*

Readers who are interested in further exploration of the topics covered in this book will find the bibliography helpful. The numerous articles and texts cited will direct readers to a more thorough discussion of the subject.

Before implementing any of the recommendations in this text, the authors strongly encourage the reader to consult legal counsel. The authors assume no responsibility for any harm this material may cuase to the reader's income, practice, or reputation.

Acknowledgments

We, the authors, would like to thank the numerous people who helped in the design and content of this book. First, we wish to thank the leadership of the American Association for Marriage and Family Therapy, who supported our endeavor. Specifically, Steve Preister and Michael Bowers reviewed various chapters and offered helpful comments.

We also thank the professionals who contributed their expertise and personal knowledge on licensure and state examining boards: Thomas E. Clark, Ph.D., Mattie Canter, Ph.D., Evelyn Hight, M.S., Carl Johnson, M.A., and Robert Lee, Ph.D. Special thanks go to Thomas Baaker, Esquire, for his indepth assistance with the legal chapters. We also recognize Ronald Aldridge, D.S.W., and Douglas Bowers, Ph.D., for their help in assembling information regarding the military practice of marriage and family therapy.

A number of individuals reviewed this book at various stages for Allyn and Bacon. We thank the following professionals for their suggestions: Thomas E. Clark, Wake Forest University; Vincent D. Foley, Ph.D., Jamaica, New York; James C. Hansen, State University of New York--Buffalo; and James R. Hine, The University of Arizona.

Finally, we sincerely thank our spouses, Kerry Vesper and Jeanette Coufal, who provided many hours of support and understanding in the writing and rewriting of this text.

CHAPTER ONE

Introduction

The field of marriage and family therapy is now recognized as a vital mental health discipline. Until recently, marriage and family therapists identified themselves as psychiatrists, psychologists, social workers, or counselors who specialized in the treatment of marriage- and family-related problems. Placement under the umbrella of these disciplines meant the marriage and family therapist had no separate identity and therefore no specific guidelines by which to practice.

Fortunately, this lack of a separate identity is changing with the implementation and proliferation of national and international university graduate programs and free-standing institutes in marriage and family therapy. Accordingly, these programs are establishing standards for service delivery, treatment methodology, and ethical principles. Hence, there is a need for a text devoted to describing and discussing the standards of ethical, legal, and professional practice in marriage and family therapy.

The material contained in this book is taken from numerous sources: existing texts, articles in professional journals, academic courses in marriage and family therapy, and state regulatory board officers and practitioners struggling with ethical, legal, and professional practice issues specific to marriage and family therapy. Laws governing the practice of marriage and family therapy are evolving and as yet are not specific to the discipline. Therefore, legal guidelines for the profession are generic in nature. Attorneys with expert knowledge in family law, administrative law, and malpractice assisted the authors in preparing portions of the book pertaining to the law and its ramifications for the marriage and family therapist.

Finally, the rules of conduct for the educator, researcher, and practitioner are now specific to the discipline. Initially, the guidelines for ethical practice were derived from existing ethics codes developed for other mental health disciplines. While all the disciplines have a common heritage, there are fundamental differences in the methods or procedures by which

marriage and family therapists carry out treatment compared with other
practitioners. Consequently, an ethical code for marriage and family therapists must address issues specific to marriage and family therapy. That
code has emerged, and it is upheld by law and the disciplinary committee
of the American Association for Marriage and Family Therapy.

Ethics in Marriage and Family Therapy

Ethics, morality, and values are fundamental characteristics of the therapeutic process. The foundation of the profession involves responsibility to
clients and colleagues, promotion of professional competence and integrity, confidentiality, and the absence of deceit or exploitation in the
therapeutic relationship. Each of these values is morally important and,
when values conflict, difficult to maintain. Such problems in treatment delivery present ethical dilemmas for the marriage and family therapist.

How does the therapist promote ethically competent treatment when
his or her values and morals are challenged by the client's lifestyle? For
instance, a therapist who strongly believes in promoting marriage and
family, discourages divorce, and denies that alcoholism is a family problem may be blinded by the marital problems depicted in the following
case.

Case One

Denial

An alcoholic spouse who denies her drinking problem is verbally, emotionally, and physically abusive to her nonalcoholic husband and children. The woman stays absent from her home for extended periods of
time. During those absences, she cohabits with men she meets in various
bars. Her spouse denies that alcoholism is a factor in her irresponsible
behavior. In fact, the husband believes that if he waits long enough and accepts her behavior without argument, she'll return to the family and re-
sume her familial responsibilities. When she goes on a binge, he covers for
her by telling the children that their mother is away on a business trip or
visiting friends.

The treatment issues of this case include the spouse-in-denial, the
children, and the absent wife. Does the therapist tell the children about the
mother's behavior? Does the therapist collude with the father about the
possibility of reconciliation? Does the therapist attempt family therapy
without the mother present? Does the therapist deny the impact of the
alcohol-related behavior on the family system?

Personal values play an important role in answering these treatment questions. Objective, valueless therapy does not happen—ever. Therapists are emotionally invested in their values and act in accordance with what they believe. As this case illustrates, the clinician is fraught with treatment issues, moral dilemmas, and a probable clash between his or her values and those of the client. The only method by which marriage and family therapists can safeguard the intrusion of their personal values and morals into the therapeutic process is to confront and challenge their belief systems, feelings, and family-of-origin issues. Otherwise, the therapist's personal philosophy of life will invariably find its way into the therapeutic relationship and possibly compromise or violate ethical standards.

When conflict occurs because a therapist's values are in opposition to client values or ethical standards, the wise course is to discuss these issues with a supervisor or unbiased colleague. If resolution cannot be achieved, the therapist must strongly consider transferring the case to a colleague who can accept the client without prejudice. To feign acceptance of a client or to terminate a client before treatment is completed is a violation of the ethical principles regarding responsibility to clients.

Professional Codes of Ethics

Most of the health care professions have codes of ethics that provide general guidelines for professional rules of conduct. These codes deal with culturally and professionally based standards of behavior between therapists and their clients, colleagues, and the public. The codes define basic principles dictating the professional practice of therapy. Codes also yield some assurance that therapists will perform professional duties within established and acceptable standards. Finally, codes of ethics give therapists a vehicle for professional identity by differentiating their discipline from others.

The statements found in codes include:

1. specific responsibilities assigned to the therapist, client, student trainee, researcher, and educator;
2. competencies specific to the application of general ethical principles in professional practice;
3. reiteration of certain universally accepted practice standards (e.g., confidentiality);
4. principles to which the profession aspires;
5. a statement of responsibility of the members of the profession to report code, civil, or criminal violations;
6. a statement regarding financial arrangements with clients; and

7. specific responsibilities regarding advertising and marketing the profession.

A professional code and its accompanying procedures cannot assure high-quality treatment. These documents are merely frameworks for professional responsibility. The burden of adhering to the code depends upon the individual therapist's sense of ethical integrity and responsibility. Therefore, codes and ethical procedures are limited in terms of enforcement of professional accountability.

In a profession where there are divergent opinions regarding therapeutic approaches to treatment, it is difficult to apply professional standards of practice in a uniform manner. Though most family therapists adhere to systems theories, other treatment modalities exist. Furthermore, since research is far from conclusive on the most effective treatment methods, various theoretical approaches and methodologies are arguable and defensible. This reality makes treatment a personalized process applied by a therapist with specific training, knowledge, values, and beliefs.

Codes of ethics cannot deal with each therapist's treatment application. Codes address more universal standards of practice. Since treatment methods are not static, therapists and researchers are constantly developing and refining therapeutic models. At times, this ongoing developmental process outpaces revisions in ethical codes. (It is essential for professional organizations to constantly monitor actual practice and rewrite codes according to the most up-to-date standards of service delivery.)

Codes of ethics address topics that are relevant to professional practice and education. Oversights or inclusion of less germane material are not unusual, since codes are designed by members of the organization who volunteer time to sit on ethics committees. Some members may feel one topic is more important than another. Consequently, one specific issue may be given more emphasis than another. For example, the codes of some disciplines carefully delineate guidelines for conducting research, while others grant it sparing attention.

Codes are written in general rather than specific terminology, since statements that are too specific can be inhibiting. Codes attempt to overcome this problem by stating general principles, which are then defined by subprinciples. The American Association for Marriage and Family Therapy (AAMFT) uses this method in its *Code of Ethical Principles* (1988). For example, Principle 7 states:

Advertising Marriage and family therapists engage in appropriate informational activities, including those that enable lay persons to choose marriage and family services on an informed basis.

Subprinciple 7.10 states:

Marriage and family therapists may not use the initials AAMFT following their name in the manner of an academic degree.

Certain problems are inherent in the application of codes, including (a) problems in code enforcement, (b) discrepancies between ethical codes and legal practice, (c) limited code topics, and (d) ambiguous or vague language. It is not until after a complaint against a member is received that a code and its accompanying procedures can be implemented. An organization is dependent on its members to adhere to the code and on the public to inform the organization of violations. The AAMFT has a membership in excess of 20,000. In 1986, the number of complaints resulting in formal cases before the Ethics Committee numbered less than 50. By 1989, the committee was reviewing approximately 70 to 75 cases at each of its quarterly meetings. The increase in charges resulted from more attention given to the importance of ethics and professional practice, both in professional publications and public media. The recent spate of articles, coupled with radio and television coverage on therapists' sexual improprieties with clients, has heightened public awareness of appropriate client-therapist interaction.

Recently, Brock and Coufal (1989) completed the first nationwide study of marriage and family therapists' clinical behavior. The findings provided good information on how closely AAMFT clinical members adhere to the AAMFT ethics code. Although the results showed that all the codes were violated by at least a few respondents, overall the code provided guidance on clinical practice that was accepted by practitioners. The findings were shared with the AAMFT Ethics Committee to provide information on portions of the code in need of revision or development.

Membership in an organization requires academic knowledge and practical awareness of standards of service delivery. Therapists cannot expect a code to define each and every complexity that arises in treatment and collegial interaction. Codes are guidelines delineating methods of conduct under certain conditions. They carry forth the tradition of a particular profession's behavior and response to the public.

Legal Issues in Marriage and Family Therapy

Each state has specific laws and legislation regarding mental health treatment. No uniform codes or national legal standards pertain exclusively to marriage and family therapy. Furthermore, inconsistencies within state laws complicate treatment by health care professionals. These factors make the delivery of service risky and confusing.

As mentioned earlier, the practitioner may look to a code of ethics for standards of practice. However, the code may be too broad based and even at odds with legal standards. /This dilemma places the marriage and family therapist between what treatment dictates and what the law mandates. For example, a couple may seek therapy for the father's child-abusing behavior. In many states, the therapist is bound by law to inform Child Protective Services of the offense, regardless of the circumstances under which the knowledge of the abuse is obtained. Thus, the therapist must inform the client of the ramifications of his or her admission of child abuse. The client may take this information as a threat to confidentiality and personal freedom and opt to drop out of treatment or never tell the therapist the essential material needed to resolve family problems. Similar conflicts occur when a therapist learns that a family member is a drug pusher. It certainly is no surprise that the family therapist can be caught among treatment implications, ethical decisions, and legal consequences in many therapeutic situations.

An even more complex dilemma arises when an attorney or court orders a therapist to reveal information obtained in the context of therapy. Some states do not grant therapists the right to confidentiality. In these states, a therapist may become caught between the legal system and the dictates of good therapeutic practice. Since it is highly unlikely that the marriage and family therapist can avoid the implications of laws in the delivery of treatment, it is imperative that he or she be familiar with both basic family and malpractice law in his or her state.

One very positive way by which marriage and family therapists can become active in family law is by becoming involved in lobbying, legislation, and education of elected officials. Since laws are developed by legislators in response to their constituents, the marriage and family therapist can be at the forefront in the development of bills relating to health and human services.

In fact, states are more involved in social and familial problems than in past decades. Issues concerning drug and alcohol abuse, sexual and physical abuse, and incest and family violence are addressed in numerous state laws. Even law enforcement officials have been directed to place more emphasis on domestic issues. As new laws are enacted and law enforcement gets involved in areas that used to be the realm of the counselor or therapist, the fields of law and marital and family therapy draw closer together. It is as vital for legislators and law enforcement personnel to understand the place of marriage and family therapists in today's society as it is for marriage and family therapists to review, understand, and abide by the established laws of their respective states. Not to do so is a basic disservice, both to the client and the profession.

Ethics versus Legalities in Clinical Practice

Ethics examines human conduct in the context of a given environment. It explores responses made from a moral, decision-making orientation rather than a factual basis. As such, ethics are used to set standards for evaluation and problem solving in interpersonal situations.

Legalities address principles of law that are specific and binding. Each state has legal statutes that delineate therapeutic practice. Failure to abide by the laws can result in civil and criminal action against the offender.

The marriage and family therapist may find himself or herself in a difficult situation when the dictates of clinical practice oppose legal standards. Such dilemmas have occurred in cases involving custody, adoption, divorce, and other areas of marriage and family therapy practice. Consider the following example: *Olson* v. *Flinn* (1986).

In Mississippi, a stepfather's adoption of his wife's daughter terminated court-ordered visitation rights of the paternal grandparents. The paternal grandparents then sued to continue visitation with their granddaughter. The court held that adoption severed the child's previous familial relationships with *all* members of the natural father's family. Hence, the natural, paternal grandparents were no longer considered the child's relatives.

As this case suggests, the law must be served, despite the emotional well-being of the child. Marriage and family therapists are aware of the significance of emotional bonding to both the parents and grandparents. Such court action in this case is certain to emotionally disrupt the child and the grandparents. Nonetheless, a marriage and family therapist must accept the court ruling and proceed on that basis. If the therapist works with the child's family, the issues of emotional bonding and loss must be addressed. If the therapist treats the grandparents, discussion of the legal action, along with permission to ventilate feelings and acceptance of the court action, are needed.

This situation poses multiple triangulation problems among the court, grandparents, and family. Ethical dilemmas surface in light of probable psychological trauma that the court action may precipitate in both the child and the grandparents. Finally, problems of powerlessness may arise in the therapist, who may feel constrained by the court decision.

Therapists are very familiar with clients who vacillate about divorcing or remaining married. These individuals have difficulty making decisions and often feel guilt and/or fear about being alone. Consequently, such individuals commonly separate and reconnect with their partners numerous times. In some extreme cases, these individuals never legally end the marriage.

A case dealing with this issue came before the Virginia Supreme Court (*Kizer* v. *Commonwealth*, 1984). The court ruled that the plaintiff's husband could not be charged with rape because his wife's "vacillating" conduct misled him into believing that the marriage still existed. The court said that the wife failed to demonstrate objectively that she no longer considered the marriage viable.

This court action assumes that the vacillation is controllable. Unfortunately, these individuals were not able to sustain independent living arrangements for numerous reasons. The ambivalence exemplified by this couple led to blurred boundaries, mixed messages, and emotional impasses that prohibited personal growth and decision making. Courts do not consider these factors when rendering judgments. Thus, the vacillating client becomes the victim of his or her own psychological history.

These cases demonstrate the conflicts that the marriage and family therapist faces when working with difficult family problems that become confounded because of legal decisions. In all instances, the therapist must abide by the legal ruling, even though the judgment may be harsh or psychologically damaging. To effectively cope with such instances, a therapist must develop ways to embrace the court decision while facilitating health for the family. Such a task stretches and challenges the creativity of even the most senior therapist, especially when he or she feels confident about having delivered appropriate and ethically sound treatment.

By accepting the court decree and working with the family to live within the dictates of the verdict, the practitioner may experience internal conflict and self-doubt, since the law and ethical treatment may differ. If solutions elude the various therapeutic orientations, colleagues and supervisors should be consulted on treatment strategies. If treatment intervention is not possible, the therapist should tell the client, rather than give the family false hope. Sometimes, the best treatment the therapist can offer is acceptance of the situation.

Such interventions may violate the marriage and family therapist's own conscience. After all, treatment is delivered to enhance personal and familial interaction through honest, direct communication. By teaching clients to accept the court decree, the clinician is preparing them to live with the reality that life is at times confusing, unfair, and immutable. Given that reality, the client learns that there are times when even the most healthy behaviors cannot bring about either just or desired results. In other words, the context of the situation dictates treatment and behavioral actuality to both the therapist and the client. In truth, what results can be termed *contextual ethics,* which can be somewhat different than *professional ethics.*

Professional Practice Issues in Marriage and Family Therapy

Professional practice encompasses standards of service delivery, regulatory concerns, and facilitation of treatment. Ethics and legalities are major factors in providing professional treatment. General professional practice issues address similar areas to those in the ethical codes: exploitation of clients, recordkeeping, standards of service delivery, appropriate credentials and clinical experience needed to practice, and guidelines for advertising.

But there are other issues. For the private practitioner, there are the concerns of how to establish a private practice, market and bill clients, and link with the existing professional community. For those practitioners who work for public agencies, professional practice involves working with other disciplines whose orientations may not be sympathetic to a systemic framework. For example, the therapist who works with domestic violence cases most likely will deal with law enforcement personnel who generally perceive the individual as being their responsibility, rather than the family system.

Clinicians working in private agencies may encounter professionals with similar theoretical orientations. However, the financial personnel of these agencies are less concerned with client welfare and more concerned with the preservation of the agency. Hence, there may be emphasis on issues such as the budget, documentation of services, the client's ability to pay, limitation on treatment of low-income people, justification of full- and part-time positions, and adherence to policies specific to the private agency, institution, or hospital.

Professional practice covers a spectrum of issues, many of which are not directly related to treatment. It is these divergent areas that can tax the therapist and make service delivery stressful. Seldom are these issues addressed prior to entry into the profession. The intent of this text is to alert the practitioner to the business of marriage and family therapy.

Conclusion

Practicing marriage and family therapy is both challenging and perplexing. A therapist is required to fully engage in the client's world, while being

detached enough to conduct effective intervention strategies. This dual reality that a therapist encounters with every client demands an active mind,
one capable of balancing the work that takes place in the office with the
development and facilitation of acceptable strategies to intervene in a dysfunctional system.

In addition, the marriage and family therapist must add at least two
more levels of awareness to every therapeutic interaction: ethical practice
and the legal ramifications of that practice. As the cited examples indicate,
therapy is subject to scrutiny by the public, the legal system, colleagues,
and clients. Although such intense observation helps to define the profession publicly, it also serves to target it for criticism. As the following chapters will reveal, the practice of marriage and family therapy is being
regulated and legislated by individuals who are not necessarily cognizant
of the standards of the profession. Therapists are being held accountable
for being able to predict the behavior of individuals who may be a danger
to society or to themselves. Treatment professionals are also being held
responsible for notification of authorities in cases of possible or perceived
child and elderly abuse. The therapist is becoming an agent of society.
This is certainly a dubious honor.

The judicial system, however, perceives the therapist as an expert in
the field of human behavior. That expertise may be construed by some to
be more specific and defensible than is truly possible. Therapists are aware
of intervening variables that cause people to behave in unpredictable ways.
Yet the expert witness is expected to account for these variables and accurately determine a client's future behavior. Thus, the profession has created
yet another duality for the clinician: treatment agent and protector of the
public good.

Treatment dilemmas are usually baffling and thorny. They pose questions involving values, morals, and laws. The trained marriage and family
therapist must be thoroughly familiar with the ethical codes, the laws of the
state in which he or she practices, and the professional standards of the lo-
cale in which he or she works.

The case examples presented in the succeeding chapters are designed to challenge the reader and illustrate how ethics, law, and professional standards can be applied to assist the clinician in making decisions
that are both beneficial to the client and within the limits of legal statutes
and ethical codes. Certainly, numerous approaches can be taken with any
client. The difficulty occurs in designing and implementing a treatment
plan that is ethical, legal, and beneficial for that individual.

CHAPTER TWO

Ethics in *did read* Clinical Practice

The practice of marriage and family therapy is constantly changing. The evolution of theoretical concepts, a new awareness of the different aspects of family functioning, and the development of innovative therapeutic procedures require new clinical behavior. Also, for the most part, marriage and family therapy has not been researched in terms of assessing techniques and outcomes; thus, there is minimal consensus as to what constitutes appropriate therapist-client roles and responsibilities. Ethical dilemmas emerge because of these differences, ranging from who is the client (individual or family) to issues of confidentiality to the relevance of indirect (paradoxical) approaches in therapy.

In this chapter, the specific ethical problems faced by marriage and family therapists are explored and the generally agreed upon areas of responsibility are outlined. Primary topics include:

1. the application of the ethical principles of client autonomy;
2. the therapist responsibility to do no harm;
3. confidentiality;
4. therapist's competence and integrity; and
5. the therapists's responsibility to colleagues, students, employees and the profession.

Commonly encountered ethical dilemmas are explored through case studies, and suggestions for resolving them are addressed. Included are hypothetical cases as they may have been reviewed and adjudicated by an ethics committee of a national human service organization.

Ethical Dilemmas
in Marriage and Family Therapy

Marriage and family therapy is a unique treatment modality because its practitioners assume that if an individual is to change behaviors, the system in which he or she operates must also change. Treatment is directed at the network of relationships in which family members interact. Because of this focus, the marriage and family therapist deems the client as the entire family, rather than one member of that social system.

This systemic approach creates a dilemma for the therapist who employs standards set by existing codes of ethics because most codes designate the individual as the client, who may or may not be viewed in the context of a relationship. The American Association for Marriage and Family Therapy (AAMFT) recognized this problem and addressed the issue in its September 1985 revision of its *Code of Ethical Principles*. Principle 2, *Confidentiality*, states:

> Marriage and family therapists have unique confidentiality problems because the "client" in a therapeutic relationship may be more than one person. The overriding principle is that marriage and family therapists respect the confidences of their client(s).

When the client is the family, it is difficult to promote the concept of autonomy. After all, each person's behavior affects the system and ultimately the individuality of the members that comprise it.

The marriage and family therapist engages the client by moving individuals into an awareness of self in relationship to others. With the recognition of familial interaction, family members come to understand their own behavior and its impact on others. The therapist points out differences in value systems and perceptions and then assesses family members' desires to reevaluate and change family dynamics.

Exploring the differences among family members may lead to anger, frustration, and withholding or rejecting love. Intrafamilial alliances may be challenged or broken, and autonomy may be lost. People caught in these dynamics and feelings often strive to protect themselves at the expense of others. Is the therapist facilitating autonomy for the client when invoking such self-oriented reactions? Remember, the client is the family.

The therapist must lead the family into health, even though the path may detour from client autonomy. For example, a father who abuses his two sons is threatening the well-being of the family. The therapist dealing with this dilemma realizes that the father needs specific treatment for his abusive behavior. The mother needs assistance in overcoming her feelings of helplessness, and the sons need work in dealing with their anger, negative self-image, and hopelessness. To rehabilitate this family will require empowering the mother, disengaging the father from his enmeshed relationship with his boys, and relieving the emotions of the sons. While this process unfolds, there will be times when various family members will be denied autonomy. Father will be informed of the therapist's requirement to involve Child Protective Services as a result of his physical assaults on the children; Mother will be overly empowered to safeguard the children, perhaps at the expense of personal time and growth; and the children will be directed to review their behavior in relationship to the family system.

(At times, the goals of the therapist vary considerably from the goals of the client.) A couple who believes that their delinquent oldest child is the only problem in the family may want the therapist to "fix" the child and disregard any other family discord. The therapist who attempts to treat such problems with a systemic approach frequently encounters disgruntled parents who attempt to sabotage therapy. In such instances, the therapist must remember that his or her ethical responsibility is to the client, which is the family. Therefore, if the client is not benefiting from systemic family therapy, the therapist must review treatment goals with the client and determine whether to continue or refer to a nonsystems therapist.

The problems in this case are addressed in three of the subprinciples in the *AAMFT Code of Ethical Principles for Marriage and Family Therapists*. Subprinciple 1.5 states:

Marriage and family therapists continue therapeutic relationships only so long as it is reasonably clear that clients are benefiting from the relationship.

Subprinciple 1.6 states:

Marriage and family therapists assist persons in obtaining other therapeutic services if a marriage and family therapist is unable or unwilling, for appropriate reasons, to see a person who has requested professional help.

And finally, Subprinciple 1.7 states:

Marriage and family therapists do not abandon or neglect clients in treatment without making reasonable arrangements for the continuation of such treatment.

Adhering to a systemic approach means that the therapist addresses the client problems differently than traditional individual treatment approaches. Families seeking assistance for their difficulties must be informed of the therapist's orientation and the reason for that approach. Furthermore, the therapist must keep therapeutic parameters clearly defined throughout the therapeutic relationship. By doing so, the marriage and family therapist demonstrates direct, honest communication and appropriate interactional behavior. It also gives the client the right to determine whether to remain in treatment, as designed by the marriage and family therapist, or to seek assistance from a nonsystems clinician.

Some new treatment techniques employ indirect methodologies. Such procedures take away client autonomy and the ability to make an informed decision regarding treatment.

Paradoxical and strategic approaches enable the therapist to control and direct treatment without client awareness. O'Connell (1984) uses "promise of treatment" as an opening strategy for therapy. This method elevates client expectancy for problem resolution, which makes the client more amenable to change. This procedure does not provide specific criteria for the types of clients with whom it is effective nor does it provide specific steps to follow for administration. Rather, the creativity, experience, and artistry of the therapist are relied upon to deliver the intervention.

In employing the technique, O'Connell initially informs the client that the results of treatment are positive and that upon completion of treatment the client will feel and think in a more healthy manner. The client is led to believe that maximum benefit will result from treatment but is never informed about what is actually being done. The client is simply the recipient of treatment that frequently results in positive change. This strategy clearly prohibits client autonomy yet creates positive outcomes. Justification under a code of ethics is difficult, since this method is rooted in the client's lack of knowledge of psychotherapy.

Clients, of course, never know for sure what their therapist is really observing or doing. The therapist can watch certain movements, hear repeated phrases, and note common familial interactions but withhold comment until such recognition is appropriate in the therapeutic process. Further, the therapist may miss client cues and in so doing divert, dilute, or inadvertently prolong treatment. When this occurs, is the therapist deliberately denying client autonomy?

There is no clear rule that speaks to what a therapist should do to promote client autonomy. Remember, ethics deals in "shoulds" and "oughts," which are merely guidelines by which to administer treatment. Haley (1987) speaks to this point when he says, "An obvious solution is to encourage clinicians to be sensible and not share all with their clientele. When the clinician concedes that he keeps private views to himself and offers his ideas to his clients only with care and circumspection, then free presentation of ideas among clinicians will do less harm" (pp. 236–237).

Theories and procedures are methods by which a therapist carries out treatment. Based on therapeutic knowledge and experience, the therapist attempts to intervene in a dysfunctional system. The relationship of the therapist to the family system creates a new system in which behavioral change and insight become acceptable. Ideally, the therapist attempts to be as careful and thoughtful as possible. However, at times, treatment involves interventions that may create pain or anxiety among family members. Such procedures require a therapist's full understanding of the skills required to implement the treatment.

The depth of the emotional pain encountered during the intervention may not be fully known to the client, but the therapist must be keenly aware of the probable consequences of using the procedure. For example, therapeutic intervention with an alcoholic family system requires gathering many of the significant people in the alcoholic's life, coaching them to tell the alcoholic about his or her dysfunctional behaviors, and then convincing him or her that immediate treatment is essential. When this approach is used, people may be scared to confront not only their loved one—the alcoholic—but also their personal anger and resentment toward him or her. The alcoholic may become enraged at the confrontation and rail at the well-meaning therapist and significant others. The volatile feelings that can ensue may upset everyone for quite some time.

In such a case, has the therapist maintained the ethical position to do no harm? At the moment, it may seem that the intervention is more painful than living in the alcoholic system. Should the therapist comfort the members of the alcoholic system? Must the therapist remain firm with the alcoholic, who may be devastated by the confrontation? The conscientious therapist knows the methodology, theory, and facilitation skills needed to perform the intervention. The therapist also knows the expected results of the technique and how to direct treatment to achieve the desired goal. To conduct the intervention without preparation and knowledge can be more harmful to the client than the intervention itself. Thus, it is the ill-prepared therapist who acts unethically and harms the client.

Is Family Therapy Indicated?

Discussion so far has centered on treatment of the family system as a unit. At times, however, working with the family may be counterproductive. When one member of the system uses therapy as a way to get out of the relationship or change the partner's values or beliefs, the therapist must be cautious. In this situation, the client's unstated goal is disintegration of the system. Should the therapist accept the challenge of keeping the relationship intact, dissolving the relationship or defending one person's belief system as better or more viable than that of the other?

Emphasis on the relationship in these cases will serve to heighten the hopes of the offended partner while angering the one who wants to termi-

nate the relationship. Accepting the challenge to alter an individual's belief system can lead to disaster, both in the therapeutic setting and in the
client's personal life. The therapist is a powerful authority and is given cre-
dence by those who seek treatment. Thus, the therapist who advocates a
specific religious, sexual, or personal lifestyle may create cognitive and
emotional disharmony in the individuals seeking treatment.

The AAMFT addresses these issues in its *Code of Ethical Principles*
(1988). Subprinciple 1.4 says:

> Marriage and family therapists respect the right of clients to make
> decisions and help them to understand the consequences of these
> decisions. Marriage and family therapists clearly advise a client that a
> decision on marital status is the responsibility of the client.

The *Ethical Principles of Psychologists* (APA, 1981) also address the
potential influence a therapist may have on directing client thinking. Principle 1f reads:

> As practitioners, psychologists know that they bear a heavy social re-
> sponsibility because their recommendations and professional actions
> may alter the lives of others. They are alert to personal, social, orga-
> nizational, financial, or political situations and pressures that might
> lead to misuse of their influence.

Responsibility to Clients

Codes of ethics among all major professional associations address the issue of therapist responsibility to clients. The *Code of Ethics of the National Association of Social Workers* (NASW, 1980), Principle IIF, states:

> *Primacy of Client's Interests* The social worker's primary respon-
> sibility is to clients.

The *Ethical Principles of Psychologists* (APA, 1981), Principle 6, is
more encompassing but affirms the primacy of the client's welfare as
essential.

> *Welfare of the Consumer* Psychologists respect the integrity and
> protect the welfare of the people and groups with whom they work.
> When conflicts of interest arise between clients and psychologists'
> employing institutions, psychologists clarify the nature and direction

of their loyalties and responsibilities and keep all parties informed of their commitments. Psychologists fully inform consumers as to the purpose and nature of an evaluative, treatment, educational, or training procedure, and they freely acknowledge that clients, students, or participants in research have freedom of choice with regard to participation.

In most codes of ethics, numerous subprinciples clarify a therapist's responsibilities to clients. Each subprinciple discusses relevant therapeutic issues related to clients' rights. Virtually all codes prohibit discrimination based on race, sex, religion, or national origin. Similarly, sexual intimacies with clients, students, or employees are unethical. The *AAMFT Code of Ethical Principles for Marriage and Family Therapists* (1988) speaks to both of these issues in Subprinciples 1.1 and 1.2.

1.1 Marriage and family therapists do not discriminate against or refuse professional service to anyone on the basis of race, sex, religion, or national origin.

1.2 Marriage and family therapists are cognizant of their potentially influential position with respect to clients, and they avoid exploiting the trust and dependency of such persons. Marriage and family therapists therefore make every effort to avoid dual relationships with clients that could impair their professional judgment or increase the risk of exploitation. Examples of such dual relationships include, but are not limited to, business or close personal relationships with clients. Sexual intimacy with clients is prohibited. Sexual intimacy with former clients for two years following the termination of therapy is prohibited.

Dual Relationships

The concept of dual relationships receives considerable attention in most ethical codes. A dual relationship refers to interactions in which a client, student, or supervisee may be at risk for expoitation by the therapist or supervisor. Code provisions dealing with dual relationships are frequently in the area of sexual relationships with clients, students, employees, and supervisees. It is noted in most codes but is not always defined beyond the scope of the explanation given in the AAMFT Subprinciples 1.1 and 1.2, stated above.

Dual relationships are more suspect in the therapeutic environment than in other work-related situations. Because therapeutic relationships can elicit feelings and create dependency on the therapist, clients may be vulnerable to exploitation. Other professional relationships do not create such dependency and generally are not as potentially manipulative and influential. While dual relationships are not prohibited for marriage and family therapists, the AAMFT code encourages avoidance of such relationship when possible; when dual relationships must exist, as when a student is also an employee in a university setting, the marriage and family therapist must exercise extreme caution. For example, if a therapist's client is a stockbroker who during the course of treatment talks about a stock that is certain to pay off, the therapist should not employ his or her client to act on the information. If the same information were discussed between the broker and her hairdresser, however, the hairdresser could use the information and invest with the broker on that particular item.

Each therapist must make a determination given the situation. The therapist's training and theoretical framework play a vital part in defining what constitutes a dual relationship. For the psychoanalytically trained therapist, obtaining therapy and supervision from an analyst is not considered a dual relationship. However, for systems therapists, supervision and therapy must be administered by two different therapists, since the nature of this relationship can become exploitive if either party chooses to violate professional boundaries.

Another area of contention is the length of time a therapist and client must remain apart until a friendship or intimate relationship may occur. Again, the more classically trained therapist may subscribe to never altering the relationship between client and therapist, while the more humanistically oriented therapist may place a specific time limit on redefining the relationship.

Each therapist is urged to review his or her respective professional organization's code of ethics to determine the guidelines on dual relationships. If the code is unclear, the individual should check with the professional affairs department of the national office. The AAMFT code clearly states that therapists are not to become sexually involved with clients for at least two years following termination of treatment. In the authors' view, all psychotherapists would be wise *never* to become romantically involved with clients—once a client, always a client.

The primary goal of treatment is to empower the client to be personally responsible. To this end, the therapist teaches the client to recognize that therapy is designed to rectify unsuccessful behaviors. Clients learn that most behavioral consequences are a result of personal responses to given situations. With this knowledge, the client develops more successful methods of problem solving and decision making. The ability to select the appropriate response creates self-determination and enhances esteem. The *Code of Ethics of the National Association of Social Workers* (1980) underscores this concept in Principle IIG:

Rights and Prerogatives of Clients The social worker should make every effort to foster maximum self-determination on the part of the client.

Duty to Refer

All codes contain provisions recognizing that the therapeutic relationship is deeply personal and unique. Although most client-therapist relationships are positive and fulfilling, some simply do not work. When there is a clash, either because of personalities or therapeutic style, the therapist is advised to refer the client to another therapist. Never should the therapist abandon or neglect the client. The American Psychological Association's *Ethical Principles of Psychologists* (1981) make this point very strongly. Principle 6e says:

> Psychologists terminate a clinical or consulting relationship when it is reasonably clear that the consumer is not benefitting from it. They offer help to the consumer to locate alternative sources of assistance.

Therapist responsibility to clients is complex. It requires the therapist to assess the client's psychological needs, employ the necessary therapeutic strategies, respect the dignity of the client, empower the client to be self-determinant, and terminate treatment upon attainment of therapeutic goals. When circumstances prohibit the therapist from providing quality standards of practice, he or she is advised to transfer or refer the client to another treatment source.

These requirements are not beyond the skills of an experienced marriage and family therapist. However, in some instances, the client may not comply or may become argumentative. Such situations can tax a therapist's ability to correctly employ beneficial treatment methodologies. In fact, extremely difficult clients may threaten the therapist's self-esteem and sense of professionalism. If a therapist remains caught up in this struggle for power and control, he or she may end up practicing unethically and be open to censure by colleagues.

The most appropriate method to correct this difficulty is to seek consultation and/or supervision on the case. If necessary, the therapist should have the consultant sit in on the therapy session to act as a senior therapist and advisor. When all else fails, the therapist should refer the client to another therapist. Remember, the therapist's responsibility to clients means respecting their ability to accept the consequences of their behavior and to admit the limits of his or her ability to work with them.

Confidentiality

The marriage and family therapist must clarify his or her position on confidentiality at the beginning of treatment. Wendorf and Wendorf (1985) suggest that the easiest way to relate the rules of confidentiality is to inform the family that shared information from all sessions will be used to benefit the health and welfare of the system. Thus, the family must bear the responsibility of what to say. Material obtained in individual sessions may then be related to the entire system when the therapist deems it appropriate. Brock and Barnard (1988) recommend a similar approach in the initial session in which clients are told that the therapist will determine how and when any information will be shared with all members of the relationship system and that the therapist will not collude or keep secrets with any family member.

Information shared in the therapeutic relationship is privileged and not to be used against the client. However, in certain legal circumstances, a therapist is bound to provide confidential information. Corey, Corey, and Callahan (1984) identify these instances as

1. when the therapist is appointed by the court;
2. when there is a suicide risk;
3. when a malpractice suit is initiated against the therapist;
4. when a client's mental health is questioned as part of a civil action;
5. when a child is a victim of a crime;
6. when the client is a danger to himself or others;
7. when the client needs hospitalization; or
8. if the client expresses the intent to commit a crime that will endanger society or another person.

The therapist is faced with a complex dilemma, since the role of the treatment agent is to elicit the client's dark thoughts and desires. Commonly, these feelings are filled with intense negativity and a wish to do harm to another person. It is the therapist's task to ascertain what is fantasy and what is probable reality. It is not unusual for a therapist to hear a spouse state a desire to harm or even kill a family member, whether covertly or directly expressed. After the urges are uttered, the therapist must assess the severity of the threat and determine the degree of reality it represents. Unfortunately, waiting to quantify the threat may be dangerous.

Codes of ethics are unclear on this issue because therapist judgment is required. Should therapy continue, or should the police or other family members be informed of possible danger? Legally, the therapist may be bound by state laws to inform the threatened person, despite the effects of breaking confidentiality on the client-therapist relationship.

More problematic are the threats expressed during sessions that are disregarded or belittled by the threatened individual accompanying the distressed patient. Does the therapist leap to the protection of the person, inform the authorities, or collude in the denial? In this situation, has the therapist met his or her duty to warn if he or she has informed the threatened person or significant other in the therapy session? Now an ethical dilemma becomes a legal consideration that might jeopardize the therapeutic relationship. Psychologist/Attorney Donald Bersoff (1976) acknowledged this problem when he stated, "Therapists may find themselves in insolvable conflicts as they attempt to reconcile their own personal morality and training regarding confidentiality, the vague remedies of their professional codes of ethics, . . . and the developing legal requirements that demand . . . balancing between the client and public interests" (p. 272).

The standard of confidentiality—and when it is appropriate to break it—is likely to be debated for a long time. Since guidelines are unclear, it is difficult to know when justifiable infringement of confidentiality is permissible. The use of a systems approach means that every member of the system may have to negotiate confidentiality needs to obtain a healthy family. As Kottler (1983) stated, "Once people decide to pool their resources and work toward a common purpose, individual needs are necessarily shelved in favor of what is good for the majority. This compromise ensures that none of us gets exactly what we want, although most people get a little bit of what they are willing to accept" (p. 288).

Professional Competence and Integrity

The profession of marriage and family therapy promotes the health of the family system. The treatment person is a competently trained individual whose primary goal is the advancement of client welfare in a nonexploitive environment. For this reason, the therapist must be open to use of referral sources, alternative treatment methodologies and continuing education. As stated in the *AAMFT Code of Ethics* (1988), Subprinciple 3.4:

> Marriage and family therapists seek to remain abreast of new developments in family therapy knowledge and practice through both educational activities and clinical experience.

Subprinciple 3.6 encourages the marriage and family therapist to expand the treatment possibility. It notes that marriage and family therapists have specific competencies and advises the therapist to stay within his or her realm of knowledge.

Marriage and family therapists do not attempt to diagnose, treat, or advise on problems outside the recognized boundaries of their competence.

There are many ways in which therapists can compromise professional integrity and act unethically. Such behavior may be due to a general lack of moral commitment to the field and/or a haphazard manner of practice. For example, the therapist who fails to keep up with educational developments may employ inappropriate theoretical frameworks or faulty facilitation skills. In fact, the therapist who is not concerned about his or her professional integrity may be ignorant of the effects of his or her behavior on the client. The impaired therapist who continues to practice can actually use faulty judgment that may severely damage the client. Many codes address this issue clearly.

The *Ethical Principles of Psychologists* (APA, 1981), Principle 2f, states:

Psychologists recognize that personal problems and conflicts may interfere with professional effectiveness. Accordingly, they refrain from undertaking any activity in which their personal problems are likely to lead to inadequate performance or harm to a client, colleague, student or research participant. If engaged in such activity when they become aware of their personal problems, they seek competent professional assistance to determine whether they should suspend, terminate, or limit the scope of their professional and/or scientific activities.

For the most part, therapists are concerned with the well-being of their clients. However, a few choose to act outside ethical practice standards to make financial gains or to feel mastery over others. These individuals harm the profession by hurting clients and in so doing diminishing the credibility of all practitioners in the eyes of the consumer. Many therapists recognize these inadequate practitioners but do not take the time or dare to confront their unprofessional colleagues. This veil of silence perpetuates incompetency and tacitly accepts the negligence of poor-quality service. Certainly, it is difficult and uncomfortable to confront the unethical and incompetent practitioner, but the acceptance of substandard treatment harms both clients and professionals.

Some therapists are not aware that their practice is below standard until a colleague or a client questions their treatment. The following example, indicates how a therapist can get enmeshed in trying to help a fragile client overcome major emotional difficulties.

Case One

Professional Competence and Confidentiality

Sharon Tine sought relationship counseling from Sol Heard. Sharon had been in a triangular relationship with Jim for five years. Jim was married to Anne, Sharon's best friend. He confided to Sharon that Anne was an unacceptable partner and that he would divorce her as soon as he corrected his financial problems. Sharon believed Jim and looked forward to marrying him.

When Sharon sought Sol's help, she was very upset, confused, and totally distraught because of Jim's inconsistent behavior. She wanted to overcome her passivity and mood swings. Sol taught her to be assertive and direct. Each time Sharon attempted to assert herself with Jim, he'd pull away and threaten to return to his wife.

Although Sol did not have permission to contact Jim, he felt compelled to protect his client from Jim's manipulative behavior. After speaking with Jim, Sol informed Sharon of his actions. Sharon became enraged both with her therapist for betraying her confidence and with her lover for being willing to talk with Sol. Lonely and conflicted, Sharon called Anne to inform her about the affair. Anne confronted Jim with the information. He admitted guilt and suggested that he, Sharon, and Anne meet with Sol. Jim then called Sol and requested a joint appointment. Sol agreed. The session was a disaster. Jim left before the session ended, Sharon became immobile and unable to speak, and Anne fled in tears.

Sol called Sharon after the appointment because he felt the need to assess her mental status. He offered to meet with her on an emergency basis. Sharon willingly accepted. After the session, Sharon felt relieved and vowed to continue treatment with Sol. Eventually, Jim resumed his relationship with Sharon, and everything returned to status quo.

Over the next few months, Anne became disenchanted with the marriage and filed for divorce; Jim began dating numerous women; and Sharon moved to another town. Sharon experienced extreme stress and weight loss. Because of her unhappiness, she reconnected with Jim. Jim felt Sharon's distress warranted his contacting Sol. Sol responded candidly. Sharon found Jim's notes from the conversation and confronted him. Although Sharon understood Jim's concern, she again felt betrayed by Sol. As a result of the discovery, Sharon filed a complaint with the ethics committee of the national organization to which Sol belonged.

The committee reviewed the case thoroughly. Sol was asked to explain his interaction with Sharon. Basically, he corroborated Sharon's story. Sol believed he acted in the therapeutic interests of his client. He cited making himself available to her whenever she required his assistance. He felt his meeting with Jim was appropriate, even though he had not spoken with Sharon about it beforehand. Sol's reason for the meeting was to clarify Jim's intentions and hopefully convince him to stop lying to Sharon. He justified his emergency meeting with Sharon by saying that it would create less stress and help assure her of his concern for her welfare.

Based on the information provided here, Sol clearly violated several ethical principles:

1. respecting the rights and dignity of the client;
2. promoting the welfare of the client;
3. maintaining confidentiality;
4. avoiding dual relationships; and
5. providing competent and responsible service.

Since Sharon was the only identified client in the case, Sol was ethically bound to assist her in reaching a personal decision as to the outcome she wanted to realize with Jim. Furthermore, the therapeutic relationship between Sharon and Sol was damaged when Sol called Jim and then later met with Jim, his wife, and Sharon. The rupture in the therapeutic relationship and the fact that Sol yielded to a joint session that he knew was potentially harmful took therapeutic control away from Sol. A breach of confidentiality occurred because Sol shared information with Jim about Sharon's unhappiness and stress. Finally, because Sol violated boundaries between personal concern and therapeutic relationships with Sharon, he created a dual relationship that proved destructive for all concerned. The results of this case indicate that while Sol sought to provide professional service to Sharon, he acted below the professional and ethical standards of the profession.

As the description above points out, Sol did not believe his actions were unethical. Like many therapists who seek to help others overcome problems, Sol genuinely cared about Sharon's welfare and felt committed to his treatment with her.

Ethics committees do not seek to harm therapists found in violation of code provisions; rather, they work to keep the profession and its practitioners abreast of standards of treatment in the field. It is the intention of these committees to define practice standards for professionals and protect the public from unethical practices by clinicians. The best interests of both the professional community and the public are served when the actions of the ethics committees create more effective therapists by heightening the awareness of professional and ethical practice of marriage and family therapy.

Responsibility to
Students, Employees, and Supervisees

Codes of ethics are relevant for both client and colleague. All codes underscore the importance of treating students, employees, and supervisees with the same professionalism as clients. Each subprinciple stresses the importance of collegial relationships and fairness to employees, supervisees, and students. The AAMFT code (1988) devotes Principle 4 to these issues. It states:

> Marriage and family therapists do not exploit the trust and dependency of students, employees and supervisees.

It is understandable that Subprinciple 4.1 is very similar to Subprinciple 1.2 (see page 17). It admonishes the therapist that he or she is an authority figure who has the potential to influence and mold the trainee or employee. Subprinciple 4.1 states:

> Marriage and family therapists are cognizant of their potentially influential position with respect to students, employees, and supervisees, and they avoid exploiting the trust and dependency of such persons. Marriage and family therapists, therefore, make every effort to avoid dual relationships that could impair their professional judgment or increase the risk of exploitation. Examples of such dual relationships include, but are not limited to, provision of therapy to students, employees, or supervisees, and business or close personal relationships with students, employees, or supervisees. Sexual intimacy with students or supervisees is prohibited.

Generally, students and supervisees rely upon the clinician to teach them appropriate methods of treatment and intervention. After all, the senior therapist has both the theoretical knowledge and the actual work experience to share. Since it is expected that the trainee will err, the therapist must be available to the student and supervisee.

Unfortunately, some trainee placements are more oriented to service than to supervision, and trainees are expected to be fully skilled and knowledgeable immediately. This presents a danger to the client and an injustice to the student or supervisee. Supervising therapists are responsible for providing ongoing staffings and case reviews, as well as practical strategies for therapeutic intervention. When such assistance is lacking, there is great potential for an ethical violation. The following case illustrates the problems that can occur when students, supervisees, and employees are not given direction by a marriage and family therapy supervisor.

Case Two

Responsibility to
Students, Employees, and Supervisees

Dr. Marla Kory was a senior clinician at Verde Valley Mental Health Center. In this position, she was responsible for ten client hours per week and supervision of four junior marriage and family therapists and two marriage and family therapy doctoral interns. Because the clinic was underfunded and understaffed, Dr. Kory and her staff frequently worked excessively long hours for weeks on end.

In an effort to boost funding, the mental health center obtained a new grant to provide crisis coverage for the domestic violence unit of the Verde Valley Police Department. These cases were extremely volatile and complex. Dr. Kory provided training for the staff and interns. The material covered both theoretical constructs and treatment methodologies specific to domestic violence. Most of the staff attended the training workshops and participated in role-playing activities to simulate the actual counseling situations that might arise. By the time the first clients were referred by the police department, the staff and students appeared thoroughly trained.

Because caseloads were very full, Dr. Kory permitted Jack Kinzer, a doctoral student, to receive the first domestic violence referral. Before meeting with the family, Jack reviewed his notes and talked with Dr. Kory about possible treatment strategies. During supervision, Dr. Kory was aware of Jack's inexperience with these cases but decided that he should be given the opportunity to work with a family.

When the Morton family appeared for their first session, Jack welcomed them into his office, attempted to build rapport, and assessed the severity of their problems. As Jack got further into the session, he became increasingly protective of Mrs. Morton and the children. Although he had a treatment plan to follow, he found himself caught up in the anguish of the mother and children and decidedly antagonistic toward Mr. Morton. By the time the therapy session ended, Mr. Morton was very agitated and argumentative. Jack ended the session without dealing with Mr. Morton's obvious uneasiness.

That night, Mr. Morton assaulted his wife and children. He blamed his wife for having colluded with the therapist. Mrs. Morton called the Verde Valley Mental Health Center for help. The therapist on duty failed to return Mrs. Morton's call for several hours. By the time he did, Mrs. Morton was severely bruised and emotionally traumatized. Mrs. Morton informed the on-call therapist of her wounds and anger with Jack for having ruined her marriage. The on-call therapist listened but did not refer Mrs. Morton for medical treatment. By morning, Mrs. Morton was hospitalized as a result of her injuries. Child Protective Services was called by the hospital social worker, and the children were placed in an emergency foster home.

A local news reporter who happened to be in the emergency room when Mrs. Morton was brought in overheard the story. The next day, the headlines read, "Verde Valley Mental Health Center Incites Family to Violence."

This case presents numerous ethical problems. Many of these problems occurred because of the staffing problems at the mental health center. Nonetheless, the center and Dr. Kory were accountable for the errors that transpired. As the senior therapist who supervises the students and employees, Dr. Kory was legally responsible for the actions of these individuals. Therefore, the errors that Jack Kinzer and the on-call therapists made were legally and ethically their responsibility, as well as that of Dr. Kory.

Subprinciple 4.2 of the *AAMFT Code of Ethical Principles* (1988) states:

> Marriage and family therapists do not permit students, employees, or supervisees to perform or to hold themselves out as competent to perform professional services beyond their training, level of experience, and competence.

Students and employees depend upon their supervisors and employers to act professionally responsible. Despite the disruptions and crises that occur throughout working hours, a supervisor and/or employer is ultimately responsible for the actions of the individuals within the work environment. Furthermore, the supervisor and/or employer has the authority to promote or terminate a student, supervisee, or employee. Thus, these individuals are reliant on the supervisor and/or employer for their graduation or livelihood. Such a position makes them liable for exploitation. The trained supervisor and enlightened employer understand this delicate balance and the potential it leaves for acting unethically.

Responsibility to the Profession

Responsibility to the profession is an extremely important section of all codes, since it is this principle that keeps the profession alert to its impact on colleagues and the public. It declares to society that marriage and family therapists are mindful of their influence on the lives of others and will police themselves to assure high-quality services.

Principles addressing responsibility to the profession also pertain to presentations of information through broadcast media and publications.

The *Ethical Principles of Psychologists* (APA, 1981) public statement principle is very specific about professional responsibility when publicly representing the profession. It delineates not only the methods by which psychologists may represent themselves to the public but also the way in which information may be provided about the profession.

> Public statements, announcements of service, advertising, and promotional activities of psychologists serve the purpose of helping the public make informed judgments and choices. Psychologists represent accurately and objectively their professional qualifications, affiliations, and functions, as well as those of institutions or organizations with which they or the statements may be associated. In public statements providing psychological information of professional opinions or providing information about the availability of psychological products, publications, and services, psychologists base their statements on scientifically acceptable psychological findings and techniques with full recognition of the limits and uncertainties of such evidence.

Fees and Advertising

On June 27, 1977, the United States Supreme Court ruled against state laws that prohibited attorneys from advertising. In a landmark decision, *Bates* v. *State Bar of Arizona* (1977), Justice Harry E. Blackmun wrote the majority opinion, which stated, "Assertion that advertising will diminish the attorney's reputation in the community is open to question. . . . In fact, it has been suggested that failure of lawyers to advertise creates public disillusionment with the profession."

This decision has had far-reaching implications for all the professions. Accordingly, most state and national associations have drafted new rules regarding advertising. Although some organizations have simply restricted the profession from false and misleading advertising, others have adopted stricter codes prohibiting the use of guarantees of treatment outcome, discounts for services, or free consultations. Furthermore, these revised codes forbid professionals from engaging in comparative or outrageous advertising.

Because of the proliferation of professionals in the marketplace, there is increased competition for clients and income. Many therapists who see marketing as a vehicle to increase caseload are developing innovative marketing strategies to entice clients into treatment. Indeed, this venture into advertising the profession has been encouraged by the Federal Trade Commission (FTC), which assumes a highly aggressive stance against curtailing competition in the professions. It has successfully filed suit against professional health service associations, alleging restraint of trade for restrictive advertising codes of ethics.

Since one out of every eleven dollars is spent on health care services, the government is inclined to keep the pressure on the professions to keep costs of treatment fair. Competition is the prime method to contain costs. Thus, the local, state, and national regulatory arms of the government can be expected to continue their investigations into health care professions whose codes permit or encourage restraint of trade.

The August 1988 revision of the *AAMFT Code of Ethical Principles* deals specifically with the issues raised by the FTC. Principle 7 states:

> *Advertising* Marriage and family therapists engage in appropriate informational activities, including those that enable laypersons to choose marriage and family services on an informed basis.

The guidelines for fee setting and advertising stipulate what a marriage and family therapist must do to provide access to accurate information regarding professional qualifications of practitioners, treatment outcomes, and products or services provided. These guidelines also stipulate what the therapist cannot do. Subprinciple 7.3 specifies what advertising information is acceptable practice among marriage and family therapists.

> Marriage and family therapists assure that advertisements and publications, whether directories, announcement cards, newspapers, or on radio or television, are formulated to convey information that is necessary for the public to make an appropriate selection. Information could include: (1) office information, such as name, address, telephone number, credit card acceptability, fee structure, languages spoken, and office hours; (2) appropriate degrees, state licensure and/or certification, and AAMFT Clinical Member status; and (3) description of practice.

Subprinciple 7.4 of the AAMFT code (1988) states:

> Marriage and family therapists do not use a name which could mislead the public concerning the identity, responsibility, source, and status of those practicing under that name and do not hold themselves out as being partners or associates of a firm if they are not.

The following case example illustrates a violation of this subprinciple.

Case Three

Truth in Advertising

Tanya Boyd received her master's degree in marriage and family therapy in 1984. For the next two years, she practiced as a clinician in Portland, Oregon. While building her practice, she became interested in financial and estate planning. She read numerous articles and attended seminars in finance. She did not, however, take any qualifying examinations to make her a certified financial planner.

Nonetheless, Tanya felt qualified to assist her clients in financial management. Because she had friends at a local investment firm, she referred clients to them. She began to tell her clients that she was affiliated with the brokerage house and that she was recognized by the investment personnel as quite knowledgeable in financial planning. Many of her marriage and family therapy clients thought her services were an extension of the investment company. Tanya did nothing to challenge that impression. Tanya thought that since she derived no financial remuneration for her referrals to the brokerage company, she did not violate her profession's advertising guidelines.

Of course, Tanya's assumption was incorrect. Her silence allowed the clients to develop a belief about her competence as a financial and estate planner and about her affiliation with the investment firm. Tanya should have directed the clients to certified financial planners when such a referral was indicated. She also should have informed the clients that her specialization was marriage and family therapy, not financial and estate planning.

The various principles and subprinciples of the codes of ethics are the standards of practice for the profession. The ethical marriage and family therapist recognizes that the guidelines may not always be easy to follow or blatantly specific. However, the framework that the codes provide gives the practitioner a realistic and usable model by which to deliver treatment. Finally, the codes sensitize consumers to the practice of marriage and family therapy and familiarize them with acceptable service delivery. Without the codes, the profession would have no standards by which to operate and would be open to control by any individual or organization.

The Investigatory and Adjudication Process

Ethics committee members review cases for proper treatment approach and strategy, as well as ethical standards. Procedures for handling ethical

complaints assist committee members wrestling with discrepancies between the perceptions of the complainant and the therapist. The procedures that define the basis and scope of authority of the ethics committee
act as the map in the management and direction of a case. Generally, the
bylaws of an organization set forth the rights, duties, and membership of
the ethics committee. The bylaws of the American Psychological Association are stated in the *Rules and Procedures*. They note the responsibility
and objectives of the committee. Section 1.1 delineates the following responsibilities:

1.11 Formulate principles of ethics for adoption by the Association;

1.12 Receive and investigate complaints of unethical conduct of Fellows, Members, and Associates (hereinafter members);

1.13 Resolve complaints of unethical conduct or recommend such
other action as is necessary to achieve the objectives of the Association;

1.14 Report on types of complaints investigated with special description of difficult cases;

1.15 Adopt rules and procedures governing the conduct of the
Ethics Committee (hereinafter the Committee).

The *AAMFT Procedures for Handling Ethical Matters* (1988) define
the roles of the Ethics Committee:.

One role of the Ethics Committee is to investigate complaints of violations of the Code . . . and, if violations are found, to take action by
mutual agreement with the member involved, or to propose disciplinary action.

Finally, the procedures lay out the actual course of action that the
committee must follow once a complaint is initiated. Violation of the procedures can invalidate an investigation and cause the case to be dropped.
The procedures are an integral part of the investigative process of the
Ethics Committee and a protective mechanism for the complainant and
the accused member.

Reviewing a case from initial presentation to adjudication will clarify
how the procedures enable ethics committees to enforce their codes of
ethics. The following simulated case is comparable to those that come before ethics committees and state boards regulating human service clinicians.

Case Four

Investigation and Adjudication

No complaint may be considered unless it is written and signed by the complainant. Generally, the initial letter of complaint does not identify specific code violations. The following is an example of a letter alleging a complaint.

June 20, 1989

American Human Services Association
2111 Kiem Street
Suite 189
Philadelphia, PA

Dear Ethics Chair:

My wife and I have been in therapy with Dr. Martin Stone for 14 months. During that time, he has told us that we have a terrible marriage and that we should get divorced. He offered my wife a job and a cosignature on a loan to help her separate from me. In fact, he told the local bank manager of his intention to arrange a loan for my wife.

My wife doesn't want to leave, but she believes that Dr. Stone knows what's best for us. I think Dr. Stone is overly involved with our marriage and in particular, my wife. He's even called her on weekends to make certain that she is all right. I think Dr. Stone is destroying our marriage and causing my wife to lose her love for me. I don't know who else to turn to for help. Since he's a member of your organization, I thought you might be of assistance to me.

Thank--you.

Sincerely yours,
Perry Brigham

When a letter is received at the national office, it is typically forwarded to the organization staff member assigned to the ethics committee. The staff member notes the content of the letter and then checks to see if the complaint is made against a member of the organization. If not, a letter is sent ex-plaining the therapist is not a member of the organization, and the com-plainant is referred to another organization or the state licensing board. When the complaint involves a member, staff then confer with both the ethics committee chair and legal counsel to determine if the complaint appears valid and if code violations appear to have occurred. If so, a letter similar to the following one is sent to the complainant.

PERSONAL AND CONFIDENTIAL
CERTIFIED MAIL
RETURN RECEIPT REQUESTED

June 30, 1989

Perry Brigham
1467 N. Sierra Drive
Pinetop, New Mexico

Dear Mr. Brigham:

You recently wrote the Ethics Committee of the American Human Services Association to formally file an ethical complaint against one of our members, Dr. Martin Stone.

In order for the Ethics Committee to proceed with the case, it is essential that you give the committee permission to use your name and the information you provided when we contact our member about the complaint and when the Committee deliberates the case. Therefore, I ask that you sign the enclosed "Waiver of Privilege and Authorization to Release Information" form, and return it to me at your earliest convenience. Also, please give the Ethics Committee permission to use your name in the manner described above. Please address all your correspondence regarding this matter to Thomas Harrell, Ph.D., Chair, AHSA Ethics Committee, in care of Sydney Kincaid, staff assistant to the Ethics Committee, the American Human Services Association, 2111 Kiem Street, Suite 189, Philadelphia, PA.

If you return the signed waiver, the Ethics Committee can consider your complaint. The Ethics Committee will then determine whether the complaint states factual allegations that, if proven, could constitute a violation of the code. The committee will be in touch with you as the case proceeds.

Thank you for bringing the case to the attention of the American Human Services Association. Our association strives to maintain the highest standards of professional practice, and we endeavor to uphold principles of ethical and professional practice.

Sincerely yours,
Sydney Kincaid
Staff Assistant, ASHA Ethics Committee

At this point, some complainants choose to withdraw the complaint because they do not want the member to know of their allegations. Some may fear reprisal; others are not certain that their complaint is valid. To proceed, however, the waiver must be signed. This policy may seem unfair to the victim, but until the allegations have been proven, the Ethics Committee has no reason to believe anyone has been victimized. The rights of the accused therapist must be protected also. How else can the accused know the allegations well enough to defend himself or herself?

If the complaint letter is too vague, the staff assistant will request specific information from the complainant, such as the people involved, the time and place of the violation, and/or more detailed accounts of the actual charge. (The Ethics Committee is charged with the responsibility of protecting the rights of all involved in a complaint.) The charged member is considered innocent until substantive information can prove otherwise. The complainant is accepted as being forthright in his or her assessment of the situation unless information reveals that he or she is arbitrary and vindictive. The committee reviews each case thoroughly. In doing so, it remains open to evidence presented from all sides.

Let's assume that Mr. Brigham returns the waiver and authorization form. The Ethics Committee chair notifies the member of the complaint in a letter that specifies the principles and/or subprinciples of the code that may have been violated. Enclosed with the letter is a copy of the complaint letter, as well as a copy of the code and the procedures pamphlets. The member is directed to respond to the charges within 30 days after receiving the complaint. The following letter is an example of what might be sent to the member.

PERSONAL AND CONFIDENTIAL
CERTIFIED MAIL
RETURN RECEIPT REQUESTED

July 10, 1989

Dr. Martin Stone
459 Calle del Norte
Pinetop, New Mexico

Dear Dr. Stone:

I am writing to you in my capacity as the Chair of the Ethics Committee of the American Human Services Association.

The committee recently received a letter of complaint against you from Mr. Perry Brigham. A copy of his letter of complaint is enclosed, as are copies of his written permission to release information and to use his name, the *AHSA Code of Ethical Principles,* and the *AHSA Procedures for Handling Ethical Complaints.*

The committee has determined, if proven, Mr. Brigham's allegations could constitute a violation of the code. Consequently, the Ethics Committee has directed me to write you, delineating the allegations and the alleged code violations:

1. Subprinciple 1.9 of the *Code of Ethical Principles,* which states:

> Human Service therapists respect the right of clients to make personal choices and help them to understand the consequences of these choices. Human Service therapists clearly advise a client that a decision regarding marital status is the responsibility of the client.

This alleged violation is stated in the complainant's correspondence when he alleges that you told him and his wife that they had a terrible marriage and should get a divorce.

2. Subprinciple 2.3 of the *Code of Ethical Principles,* which states:

> Human Service therapists do not use their professional relationship with clients to further their own personal or professional interests.

This alleged violation is stated in the complainant's letter when he says that you offered his wife a job.

3. Subprinciple 2.4 of the *Code of Ethical Principles,* which states:

> Human Service therapists are aware of their potentially influential position with respect to clients, and they avoid exploiting the trust and dependency of such persons. Human Service therapists therefore make every effort to avoid dual relationships which might impair the clinician's professional judgment and objectivity.

This alleged violation is stated in the complainant's correspondence when he notes that you notified a bank manager of your intent to sign a loan for his wife.

4. Principle 3 of the *Code of Ethical Principles,* which says:

> Human Service therapists respect the confidences of their clients and treat all information received in the therapist-client relationship with utmost discretion.

This alleged violation is stated in the complainant's correspondence when he notes that you notified the bank manager that Ms. Brigham was your client and that you intended to cosign a loan for her.

5. Principle 4 of the *Code of Ethical Principles,* which states:

> Human Service therapists are committed to advancing the well-being of families and individuals. Therefore Human Service therapists respect the rights of those persons seeking their assistance. Human Service therapists make concerted efforts to deliver appropriate services.

This alleged violation is identified in the correspondence that says that you called the Brigham family on weekends and caused the marriage to be destroyed.

Please respond to these allegations in writing within 30 days of receipt of this letter. Failure to respond within 30 days may result in termination or further action against your AHSA membership.

The Ethics Committee will meet August 26, 1989, in Philadelphia, PA. At that time, the particulars of Mr. Brigham's complaint and your response will be reviewed. If further information is needed, I, as chair, will write to you within 30 days after the meeting. If the committee reaches a decision, you will be notified within one month after the meeting.

Please address all your correspondence regarding this matter to me, Thomas Harrell, Ph.D., Chair, AHSA Ethics Committee, in care of Sydney Kincaid, Staff Assistant, AHSA, 2111 Kiem Street, Suite 189, Philadelphia, PA.

Sincerely,
Thomas Harrell, Ph.D.
Chair, AHSA Ethics Committee

Obviously, when Dr. Stone receives this letter, he will be upset. Letters of complaint from ethics committees are written in formal, legal styles, detached and ominous. For awhile, Dr. Stone may ponder how to appropriately respond to the letter. If he is wise, he will seek advice of legal counsel, talk with colleagues, or call a therapist for some help in stress management. Unfortunately, clinicians in these situations do little to contact their colleagues because of shame and embarrassment, which serves to isolate them and evoke a great deal of obsessive thinking and anxiety. Such behavior can cause a therapist to respond too quickly or haphazardly to the request-for-response letter.

When such a letter is received, the accused member should take time to read it thoroughly, review casenotes, talk with senior colleagues, and consult legal counsel who understand national organizations' ethics committee action. The request for a response within 30 days allows the therapist enough time to calm down and approach the situation in a more reasoned manner. At this point, time may seem to rush by, thus encouraging knee-jerk response. If faced with an ethics inquiry, it is best for therapists to take at least a week before drafting a response. They should read and reread the response. A trusted colleague or attorney should also read the letter. The therapist should take suggestions, rewrite, and then write the formal response to the committee. After all, the response is the first defensive action that the accused must take. Therefore, it is wise that the response be well planned and thoroughly thought out.

Dr. Stone's response reflects the seriousness of the charges. His professionalism and respect for his investigative colleagues are apparent in his letter, which follows.

July 25, 1989

Thomas Harrell, Ph.D.
Chair, AHSA Ethics Committee
2111 Kiem Street
Suite 189
Philadelphia, PA

Dear Dr. Harrell:

I am responding to your letter of July 10, 1989. In that letter, you identify several possible ethical violations that I may have incurred in the treatment of the Brigham couple. I will list each allegation individually and respond accordingly.

Subprinciple 1.9 The Brigham's do have a very destructive marriage. Mr. Brigham is a compulsive gambler who has spent the family's income. The family is on the brink of bankruptcy, and there appears to be no way for the couple to survive financially. I realize that it is the client's responsibility to make a decision about their marriage. Therefore, I refrain from telling client's what to do about staying married. I told Mr. Brigham that he had to stop gambling or he'd "lose his marriage." That might be why he thinks I told him to get divorced. I also informed him that compulsive gambling is an addiction and can destroy relationships and love. He may have interpreted this as my saying that the marriage is terrible.

Subprinciple 2.3 Ms. Brigham is a bookkeeper who hasn't worked in several years. I thought she might work temporarily in my office. I figured she could brush up on her skills, and we could trade her bookkeeping time for therapeutic hours. It was to be a barter situation. That would help with the financial burden and ensure that the couple could continue in treatment.

Subprinciple 2.4 The topic of my cosigning a loan came up during one of our sessions. Ms. Brigham raised the topic. She thought that since I was her employer, I could vouch for her financially. Her husband thought that was a very good idea. He wanted to get a loan the next day. I told the couple that was impossible. I do not cosign loans, even for family members. Mr. Brigham was angry with me for not lending support. He left that session enraged. He stated, "You are a rich doctor who could certainly afford to cosign a small loan for people who are less financially fortunate." It was a very difficult session. I have thoroughly documented it. If you would like my casenotes, I will send them to you.

Principle 3 I did call the local bank manager about the Brigham's because I was afraid that they would say that I was going to cosign a loan for them. It might interest you to know that the bank manager is my sister-in-law. I did tell her about the Brigham's, but I did not tell her they were my clients. The intent of the call was simply to tell her that I would not cosign on a loan.

Principle 4 I returned Ms. Brigham's phone calls whenever she called. Since her marriage is so stressful, she called frequently. One weekend, Mr. Brigham flew to Las Vegas and spent their entire savings account. He was wagering the home mortgage when she called. She was frantic. I spent at least one hour on the phone with her. During that time, her husband placed an emergency call through the long-distance operator. When the operator cut in on our conversation, Mr. Brigham learned that his wife was talking to me. He has mentioned that phone call numerous times. It is his belief that I was romancing his wife. Although we've talked this through, he still is leery of my intent.

I hope this clarifies your request for information. Should you have any further questions, please don't hesitate

to ask. Also if you would like, I can send you the names of a
number of people who will vouch for my character and skill as
a marriage and family therapist.

Sincerely yours,
Martin Stone, Ph.D.

This letter certainly gives a different picture than that presented by
Mr. Brigham. The chair is faced with conflicting evidence and must gain
further information. (An investigating subcommittee is created to obtain
additional evidence before submitting the case to the full Ethics Committee for a decision.) The subcommittee is usually composed of three members of the Ethics Committee. The subcommittee develops a list of persons
who should be interviewed and a set of questions that must be addressed
to fully understand the case. Likely questions for this case might include
knowledge of Mr. Brigham's compulsive gambling, Dr. Stone's hiring practices regarding previous clients, Dr. Stone's discussion with the bank manager, and Dr. Stone's clinical practice skills and methodology. Individuals
for potential interviews might include Ms. Brigham, the bank manager, Dr.
Stone's office personnel, and a character reference from Dr. Stone's list of
possible resource people. Certainly, it would be advantageous to obtain Dr.
Stone's notes from the therapy session that caused Mr. Brigham's upset.
Although the interviews may be done by telephone, it is generally more
practical to obtain the information in writing. The material can be distributed to the committee members for deliberation at the ethics meeting.
     The following responses give an idea of the types of answers the sub-
committee might obtain from the interviewees.
     Ms. Brigham told the subcommittee that Dr. Stone was a very compe-
tent marriage and family therapist. She knew that her husband's excessive
gambling was bad for the family, but she never felt that Dr. Stone encouraged or directed her to leave her husband. She said that Dr. Stone believed that the marital problems were caused by both of them. She acknowledged that her husband was very angry with Dr. Stone for talking to
her on the weekends. However, Ms. Brigham confirmed that she initiated
the calls to Dr. Stone. She was very happy with her working arrangement
with him. Her bookkeeping skills have sharpened, and she will look for a
full-time job within the month. She said that the barter situation had been
very helpful to her because it enabled her to continue therapy. Above all
else, Ms. Brigham wanted the committee to know that Dr. Stone was a gentle, kind man who had her family's best interests in mind.
     Lenore Janing, the bank manager, said her brother-in-law did call her
regarding someone who might ask him to give a character reference regarding a loan application. She was certain that Dr. Stone did not identify

the person or the nature of his relationship to the person. She added that Dr. Stone was a financially responsible person and was active in the local church.

Sally Myers worked for Dr. Stone. She had been his secretary for a number of years. She confirmed that Ms. Brigham had worked in the office for the past three months. Sally added that Dr. Stone routinely barters with clients who cannot afford therapy. Ms. Myers added that Dr. Stone was always objective and treated Ms. Brigham as an employee.

The committee was able to obtain information about Dr. Stone from an approved supervisor in the area. Although the supervisor did not know Dr. Stone's work, the supervisor said that Dr. Stone was active in the local AHSA group and that he attended and gave clinical seminars. The supervisor did attend Dr. Stone's seminar on paradoxical intervention and found it quite beneficial.

Finally, the committee reviewed Dr. Stone's casenotes regarding the stormy session with Mr. Brigham. The notes indicated that Mr. Brigham was hostile and accusatory toward Dr. Stone. The notes pointed out that Ms. Brigham was tearful and speechless throughout the session. Dr. Stone was unable to redirect or reframe anything that Mr. Brigham said. The session ended on a very angry note, although an appointment was set for the following Tuesday.

As a result of the investigation, the Ethics Committee decided to question Mr. Brigham about the discrepancies between his statements and those of the respondents. Mr. Brigham held firm in his allegations but did concede that he was not satisfied with the results of the therapy. He continued to allege that Dr. Stone caused the deterioration of the marriage. Therefore, he felt the need for restitution from both Dr. Stone and AHSA.

After deliberation of the evidence, the Ethics Committee dropped charges pertaining to Principles 3 and 4 and Subprinciples 1.9 and 2.3. Violation of Subprinciple 2.4 was sustained because of the dual relationship that Dr. Stone maintained with Ms. Brigham. The following letter reveals the committee's findings and the method by which Dr. Stone was asked to remedy the situation.

PERSONAL AND CONFIDENTIAL
CERTIFIED MAIL
RETURN RECEIPT REQUESTED

September 3, 1989

Dr. Martin Stone
459 Calle del Norte
Pinetop, New Mexico

Dear Dr. Stone:

The purpose of this letter is to inform you of the actions
taken by the AHSA Ethics Committee at its recent meeting in
Philadelphia, PA. At that meeting, the committee thoroughly
reviewed the case and all relevant materials. The committee
decided the following:

The committee found you in violation of the following
subprinciple of the AHSA *Code of Ethical Principles:*
Subprinciple 2.4, which states:

Human Service therapists are aware of their potentially influential position with respect to clients, and
they avoid exploiting the trust and dependency of such
persons. Human Service therapists therefore make
every effort to avoid dual relationships which might
impair the clinician's professional judgement and ob-
jectivity.

Your employment of Ms. Brigham contaminated the therapeutic relationship, since it established you as an employer.
This type of relationship requires different interaction than
that of the therapeutic relationship. Therefore, it has the
potential of confusing the client in her working with you.
Furthermore, it can affect the way her husband perceives you,
since he knows that your relationship with his wife is daily
and ongoing. As such, he may misinterpret your association and
your professional intentions with his wife.

The Ethics Committee has decided to offer to settle the
case with you by mutual agreement. The terms of the settlement
the committee offers you are as follows:

You are immediately requested to cease and desist from
employing Ms. Brigham as your bookkeeper. To be certain
that you have complied with the committee's request, you
are to submit a signed and notarized letter from Ms.
Brigham and yourself that she has ended employment within
30 days after receipt of this letter. Furthermore, you
are to permanently cease and desist from employing any
clients or family members of clients.

The complainant, Mr. Perry Brigham, will be informed
of the findings and the recommendations of the Ethics
Committee.

Should you decide to adopt the settlement offered, you
must sign this letter in the space provided below and return
it to me, Thomas Harrell, Ph.D., Chair, AHSA Ethics Committee,
in care of Sydney Kincaid, Staff Assistant, ASHA, 2111 Kiem

Street, Suite 189, Philadelphia, PA. You must do this within
30 (thirty) days of your receipt of this letter.

  If you decide not to accept the terms of this settlement,
the matter will be returned to the committee for further deliberation and action.

  Please understand that your failure to respond to this
letter within 30 days will mean that the settlement offer is
withdrawn. Moreover, your failure to respond could result in
termination or further action against your AHSA membership.

Sincerely yours,
Thomas Harrell, Ph.D.
Chair, AHSA Ethics Committee

I hereby accept the terms of the settlement offered me by the
AHSA Committe on Ethics. Seen and agreed to:

_____   _____

Signature   Date

The agreement constitutes a binding transaction between the Ethics
Committee and the member. Once signed by the member, the settlement
is noted. The agreement is then entered into the membership file, where it
remains permanently.

If Dr. Stone does not contest the settlement agreement, the recommendations of the Ethics Committee become the final determination on
this matter. However, if Dr. Stone requests a hearing to appeal the committee's findings, he may ask that his case be heard before the Judicial Council
of the organization. When this occurs, the Ethics Committee and legal
counsel act as the prosecutors against the member. The member may be
represented by counsel and present all witnesses and information that he
or she feels is relevant.

The Judicial Council can overturn or uphold the Ethics Committee
decision. In most situations, the decision of the Judicial Council is final.
Only when the panel violates procedural rules can its ruling be overturned.
In such an instance, the aggrieved member may appeal the case to the
Board of Directors of the organization. At that point, the board makes a
written recommendation or may order a new hearing before the panel. Of
course, the board may opt to accept the decision of the hearing panel.

The following discussion is a summary of a judicial hearing case. It
reveals the checks and balances at work between the Ethics Committee and
the Judicial Council.

Case Five

Judicial Council Hearing

Jerry Lyon, a marriage and family therapist employed by a large counseling agency, was found to be in violation of specific ethical principles regarding sexual harassment and dual relationships with clients. Five of his female clients claimed he exploited the therapeutic relationship by asking them to date him while still under his treatment. Their allegations were substantiated through personal and witness testimony. The Ethics Committee ordered Mr. Lyon to two years of therapy and one year of supervision. Mr. Lyon refused to accept the mutual consent agreement. Therefore, he petitioned the Judicial Council for a hearing.

At the hearing, the Ethics Committee presented its findings. Mr. Lyon presented his information and rationale for not accepting the sanction. He said that the women were of age and therefore were responsible for "leading him on." He added that his experience as a clinician exceeded 20 years and that no supervisor or therapist could teach him anything new. Through further investigation, the Judicial Council learned that Mr. Lyon had been propositioning female clients for the past several years. The agency where he was employed had placed him on disciplinary probation numerous times, but his behavior remained unchanged. Ultimately, the agency terminated his position as a therapist but permitted him to remain in a nontreatment position.

The Judicial Council told Mr. Lyon he would have to comply with the Ethics Committee's findings. He refused. Consequently, the council removed him from membership status in the national organization. Their decision remained final, based on the cited code violations.

As this case shows, anyone may appeal the Ethics Committee's findings. The Judicial Council uses the Ethics Committee material but carries out its own investigations before delivering a decision. The member is permitted to restate the case and show cause why the Ethics Committee findings were unacceptable. Cross-examinations may occur, more witnesses may be called, and previous findings may be reviewed. After thorough assessment of the information, the Judicial Council adjudicates the case and delivers whatever sanctions it deems appropriate.

The procedures bring the *Code of Ethical Principles* full circle by guaranteeing the organization and membership responsibility to the public, the client, and the member. Through due process, any aggrieved individual may state his or her case before an impartial body of professionals who must follow a specific course of action. The diversity of members on the Ethics Committee and Judicial Council is essential in underscoring that these bodies cannot possibly railroad a complainant or a member. Thus, in our fictitious example, the Ethics Committee members have complied with Principle 5 of the *AAMFT Code of Ethical Principles* (1988) while adhering to the *Procedures for Handling Ethical Matters* (1988).

> Marriage and family therapists respect the rights and responsibilities of professional colleagues; carry out research in an ethical manner; and participate in activities which advance the goals of the profession.

This detailed and sometimes complicated process is designed to provide fair treatment for all parties involved in an ethical complaint. The process safeguards against arbitrary decisions by committee or council members. It also provides assurance to the public that national organizations seek to maintain high standards of practice.

Conclusion

Ethical considerations are imperative in delivering high-quality marriage and family therapy. Therapists must integrate theoretical frameworks, facilitative skills, and professional competence during every therapeutic hour. Clinicians are expected to recognize the limitations of their competence, as well as their personal biases and values. Practitioners must continually assess their knowledge and ability to deal with particular client problems. Therefore, it is wise for therapists to confer with colleagues about difficult or baffling cases and to share perceptions of what is occurring with the client, himself or herself, and the relationship between him or her and the client. Consultation and supervision benefit both the therapist and the client and are an integral part of ethical practice.

Just as therapists cannot exclude personal values and biases from the therapeutic relationship, neither can they deny the impact of their needs and personality structure on the client. Therefore, it is essential that therapists note their own areas of unresolved issues in their families of origin and personal lives. Knowledge of these issues may require personal psychotherapy and supervision to alleviate defensive responses and vulnerability. When a therapist is blind to personal issues, he or she may inadvertently commit an ethical violation by prohibiting a client from exploring his or her personal dimensions. Acknowledging such omissions is difficult. Therefore, a therapist may not know of the therapeutic errors being made. In such a situation, therapy may be used to serve the needs of the therapist more than the client.

Therapy is a deeply personal experience, both for the client and the therapist. Every client presents some aspects of self that affect a therapist's personal psychology. Thus, it is crucial that the therapist enter into a treatment relationship as an individual who is personally satisfied and emotionally healthy. When these conditions are met, ethical violations will be avoided and therapy will accomplish its goal of leading clients to successful self-exploration and increased family satisfaction.

CHAPTER THREE

Legal Issues
Facing Marriage
and Family Therapists

Generally, marriage and family therapists have reduced legal liability in comparison to physicians. However, in today's litigious society, suits are becoming more prevalent. The recent increase in malpractice insurance premiums testifies to this point. In fact, some clinicians are following their attorney's advice to avoid suits by not attempting to collect on unpaid bills and not testifying in heavily debated custody disputes. It does not matter whether the therapist is performing his or her work within legal and ethical guidelines. Unfortunately, any person has the right to sue any practitioner, regardless of how spurious the claim.

There is no formula to assure immunity from allegations and/or suits. Laws and the needs of clients are constantly changing. Individual states have different rules and procedures; therefore, each court's interpretation of the law differs. To clarify laws relating to the specific treatment of a marriage or family, therapists must consult the state statutes and rules for the jurisdiction in which they practice. Should the chapter spark questions or problems for the reader, he or she should consult an attorney specializing in the practice of family law and/or psychotherapy malpractice. Because family law and psychotherapy malpractice are highly specific subareas of the law, a general practice attorney may not be the best consultant. An attorney who specializes in the area under question will provide better service. One shouldn't hesitate to check a prospective attorney's credentials, past and present case and court experience, and attitude toward clinicians. Therapists should shop for malpractice or family law attorneys as they would a therapist for them and their families.

Legal Liability for the
Marriage and Family Therapist

Every practitioner is exposed to the potential of professional liability. To bring a charge against a therapist, the plaintiff must cite a rationale for the suit. Generally, the complaint alleges that the therapist either intentionally or unintentionally harmed the client in some specific manner. The most frequently used allegations include sexual misconduct with the client, marital disruption, faulty or negligent delivery of service, breach of contract, breach of confidentiality, failure to obtain informed consent, and negligent or abusive use of evaluative instruments and/or interviews.

When bringing these charges against a therapist, the client may claim both compensatory and punitive damages. Compensatory damages are awarded by the court to compensate a successful plaintiff for loss, while punitive damages are awarded to punish the defendant for reckless, wanton, or heinous results stemming from the therapist's actions or omissions (Cohen, 1979).

Most suits brought against therapists are based on tort law, which is centered on civil rather than criminal liability. Essentially, these laws are specific to offenses committed against an individual rather than society. The client may charge that the therapist deliberately or unintentionally caused harm through negligent acts. The measure of negligence is obtained from the standard of care given by practitioners of the same specialty in the same locality. (The concept of *locality* is changing to that of national acceptance as more accredited marriage and family therapy programs develop.) Defining *standard of care* is problematic, since there are numerous schools of thought regarding treatment of couples and families. No theoretical framework has universal acceptance by the profession. Certainly, an attorney can use a so-called expert with one theoretical leaning against another so-called expert of an entirely different orientation. It is not surprising that a court may be confused and unable to make legal decisions on evidence supplied by therapists. In fact, experienced trial lawyers have used the contradictions among treatment professionals to confound jurors and discredit the profession as nonscientific and baseless.

Schutz (1982) notes that the plaintiff must prove that the therapist did not exercise proper standards of care by failing to demonstrate (1) minimal accepted degrees of knowledge or skill possessed by other practitioners or (2) minimal acceptable degrees of care, attention, diligence, or vigilance exercised in the application of those skills. In other words, if a therapist is uncertain as to how to proceed in a case, it is incumbent upon him or her to obtain supervision or direction from a senior colleague. To deliver treatment using the "seat-of-the-pants" method leaves the therapist open to charges of negligent behavior and possible malpractice.

For those marriage and family therapy practitioners who use the more proactive techniques of prescription, it is possible to breach the standard of care by prescribing the symptom or intensifying the symptom. For example, a family with a defiant adolescent may be given a paradoxical injunction to assist the teen in strongly demonstrating his or her anger and animosity toward the family. The youth may take the injunction as permission to physically abuse the parent with whom he or she is disenchanted. Such activity may bring physical and emotional harm to the adult, as well as other children within the family. Consequently, the family may claim that the therapist failed to inform them of the possible damage that could occur from the prescription and that such failure is the proximate cause for the plaintiff's injuries. *Proximate cause* means that the injury is the direct result of the therapist's treatment and that if the therapist had not made the prescription, the injury would never have happened. Of course, the attorney for the therapist could argue that the treatment conformed with acceptable standards of practice prevalent in the field of marriage and family therapy. Furthermore, the attorney could propose that the damage came from actions other than those of the therapist. Regardless of the legal arguments, the judge and jury may find such techniques puzzling and unacceptable when trying to decide if the therapist was at fault.

For the most part, therapists attempt to deliver high-quality treatment that adheres to the existing standards of care. Unfortunately, good faith and positive therapeutic rapport are not sufficient to deter a litigious client. Therapists may be unaware of their undue influence on clients until a complaint has been made against them.

Because clinicians are involved in the most intimate facets of individuals' lives, they can become the object of angry, hostile, or affectionate reactions by clients. These feelings may lead clients to imagine encounters with the therapist, bequeath the therapist money, or assume clandestine meetings with the therapist. In these instances, family members of the client may see the therapist as opportunistic, alienating affection, or conspiring against the family. It is these heightened feelings by concerned family members that can lead to lawsuits against clinicians.

Laws Impacting Clinical Practice

Laws are created to manage society. Yet laws are merely written and spoken words, which, if not enforced, do little to sustain and perpetuate a healthy society. Because laws are created by people, they contain various biases and agendas. Therefore, numerous interpretations of the law can be made. Appeals are just one indication of the way in which one court can review and even overturn another court's decision based on a different interpretation of the law. Debate over semantics, the relevance of a dated law to present societal behavior, and the constant search for a better way of life keep the justice system active and alert.

(The various laws discussed in this section are the framework by which a therapist should operate.) The laws appear global and somewhat philosophical, yet they are specific to the health care profession and relevant to the marriage and family practitioner. Some therapists may choose to avoid legal control of their profession by denying any wrongdoing. Others may be intimidated by the law and refuse to take difficult clients, such as those who may be violent or abusive.

Both reactions are naive and do not guarantee immunity from lawsuits. In undertaking work with families and couples, the therapist must pursue the best possible treatment, even if it involves taking risks. Certainly, the therapist must gather all necessary information regarding client history and behavioral responses. Only after thoroughly reviewing that information can the practitioner determine the legal liability of the case.

(At times, the law is at odds with therapeutic theory and effective treatment. Basically, the law attempts to view actions in a black-and-white framework, while therapy views human behavior as being more complex. Because of these different views, therapists and attorneys frequently argue about individual rights to make competent and informed judgments. More confusing than client self-determinism is the argument that therapists can predict and are accountable for the behavior of clients while they are in treatment.

The laws presented in this section deal with the legal dilemmas a clinician faces while treating a client. (The informed practitioner must address each client with the law in mind.) To turn away from the legal ramifications of therapeutic intervention is to deny the reality of the marketplace.

Informed Consent

The doctrine of *informed consent* was originally designed to require physicians and surgeons to explain medical procedures to patients and to warn them of any risks or dangers that could result from treatment. (The intent of the doctrine was to permit the patient to make an intelligent, informed choice as to whether to undergo the proposed treatment or procedure.) The duty to disclose information requires the physician to explain the nature of the ailment, the proposed treatment, the probability of successful outcome from the treatment, alternative treatment methodologies, and the consequences of various treatments (see *Sard* v. *Hardy* [1977]). (The purpose of the informed consent doctrine is to permit patients to use their own values and preferences in making decisions regarding medical treatment.)

The law regarding informed consent is constantly evolving. Various cases have come before the courts since the late 1950s. However, the most important case is *Canterbury* v. *Spense* (1972). The rules established from this case are used in half the jurisdictions in the United States. Basically, the case clarifies (1) what material must be disclosed to the patient, (2) how the physician must disclose the information, (3) when there is no need to obtain an informed consent, and (4) who is permitted to make the medical decision when the patient cannot.

Since information regarding informed consent deals with physicians and medical practice, marriage and family therapists and researchers must generalize physicians' practice standards to their own work with clients. In the authors' view, a clinician must inform a client of the benefits and possible risks encountered in pursuing therapy (e.g., marital disharmony, arguments and misperceptions between family members and at times the therapist, and the heightening of emotional sensitivity), just as marital and family therapy researchers must inform the participants of the procedures, possible research outcomes, probable risks, and purpose of the research. Regardless of whether the client is in therapy or a research subject, the marital and family practitioner and/or researcher must disclose the information to the client before administering services.

The Psychologist's Legal Handbook (Stromberg et al., 1988) notes four components necessary for informed consent: (1) competency of the patient, (2) disclosure of *material information,* (3) understanding by the patient, and (4) voluntary consent (p. 447). *Competency* is defined as having the capacity to understand the information that the therapist discloses. Marriage and family therapists must provide clients with basic information about treatment. Generally, this means that the therapist must inform the client of the elements of treatment—cost, possible duration, reasonable goals, risks, and realistic consequences. The explanation of treatment must be given in such a manner that a competent client can fully grasp the potential benefits and liabilities of treatment well enough to make an informed judgment as to whether to proceed with treatment. *Voluntary consent* means that the client must make the decision for treatment without duress, pressure, or coercion.

Competency is at issue if the marriage and family therapist is working with a family who has an aging, senile parent; a spouse who is mentally disabled; or a child who is under age and in need of therapy or assessment. In these instances, the therapist may be faced with dealing with the competent family members and the incompetent or underage individual.

For example, consider the following case. The adult children of an elderly woman are seeking treatment to assist them in making a decision about nursing home placement for their mother. The children are at odds with each other because of unresolved feelings about their mother, which is something she has promoted. The fact is that the mother is not able to

fully care for herself without supervised care. The adult children want therapy for the family, but it is clear that the mother is not mentally capable of
utilizing treatment. In this instance, the marriage and family therapist must
inform the adult children of the direction of therapy (i.e., alternative living
arrangements for the mother, the need for some personal reflections upon
their individual relationship with their mother) and the rationale for not
including her in the treatment process.

Competency for consent purposes means that an individual has the
right to refuse treatment. Marriage and family therapists face this problem
regularly with the noncompliant spouse. Frequently, one member of a
couple may wish to engage in treatment, while the other may be wary or
circumspect. Should the nonconsenting spouse eventually choose to dis-
engage from treatment, the therapist should inform him or her of the possible consequences of such actions to the marriage or relationship.

Competency means that the client understands the purpose of treatment, diagnostic assessment and marital or familial homework. The marriage and family therapist who uses indirect treatment methodologies may
take issue with this concept and may even be able to adequately defend his
or her position. However, the fact remains that competency is a facet of informed consent that calls into question the legal rights of clients.

Equally important are the points of *material information* and *understanding of treatment*. Some states define what a therapist must disclose so that the client can consider accepting or rejecting treatment.
Arizona law addresses informed consent for the mental health practitioner
by assessing the legal circumstances under which informed consent is applicable. In *Rodriguez* v. *Jackson* (1978), the Arizona Court of Appeals
held that "whether a physician or surgeon has a duty to warn a patient of
the possibility of a specific adverse result of the proposed treatment depends upon the circumstances of the particular case and of the general
practice followed by the medical profession in such cases" (p. 486). Thus,
the mental health practitioner must inform the client of the nature of the
problem, the treatment plan, the benefits and risks of treatment, the probability of a successful outcome, and alternative treatment plans for the
same type of problem. In other words, the clinician must follow a treatment plan similar to that utilized by colleagues treating similar cases.

If a client informs the therapist that he or she does not want to engage in treatment that may change some aspect of his or her life (e.g.,
therapy may alter a client's religious orientation or belief system), the
practitioner is bound to inform the client of all risks pertaining to that
concern, even though a prudent therapist might refrain from such disclosure. If the client asks for more information, the therapist may discuss the
impact of treatment from a broader perspective. (See *Hales* v. *Pittman*
[1978], where the court notes that the patient's instructions may expand the

scope of the disclosure required.) Armed with all the information, the client must determine the next course of action regarding treatment. Should the client then consent to treatment, he or she cannot charge the therapist with failure to inform him or her of the consequences of treatment.

Court rulings on informed consent are based on objective standards or *reasonable outcomes*. In other words, a person is considered competent to make an informed judgment regarding treatment if his or her decision is the choice that a reasonable person would make given the same alternatives. Conversely, a therapist's attorney, alleging client incompetency, must prove that a reasonable person standing in the claimant's shoes would decline the treatment offered by the clinician.

Although it is not standard procedure to obtain written consent for treatment from the client, it is good practice to use part of the initial session to inform the client of the procedures and possible consequences of treatment. The therapist who chooses to use a written, signed informed consent form is urged to have an attorney review the document for precise language.

There are four exceptions to the doctrine of informed consent. The first exception involves those situations that are life-threatening to the client. In other words, if an individual is in a major accident and is rendered unconscious and thereby unable to make a decision regarding medical treatment, the physician may proceed with prudent medical care. Courts usually do not regard mental health problems as emergencies unless the individual is blatantly violent, self-destructive, or an immediate danger to others. In such instances, it may be possible to restrain and/or administer psychotropic medication to the individual without expressed informed consent.

The second exception is when a client is deemed incompetent to consent to treatment. Since the definition of *incompetent* is vague, it is difficult to determine when to allow this exception to the doctrine. Lidz et al. (1984) distinguish two different types of incompetence: general and specific. The category of *general incompetency* applies to individuals who are actively psychotic, severely mentally retarded, unconscious, or senile. *Specific incompetency* refers to an individual's actual ability to make a decision and to understand information presented by a physician or therapist so as to be able to make the treatment decision.

Regardless of the reason for incompetence, informed consent must be given by a third party if treatment is to proceed. The question of who may give the consent and for what reason is problematic for the third party acting on behalf of the client. Certainly, if the client is a minor, it is generally accepted that a parent may give informed consent. However, if the client is an adult whose judgment is questionable or who has previously been judged incompetent but who is now stabilized, the decision of informed consent becomes knotty. The courts offer little clarity or guidance on this issue.

The third exception to informed consent is the client's prerogative. A client may waive his or her right to informed consent but only after being advised of his or her rights to be fully informed of treatment procedures and consequences. The clients may waive his or her rights by saying, "I don't want to know about those things," "Don't tell me what you intend to do; just do it," or "You're the expert; you do what you think is best for the family." When a client makes these statements, the clinician must inform him or her of the client's right to the information and to question treatment processes. The waiver of informed consent becomes valid only when the client has verbally and directly declined to hear the information and participate in the treatment decision-making process.

The fourth exception to the doctrine of informed consent is identified as *therapeutic privilege,* which permits the physician to withhold information from the patient that is deemed harmful. If, for example, the disclosure of medical information threatens a patient's ability to make a decision about medical treatment, the physician must seriously consider the manner in which he or she will share the material with the patient.

Informed consent is a difficult doctrine to apply to marriage and family therapy, since it is based on the medical model. Nonetheless, it cannot be ignored. Therapists should consider the following guidelines when initiating marriage and family treatment.

1. Provide the client with written material that states the purpose of therapy, the risks involved in treatment, and the type of treatment that is being provided (e.g., systems theory).
2. Inform the client that therapy cannot guarantee outcomes. In fact, the end result of treatment may vary considerably from client expectations.
3. Clarify that therapy involves identifying emotions, uncovering family secrets, and exposing various familial interaction patterns, which can evoke sensitivity and psychological pain.
4. Specify that the therapist will not abandon the client and will inform him or her of vacation schedules and the like well in advance.
5. Inform the client of the right to privacy and confidentiality.
6. Tell the client that should another treatment methodology be more appropriate, the therapist will inform the client and make the appropriate referral.
7. Advise the client that he or she may discontinue treatment at any time but that the therapist has the right to share his or her opinion regarding the termination of treatment.

Confidentiality

(The essence of good therapeutic practice is based on confidentiality) The successful clinician encourages the client to disclose information that may be disconcerting. To obtain such guarded information, the therapist must be able to assure the client of strict confidence. Without this assurance, it is difficult to develop therapeutic rapport or facilitate treatment. Indeed, most ethical codes for mental health practitioners thoroughly address the issue of confidentiality and provide sanctions against individuals who violate client confidentiality.

(Clients whose confidences are disclosed without authorization have legal recourse against the clinician.) The charges that a client may bring against a therapist for such a violation may include malpractice, invasion of privacy, defamation of character or breach of fiduciary responsibility. In the case of *McDonald* v. *Clinger* (1982), a patient filed suit against his psychiatrist for revealing confidential information to his wife without his authorized consent. The claimant alleged as a result of the psychiatrist's actions, he lost his wife, his job, and his financial security. These problems simply created more emotional harm, which necessitated his obtaining further psychiatric help. The court held the psychiatrist breached the fiduciary duty of confidentiality (*McDonald* at 804). This decision supporting confidentiality reinforces the stipulations of ethics codes.

(Confidentiality can be compromised by many aspects of practice today.) Request for patient information is increasing. Insurance companies, health care professionals, academic institutions, authors, and employers are but a few of the groups seeking information on mental health clients. Before responding to these requests for information, the therapist should obtain a Release of Information form from the sender (see Appendix B). As an added safeguard, the therapist should speak to the client regarding the request and if possible show him or her the material that will be sent to the requestor. This practice allows the client to make an informed judgment on the information being sought.

Confidentiality is also at issue when a case is used for teaching in a classroom or textbook or when a therapist is discussing a case with a supervisor or colleague. In fact, instances have been cited in which clients thought they recognized their cases in publications, even though names and places had been changed. The therapist would be wise to obtain a written authorization to release information.

Privileged Communications

Therapists may confuse confidentiality with privileged communication. (*Privileged communication* refers to maintaining confidences within the

legal proceedings, while *confidentiality* refers to maintaining of confidences outside of legal proceedings)(Miller & Sales, 1986). This distinction
is not universal across states. For example, the Arizona Privileged Communications Statute (§ 32-2085) reads, in part:

> The confidential relations and communications between a psycholo-
> gist certified as provided in this chapter or a person excepted from
> this chapter by § 32-2072, subsection E, or § 32-2083 and his client
> are placed on the same basis as those provided by law between at-
> torney and client. Unless the client has waived the psychologist-client
> privilege in writing or in court testimony, a psychologist shall not be
> required to divulge, nor shall he voluntarily divulge, information
> which he received by reason of the confidential nature of his prac-
> tice as a psychologist, except that he shall divulge to the [B]oard any
> information it subpoenas in connection with an investigation, public
> hearing or other proceeding.

According to this statute, the psychologist has a duty to maintain
confidentiality based on law rather than ethical standards.

Privileged communications law cites the lawsuit as the threat to client
privacy. Any individual involved in litigation can demand that a professional reveal confidential information regarding the client. By guaranteeing client privacy in a court of law, the therapist-client relationship can
remain unencumbered. Although laws vary across states, there is uniform
agreement that the privilege belongs to the client, not the therapist. Thus, a
therapist may be placed in the middle of two opposing legal claims: the
client's claim of confidentiality and the third party's contention that the
communications should be disclosed.

In *People* v. *District Court, City and County of Denver* (1986), the
Colorado Supreme Court held that communications between psychologist
and sexual assault victim/patient are privileged and thus protected from
disclosure, even when the assailant/criminal defendant wants to use the
material for his or her own defense. In this case, the defendant subpoenaed the victim's past assault records from the therapist treating the victim, contending that the victim said something to her therapist that may
be inconsistent with her trial testimony. The prosecution objected on behalf of the victim, stating that producing such documentation violates the
Colorado statutory psychologist-patient privilege. A hearing was held in
which the court ordered that the therapist produce the records for an "in-
camera" inspection to allow the court to determine the relevance of the
records. The prosecution appealed the order to the Colorado Supreme
Court, which held that the records were privileged.

Therapists who find themselves caught between client's assertion of privileged communication and court-ordered request for documentation will undoubtedly be confused about their role and obligations to both client and court. In such situations, therapists must protect themselves by hiring their own attorneys.

A client may invoke the privileged communication law in any part of a legal proceeding. It is interesting to note that privilege law does not demand that the client be a party in the litigation. The privilege simply serves to protect individuals from disclosure of personal material in legal proceedings, not from damage or loss sustained in a lawsuit. It is not surprising that the primary reason to invoke the privilege is to allay the client's fear of legal injury resulting from public disclosure of confidential material (Everstine & Everstine 1986, p. 173).

The American Association for Marriage and Family Therapy *Legal Consultation Plan Newsletter* (Staff, 1986) cites a California case, *Cutter* v. *Brownbridge* (1986), in which Cutter alleged that his therapist, Brownbridge, voluntarily signed a written declaration stating diagnostic and treatment information gained during the therapy sessions. The signed document was attached to papers filed by Cutter's exwife, who was requesting denial of Cutter's visitation rights with his children. When the court denied Cutter's visitation rights, he sued Brownbridge for disclosing privileged communications, stating that the therapist violated his constitutional and common law rights to privacy, breached an implied covenant of confidentiality based on the therapist-client contractual relationship, and intentionally inflicted emotional distress. Although Brownbridge claimed immunity, based on California statutes providing that statements made in judicial hearings could not be the basis for civil liability, the court found for Cutter. Essentially, the court identified a state constitutional right to privacy, which includes therapist-patient communications. The court found that the therapist could not rely on immunity for his statements without first asserting the privilege and seeking a court ruling on the disclosure. Without doing so first, "a psychotherapist who volunteers information concerning a patient obtained in connection with their relationship does so at his or her peril." In this instance, the therapist should have consulted an attorney before providing the requested information.

Exceptions to the Right of Confidentiality

Although marital and family therapists are ethically and legally bound to maintain the confidences of their clients, there are clearly times when disclosure of information is mandated by law. New Jersey revised statutes address confidential communications for marriage counselors (annotated section 45: 8B–29), as follows:

Confidential Communications; Waiver of Privilege

Any communication between a marriage counselor and the person or persons counseled shall be confidential and its secrecy preserved. This privilege shall not be subject to waiver, except where the marriage counselor is a party defendant to a civil, criminal, or disciplinary action arising from such counselling, in which case, the waiver shall be limited to that action.

When a clinician is ordered to testify or disclose client records by the client or by the court, he or she must comply with the request. Before doing so, the therapist should consult with his or her personal attorney to determine if the information is protected by law. It is also advisable for the clinician to speak with the client and the client's attorney to find out the exact nature of the request for records and/or clinical findings.

If the client prohibits the therapist from disclosing information to the court, the therapist may be uncertain of his or her responsibilities in the legal action. In such a case, the therapist must consult with his or her attorney to determine his or her duty in the legal process. In certain situations, privileged communication can be overturned. Although some state statutes delineate these conditions, other jurisdictions are more vague. In general, the exceptions to the privilege may include:

1. cases in which the assistance of a therapist is being sought solely for the purpose of committing a criminal or civil action;
2. cases in which the client is involved in workman's compensation litigation;
3. cases involving a malpractice action between the client and the therapist;
4. cases in which the therapist-client communication occurred because of court order (e.g., an evaluation); and
5. cases in which the client is charged with a crime.

In yet other situations, the client may automatically waive the right to privileged communications. These exceptions relate to statutory law requiring mental health professionals to disclose specific confidences regarding child or elderly abuse. Most states require physicians and mental health practitioners to report child and elderly abuse to local state protective agencies. Failure to report the observed or disclosed abuse may lead to criminal sanctions against the therapist.

Also, most states require therapists and physicians to waive confidentiality when the client introduces his or her mental condition as part of his or her claim or defense. An example of this action might involve a patient suing for mental damage as a result of an accident or altercation with the defendant.

Duty to Warn

A common exception to client confidentiality involves threats of danger or violence made by the client. Although the concept of *clear and imminent danger* is difficult to determine, the therapist must be attuned to the patient's announcement of intention or plan to harm to another individual.

The most notable case of a therapist's duty to the patient and society is *Tarasoff* v. *Regents of the University of California* (1976). In this landmark case, Prosenjit Poddar, a graduate student at the University of California at Berkeley, met Tatiana Tarasoff in square-dancing class. The two dated regularly throughout the fall. On New Year's Eve, she kissed him. Poddar, a native of India, interpreted the kiss as a sign of an engagement. Although Tatiana told him that she did not regard the kiss as an intention to marry, Poddar did not believe her. He became consumed with her lack of commitment to him. As a result of his preoccupation with the woman, friends urged him to seek therapy at the student health center, where a psychiatrist referred Poddar to psychologist Thomas Moore. During therapy, Poddar confided his intentions to harm Tarasoff when she returned to campus in the fall. Because of the seriousness of the threat, Moore notified the campus police orally and in writing that Poddar should be committed. After talking with Poddar, the police determined that he was rational and did not detain him. Subsequently, Moore's superior ordered no further action be taken against Poddar. As a matter of confidentiality, Moore's superior asked that the letter to the police, as well as certain therapy records, be destroyed. Two months later, Poddar shot and stabbed Tarasoff to death. Poddar was found guilty of voluntary manslaughter.

The parents of the victim sued the therapists at the clinic, the police, and the Regents for negligent behavior in allowing Poddar to be released from custody without notifying the family that Tatiana Tarasoff was in grave danger. The Superior Court of Alameda County held that the defendants owed no duty of reasonable care to Tarasoff. As a result of the adjudication, Tarasoff's parents filed an appeal to the Supreme Court of California, which reversed the judgment and found the defendant's therapist guilty of failure to warn. The court determined that when a therapist decides a patient "presents a serious danger of violence to another" the therapist has a duty to "use reasonable care to protect the intended victim against such danger" (*Tarasoff* at 340).

Although the *Tarasoff* decision set precedent only in California, its ramifications have been felt nationwide. Basically, it states that the therapist has the duty to protect the potential victim. In order for the therapist to actively do so, he or she must have a special relationship with the person whose behavior needs to be controlled. *Tarasoff* defined the therapist-patient relationship as "special," thus creating the therapist's duty to

take positive moves toward preventing foreseeable risks caused by the behavior of the patient.

Cheryl Simon (1988), associate editor of *Psychology Today,* notes
that psychiatrist James C. Beck of Harvard University Medical School studied a number of cases involving the duty to warn. He found a clear relationship between how a warning against violent acts is given and what
effects this has on psychotherapy. Patients were more amenable to hearing
about a therapist's duty to protect when informed of the duty in the initial
phase of treatment than when warnings were given to potential victims
without the client's knowledge. The findings of this study support the policy
of warning clients in the initial phase of therapy.

Although the *Tarasoff* case is specific to psychiatrists and psychologists, it has implications for marriage and family therapists. One of the
largest settlements in a duty-to-warn case occurred in Michigan. The
National Law Journal (Staff, 1986) noted the case of *Buwa* v. *Smith*, in
which a licensed marriage and family counselor was found guilty for failure
to warn the police or the potential victim of a client's threat to murder his
estranged wife. Indeed, the client did kill his wife and wound his brother-in-
law, which whom he had wrongfully assumed that his wife was having an
affair. The couple's four children were in the mobile home at the time of
the murder. Two of the children witnessed the killing.

A wrongful death suit was filed by the wife's estate and the four children. The two children who witnessed the murder sought damages on the
"bystander theory" of harm. The complainant's attorney argued that the
counselor had a legal duty to warn the victim, since she was readily identifiable. The attorney added that the failure to warn was a breach of the professional code of ethics for marriage and family counselors. The final
charge alleged that the therapist was negligent because of his failure to refer the case to a psychiatrist. The attorney claimed that the therapist was
not properly qualified to treat a violent patient.

The father was sentenced to 30 to 50 years for the murder of his estranged wife and a concurrent 30- to 50-year term for assault on the
brother-in-law. The court awarded $2.8 million in damages from the fa-
ther's property to the four children.

It is the task of the therapist to determine if the client presents a clear
threat to the safety of others. Balancing the duty to warn and the therapist-
client relationship and confidentiality boundaries is very delicate. In
McIntosh v. *Milano* (1979), the court found that even though the duty to
warn might make treatment less effective by breaking therapist-client confidence, it would not outweigh the public interest in protection from danger (*McIntosh* at 512–13).

The *Tarasoff* case forces the therapist to consider the ramifications
of therapeutic responsibility to the client and society in general. Therefore,

the clinician might wish to consider the following guidelines when determining the possibility of enforcing the duty to warn.

1. *Inform the client of the therapist's duty to warn.* The therapist must notify the client, preferably at the initiation of treatment, of the legal requirements to warn authorities and the potential victim if the client reveals abusive/violent threats or actions to third parties. Some malpractice attorneys advise that with extremely dangerous clients, the therapist is safer from litigation if he or she tells the client that it would be unwise to reveal any intention to do harm, rather than inform the client of the duty to warn. In other words, the (therapist may sidestep the duty-to-warn issue simply by discouraging the client from revealing anything that could be construed as threatening.)

2. *Assess the extent and development of the violent/abusive plan of action.* The (therapist must ask the client specific questions about the method by which the plan to harm would be put into action.) This includes the type of violent/abusive act that will be perpetrated, the name of the victim, the location of the intended violent act, the time when it will be carried out, the contingency plan if the initial attempt fails, and the client's sense of satisfaction with the plan.

3. *Determine the probability of the client's ability to follow through on the claim.* The therapist must review casenotes and oral history regarding the client's previous violent/abusive behavior. A client with a history of violence/abuse is more likely to cause harm.

4. *Evaluate the strength of the therapeutic relationship.* The client is more apt to permit the therapist to warn the potential victim if therapeutic rapport is well established. Although this is not always the case, a client may inform the therapist of violent thoughts as a cry for help.

5. *Document the client's plan and the therapist's intervention fully.* When working with violent/abusive clients, it is essential to note their repetitive patterns of behavior, the trigger mechanisms that cause the violent thoughts, and the interventions that are effective in quelling the ideation and/or acting out. (Documentation is also essential to safeguard the therapist against legal claims the client might make concerning breach of confidentiality.)

(Duty to warn applies equally to suicidal patients.) Lawsuits have ensued because therapists failed to take precautions to prevent suicide, either through abandonment or failure to hospitalize. Some inexperienced therapists have encountered liability because of improperly diagnosing or missing clinical cues from suicidal patients. The (primary issues in assessing therapist liability are predictability and control.) Could the therapist have foreseen any suicidal risk? Did the therapist attempt to control the client?

Since the best predictors of suicide are (1) previous attempts, (2) a plan, and (3) the means, therapists often seek this type of information from clients.

Typically, the courts are more apt to take action against practitioners whose clients are in inpatient units rather than in outpatient treatment. If a client has been actively suicidal in a psychiatric unit, the therapist is expected to note the behavior and take full precautions to guarantee the individual's safety. Failure to exercise all protective measures when a client is clearly suicidal is lack of due care.

The Acquired Immune Deficiency Syndrome (AIDS) epidemic that developed in the 1980s has presented a perplexing duty-to-warn problem for the family therapist. The therapist who treats people who have AIDS or are HIV positive is placed in conflict between the rights of the victim and the safety of those with whom the victim has had sexual contact. Although no clear legal or ethical guidelines have been established as yet, people with AIDS who engage in unprotected sex and who refuse to inform their partners of the illness certainly present a clear and imminent danger to others.

In situations where the therapist has taken a complete sexual history and is certain of the diagnosis, the marriage and family therapist should advise and inform the client of the need to inform those with whom he or she has had sexual contact. If the client refuses to engage in protected sex or inform the sexual partner(s) of his or her condition, the therapist may wish to consider notifying any identifiable person who may be in danger of contracting the disease. In jurisdictions where there is no legal duty to warn, the therapist may want to inform public health officials of the client's illness or at least seek legal advice on whether to inform a possible victim.

Because individuals presenting themselves for marital or family therapy may have both personal and interrelationship problems, the marriage and family therapist must determine the treatment plan that best benefits the client. In some instances, the family may be able to proceed in therapy while a single family member is obtaining individual therapy from another practitioner. In other cases, the family may refuse to permit individual therapy to run concurrently with family treatment; the marriage and family therapist must then make a difficult clinical decision on whether continuing family therapy is the best course. Another option is to stop family therapy in favor of referring the more distressed person to individual therapy.

Whatever the decision, the therapist must attend to the degree of distress in each of the presenting individuals. If one family member is overtly suicidal, the marriage and family therapist has the duty to warn other significant individuals within the family system of the potential risk and the possible need for hospitalization of the distressed family member.

Woody and Woody (1988) affirm the impact of public policy on therapeutic work. They note that even though concern for client violence might lead to less than ideal treatment, the clinician has a legal duty to warn and protect the client and/or the public.

> Marriage and family therapists must accept the fact that they practice in the context of a system larger than the client-therapist system. In life-threatening situations, this larger system includes persons other than the client who may be at risk, agencies of social control that may be an appropriate resource, and the society itself that mandates protection of life through law. The profession can ill afford to ignore the standard of care imposed on all mental health professionals. (p. 136)

Failure to Commit

Marriage and family therapists are typically not faced with the dilemma of committing severely disturbed individuals. At times, however, the commitment may be a most appropriate action. Family therapists will certainly experience pushy, demanding family members who feel that the only alternative for an actively ill spouse or child is hospitalization. Some families may even use or attempt to use commitment as a method of ridding themselves of the so-called family nuisance. Those therapists who work from a systems approach may be adverse to dealing with the identified patient and may want to refer the case or the individual to a nonsystems treatment agent. If, however, the therapist decides to continue working with the family, the duty to involuntarily commit a dangerous client must be understood. Unlike the duty to warn, the duty to commit arises even when there is no foreseeable victim. Certainly, the therapist may follow alternative treatment plans, such as voluntary hospitalization, day or night hospital, or daily individual therapeutic sessions. If such a decision is made, the therapist should thoroughly document his or her rationale. Indeed, to avoid the possibility of malpractice, the therapist must take every necessary precaution to assure that treatment decisions do not result in harm to the patient or others.

Compliance with the duty to commit is judged on the *psychotherapist judgment rule*, which binds the therapist to good faith and professional standards. This rule, which came from *Currie* v. *United States* (Staff, 1987), states:

> Under such a "psychotherapist judgment rule," the court would not allow liability to be imposed on therapists for simple errors in judgment. Instead, the court would examine the "good faith, independence and thoroughness" of a psychotherapist's decision not to

commit a patient (*Joy*, 692 F. 2d at 888). Factors in reviewing such good faith include the competence and training of the reviewing psychotherapists, whether the relevant documents and evidence were adequately, promptly and independently reviewed, whether the advice or opinion of another therapist was obtained, whether an evaluation was made in light of the proper legal standards for commitment, and whether other evidence of good faith exists.

The psychotherapist judgment rule attempts to avoid imposing liability on therapists who have made errors in judgment but have followed proper professional standards. The rule compels the therapist to determine if the dangerous patient is appropriate for involuntary commitment. Legally, the therapist may not be the person responsible for the actual commitment. However, the therapist must initiate the process. State-appointed authorities will make the final decision on commitment.

As a practical rule, therapists with dangerous patients should consult with other professional colleagues and document the consultation. Careful consideration must be given to the legal and professional ramifications of treating dangerous patients. All decisions regarding patient treatment must be made in good faith on the basis of a thorough review of all the relevant documentation.

The treating clinician has numerous burdens: determining the degree of danger a patient represents, warning potential victims or authorities of probable harm by the patient to himself or herself or others, assessing commitment possibilities, and maintaining therapeutic rapport. Although the law speaks to all of these issues, the various courts have ruled in many different ways on the same topics. In matters as crucial as these, every marriage and family therapist and/or researcher must have an established relationship with an attorney who knows the laws relevant to therapeutic practice.

Sexual Relations and Clients

The therapeutic relationship is a very personal one, based on trust and confidentiality. It is not coincidental that the intensity of the therapeutic relationship, especially in individual therapy, creates an intimacy that may be mistaken for a romance. The therapist must point out that the feelings the client is experiencing are part of the *transference* phenomena; not to do so is to shirk one's professional responsibility and invite problems.

The ethical and legal ramifications of sexual relations with clients are noteworthy. Most mental health professional codes of ethics prohibit sexual relations with clients, whether the sexual overture is made by the therapist or the patient. Most state regulatory boards provide for sanctions against practitioners who engage in intimate relationships with clients.

Despite the clear admonition against such practices, an interview reported in *Behavior Today* (1987) states that 7% to 10% of male therapists and about 1.5% of female therapists engage in sex with their clients. Some commentators believe these figures to be unrealistically low.

Depending on the nature of the sexual exploitation and the circumstances surrounding the therapist-client relationship, the client may have grounds for filing a malpractice suit. The courts and mental health professionals agree that sexual relationships between doctor or therapist and client is a breach of the duty to care, and thus establishing liability for civil action. There is disagreement on whether a therapist can be held liable if the sexual relationship occurred after termination of treatment, reflecting in part the sentiments of different schools of therapeutic treatment. For example, a psychoanalytic therapist may contend that sexual relationships with clients can never be initiated, while a humanistic therapist may contend that such relationships are allowable as soon as therapy has terminated.

Sell, Gottlieb, and Schoenfeld (1986) conducted a survey in which the chairs of ethics committees and the executive secretaries of the state boards of psychologist examiners were asked to list the number of complaints of sexual impropriety between psychologist and client. The findings and the actions taken were also requested. The results of the study indicated that state boards and ethics committees were very likely to rule against practitioners who engage in sexual activities with clients after termination of treatment. The duration of time that elapsed after treatment did not determine the disposition of the case. Unfortunately, the criteria for the findings were variable and determined on a case-by-case basis. As a result of their findings, Sell et al. contended that sexual relationships, even with former clients, were exploitive regardless of the elapsed time from treatment.

Few states have passed laws making sexual relations between doctor or therapist and client criminal. To bring suit against a professional, the client must show that coercion (e.g., via hypnosis, drugs) was used to lower resistance and thereby create compliance. Thus, only overt sexual exploitation cases ever result in criminal prosecution.

Marriage and family therapists who do not conduct individual psychotherapy may not be as apt to encounter these types of problems. However, several sexual relationship cases are currently being litigated because a marriage counselor had an affair with the spouse of the client (see, e.g., *Omer* v. *Edgren* [1984]; *Cotton* v. *Kambly* [1980]; *Roy* v. *Hartogs* [1976]; *Zipkin* v. *Freeman* [1968]). To date, the courts have varied on their decisions regarding whether a marriage counselor can be held liable in these instances. In states where fornication and adultery are illegal practices, therapists may find themselves under prosecution for sexual involvement with clients or spouses of clients.

In *Gasper* v. *Lighthouse* (1987), Nicole and Daniel Gasper sought the assistance of a marriage counselor. After several sessions, Daniel discovered Nicole and the marriage counselor were having an affair, which led to the couple's divorce. Daniel Gasper filed suit against the counselor, alleging professional negligence, breach of fiduciary duty, breach of contract, and intentional infliction of emotional distress. The court concluded that the plaintiff was in actuality "refitting" these torts to create an affection tort, which Maryland had abolished (*Gasper* at 1360). The court also stated that while the counselor might be subject to tort liability for not exercising reasonable care and for breach of the patient-psychiatrist contract, liability will not stand where adultery is the basis for the claim. The court also stated that the claim for breach of the marital contract could not stand because the basis of the action was destruction of the marriage (*Gasper* at 1361).

In a similar case in California, however—*Richard F. H.* v. *Larry H. D.* (1988)—the appellate court dealt with the allegations differently. The claimant alleged that a psychiatrist was negligent by deviating from appropriate standards of professional care and had committed fraud by representing that he would act in his patient's best interests when he actually used his position to seduce the patient's wife. In this case, the court agreed that the plaintiff suffered emotional distress.

Review of the various legal cases before the courts shows that the definition changes regarding who is the client and to whom the therapist owes the professional duty. Systems-oriented therapists accept the concept that the family/couple is the client and are keenly aware that sexual exploitation of one member of the system is the same as exploiting the entire system.

Although most sexual exploitation cases report therapists making overtures to clients, in some cases, the reverse has been true. These situations can be quite delicate, since the client may genuinely believe that the therapeutic relationship is an intimate, loving one that warrants sexual activity between therapist and client. Such situations are more apt to occur with individual clients who were sexually exploited in childhood, since these individuals are often uncertain about their sexual boundaries and misperceive the caring actions of the therapist. The marriage and family therapist must be gentle but firm in setting the therapeutic limits and in interpreting the probable reasons for the client's feelings and behaviors. When the therapist handles the situation properly, the treatment process can proceed with insight and growth.

Family therapy requires dealing with sexual matters. Whether these issues are specific to psychosexual development, sexual relations between spouses, or incest and sexual abuse, the marital and family therapist is apt to encounter strong emotions and misperceptions regarding the therapist-client relationship. The therapist must be prepared to deal with questions and feelings that arise in this context. This is no place for naiveté or minimal professional standards of care. Should the therapist note that he or she is becoming attracted to a client, supervision should be sought immediately. If the case becomes too problematic, the therapist should not hesitate to make an appropriate referral. The more aware the therapist, the more successful the treatment outcome, and the less prone the therapist is to liability.

Supervision

Effective supervision of students, trainees, and fellow mental health practitioners is essential for professional as well as legal reasons. The doctrine of *respondeat superior* ("let the master respond") refers to the vicarious liability that a supervisor has for any people who work under his or her direction. Marriage and family therapists who supervise others' work must attend to the treatment plan, the facilitation of treatment, and the continuation of positive therapeutic rapport between the supervisee and the client in order to avoid legal jeopardy under the *respondeat superior* doctrine.

Even though the supervisor assumes legal liability for the supervisee, the supervisee is still liable for his or her actions with the client. Therefore, if the client of a supervisee sues, full damages may be sought from the supervisor and the supervisee. Even if the supervisor is not found to be negligent, he or she may be remanded to pay damages because of secondary or vicarious liability. When this occurs, the supervisor may then sue the supervisee to recover the financial loss.

Problems may arise in supervision when the supervisor does not set a standard procedure for review of cases. This standard procedure should consist of the following:

1. a clearly defined outline of the frequency with which supervision must occur (e.g., weekly, bimonthly);
2. a method of identifying client problems;
3. careful delineation of the treatment plan;
4. description of how to implement the treatment plan; and
5. discussion of desired and expected outcomes, as well as probable pitfalls in accomplishing the treatment plan.

If at all possible, the supervisee should provide the supervisor with either a video- or audiotape of the sessions on which the supervisee is reporting. Although it is difficult to monitor, the supervisor should assess whether the supervisee is carrying out the supervisory directions. This may be accomplished by sitting in on a therapeutic session, meeting in a consultative role with the client and therapist, or observing the treatment session through a one-way mirror. From a liability standpoint, this direct supervisor/supervisee-client contact reduces the possibility of supervisee error.

Whenever supervision occurs, the supervisee must inform the client of the name of the supervisor. The supervisor should meet with the client to establish rapport, assure confidentiality, and answer any questions that the client might have regarding the supervisory relationship. At this point, the supervisor must be careful to avoid triangulation between client and supervisee, which may be the aim of some highly manipulative clients.

By far, the most legally dangerous situation occurs when a supervisor signs off on insurance documents as though he or she has been the treating therapist when in fact the supervisee has filled that role. Many insurance companies have filed fraud suits against therapists who do so. A therapist who signs off as the treating therapist is verifying that he or she actually performed the therapeutic service and thus assumes full liability for the work. This practice eliminates the therapist from any protection that merely supervising the work would have given. In order to avoid prosecution, therapists who supervise practicing clinicians must sign the insurance report noting the professional relationship with the supervisee (e.g., sign off "Terry Grove, Ph.D., supervising marriage and family therapist for Stacy McKay, M.S.W.").

Recordkeeping

The fundamental purpose of recordkeeping is to document treatment, evaluate patient progress, and note any peculiarities specific to treatment response. Previously, therapists wrote notes with little regard for actual content. In fact, most therapists kept notes brief to assure client confidentiality in the event of subpoena. However, malpractice suits have sustained decisions against therapists for keeping incomplete notes.

The general opinion on case records is that the notes must be complete enough that any clinician could immediately take over treatment with a client if the original therapist were physically or mentally unable to continue. In one case, *Whitree v. State of New York* (1968), the court said that the records were so deficient that they contributed to inadequate treatment because they did not provide direction for suitable care.

Ideally, records should provide a clear explanation of the client's problem, the mode of treatment, possible dangers in working with the client, previous treatment strategies, and whether they were effective. The material should be written so that any practitioner reading the notes can understand the quality of service and the client response to the treatment. A complete record should include all written contracts between client and therapist, release-of-information forms and notes from previous therapists, progress notes, notes pertaining to any medication, and documentation of any unusual events, such as emergencies or acting-out behavior, that may result in liability for the clinician (Hall, 1987).

Federal, state, and professional conduct regulations specify the length of time that records should be kept. Therefore, it is essential for the mental health practitioner to consult the relevant organizations to determine the duration required. A rule of thumb is that therapists should retain records for at least as long as the contents may benefit the client and for the duration of the statute of limitations for malpractice actions in the state (VandeCreek, 1986).

Good recordkeeping helps the therapist remain aware of client progress, enhancing the evaluation of the effectiveness of therapy and documenting any unusual occurrences in treatment that may be invaluable in further therapeutic work. Since inadequate documentation has been construed to mean inadequate care, the therapist is well advised to keep clear, accurate records (Stromberg, 1987).

Conclusion

The authors cannot overstate the necessity of therapists' understanding the legal issues impacting marriage and family therapy. For years, therapists have operated with little awareness of or education in legal issues. In today's society, such ignorance is dangerous; the treatment arena has changed significantly over the past fifteen years or so. In fact, laws exist that govern licensure, third-party reimbursement, patient rights, public protection from potentially harmful or dangerous patients, and professional corporations. If therapists lack awareness of these laws, they expose themselves to liability and potential disciplinary sanction. Failure to stay abreast of the state and federal laws governing the practice of marriage and family therapy is no defense against substandard practice.

Certainly, no text can inform the reader of all the rules, regulations, and laws governing marriage and family therapy. In fact, laws are constantly reviewed, revised, and developed to protect the public and assure fair and accurate treatment standards. The material presented in this chapter serves to acquaint the reader with legal issues that could affect his or her practice.

Hopefully, the information will spur marriage and family therapists to think through the rationale for their actions so that legal problems can be avoided and sound legal judgments can be made. Those who have legal questions are well advised to seek legal counsel.

CHAPTER FOUR

Working with the Courts and Attorneys

The legal system is adversarial and critical. Therapy is based on unconditional positive regard. Clinicians are taught to accept the client without prejudice. Therefore, the therapist who chooses to work forensically must have the attitude, demeanor, and personality requisite for the work. There is no question that this type of work is stressful and demanding. The therapist who engages in forensic work must not only be detail oriented and able to extract relevant facts from emotional discussions and argumentative clients; he or she must also be able to withstand the challenge of cross-examining attorneys who seek to undo the forensic therapist's testimony.

A therapist must have the right training to become an expert in forensic practice. This means knowledge of treatment as well as the laws applicable to the issues on which he or she testifies. The marriage and family therapist who is interested in forensic work can certainly find legal areas where his or her expertise is invaluable.

1. *Child custody*—Present trends in child custody litigation require an independent practitioner to assist the court in determining who is the most fit custodial parent. Clinical assessment in evaluating the parents and the children socially, emotionally, and personally is part of the marriage and family therapist's training and a logical arena in which to participate.

2. *Divorce mediation*—This field is expanding rapidly as a result of the increase in marital dissolutions. Many attorneys request the assistance of marriage and family therapists in bringing divorcing families to a more civilized resolution of an extremely painful process.

3. *Severance of parental rights*—Attorneys need accurate assessment of parenting skills and styles to determine if a child is being adequately parented. The marriage and family therapist can evaluate parental behaviors and disability factors that may make individuals unfit parents.

4. *Adoption*—Assessment of the requisite behaviors needed to parent is a major factor in determining a couple's suitability to become adoptive parents. The marriage and family therapist is cognizant of these characteristics and knows how to evaluate them objectively.

5. *Spouse abuse*—Court decisions revolve around the battered-wife syndrome. As most family therapists know, violent/abusive families are representative of a pathological system. Testimony on the factors supporting such a system and effective treatment strategies can be provided by the marriage and family therapist.

6. *Social issues*—The effects of pornography, media aggression, AIDS, child and elderly abuse, and family stability among absent or returned war veterans are just a few of the human problems on which family therapists can testify with authority.

7. *Severe psychological damage*—Clients who are involved in major accidents, medical malpractice, or posttraumatic stress suffer emotional damage that impacts on them and their family members. Therapists working with this population are aware of the time and expense these distressed individuals cost the family. Marriage and family therapists with a systemic orientation can inform attorneys of these factors as the attorney seeks to recover appropriate damages for the client and his or her family.

8. *Professional malpractice*—Although not all areas covered in malpractice are relevant to marriage and family treatment, the marriage and family practitioner can deliver expert testimony on the topics that are.

Marriage and family therapists serve the legal system best as impartial witnesses who represent their knowledge accurately and in a straightforward manner. Those who become strongly invested in one side of any issue and become advocates participate in the adversarial process and function more as the judge and jury than an expert in their field of study. It is the court's task to make the final decision regarding the outcome of the legal proceedings. To that end, the marriage and family therapist in forensic practice provides only the best up-to-date clinical, evaluative, and research information on the nature of the case.

Case Preparation

Lack of preparation is the biggest downfall of forensic therapists. It is the responsibility of both the expert witness and the attorney with whom the witness is working to prepare for all possible contingencies in the upcoming legal case. Horsley and Carlova (1983) characterize two types of witnesses: the *fact* type and the *opinion* type. The fact witness reports client history, test results, diagnosis, present condition, and possible prognosis. The opinion witness offers facts, observations, clinical experience, and knowledge of similar cases to aid the court in reaching a disposition. Although the marriage and family therapist will probably be called upon to act as an opinion witness, it is wise to check with the attorney to understand exactly how the testimony is to be used.

Familiarity with courtroom procedures is important to anyone serving as an expert witness. Nietzel and Dillehay (1986) recommend that the therapist master the techniques of courtroom testimony by rehearsing with attorneys who use both direct- and cross-examination techniques. As an adjunct to learning, they propose the use of videotaped sessions to review and modify performance when necessary. Finally, they suggest that the expert undergo the same pressure, aggressiveness, and emotional conflict in the rehearsal as he or she would on the witness stand. By mastering the art of remaining calm under strong adversarial attack, the expert witness will feel more secure in the real courtroom experience.

A thoroughly prepared expert keeps a detailed record of contact and consultations with the defendant and other interviewees. Included in the record are the dates, times, and locations of contact; names of interviewees and others present; contents of the various interviews; and any formal assessments and written reports regarding the defendant. Preparation such as this will ensure that the therapist's knowledge of the case will be presented as being orderly and precise. It also permits the witness to integrate the findings and prepare testimony that is presented in a polished narrative fashion.

The therapist should not hesitate to point out relevant information to the attorney who has contracted for expert services. After all, the therapist knows more about marriage and family theory and practice than does the attorney. The therapist should anticipate possible opposition to his or her testimony and prepare retorts working with the attorney. It might even be helpful to develop a list of terms and questions that both attorneys might use during deposition or trial proceedings. Being prepared means knowing the literature on the case, as well as the actual therapeutic history on the client. By preparing the case as fully as possible, both the therapist and the testimony will appear professional and convincing to the court.

Quite often, a deposition (formal sworn statement) is taken before a case goes to trial. A deposition is held away from the courtroom and therefore may seem to be less authoritative or official than a hearing. The deposition, however, is just as important as the hearing; to assume otherwise is a mistake. In fact, the therapist who is asked to give a deposition is bound by the same responsibilities and penalties as a witness in court. The purpose of the deposition is to acquaint both sides with the facts and arguments and to allow both attorneys an opportunity to prepare rebuttals to the material raised in the case (Horsley & Carlova, 1983). Any material presented in the deposition may be used in court. Therefore, presenting the same opinions in the deposition and in court is essential.

Sometimes, a case may not go to court for months or years. Certainly, no expert witness is expected to remember what was said over such a long period of time. In such instances, it is recommended that the therapist thoroughly review his or her deposition before testifying. If after rereading the material, the therapist has a different opinion than originally stated, he or she must inform the attorney immediately. During discussion with the attorney, the therapist must specify his or her rationale for the change of opinion. It is also wise to strategize with the attorney on how the changed information might be handled by the cross-examining attorney. It cannot be stressed strongly enough that the expert witness must be well prepared regarding case material, well coached by the attorney, and confident in the presentation of information.

Courtroom Appearance

The therapist's initial influence on the judge and jury is crucial to the impact his or her testimony will make. The courtroom is a traditional arena in which both language and dress are expected to be customary and appropriate. It is no place for flamboyant behavior, hostile language, or chicanery. Even in the face of strong attacks by the cross-examining attorney, the expert must remain poised, calm, and self-assured. An attorney's techniques to distract, distort, and incite should not instigate argumentative or passive responses from the expert, nor should he or she feel intimidated. The attorney is simply performing his or her job using the skills of the trade. Many expert witnesses come to realize that rough treatment from an attorney is a good indication that the testimony is damaging the attorney's case.

Brodsky and Poythress (1985) discuss the importance of *impression management* on the witness stand, which refers to controlling both verbal and nonverbal responses in order to make the desired impression. They propose the following behaviors to effect favorable responses from the judge and jury.

1. When called to the witness stand, convey a sense of comfort and familiarity in the courtroom by walking confidently toward the stand.
2. When giving answers to questions, begin each response with the

attorney's name (e.g., "Mr. Rogers, I assume that you . . .")

3. When responding to examination, make eye contact with the jurors. Such behavior permits the jurors to feel included in the testimony and gives the witness nonverbal feedback concerning juror opinion.
4. When delivering testimony, minimize the use of jargon or professional-specific language.
5. When speaking, use direct, unequivocal speech.
6. When responding, keep the answers brief and specific to the question.
7. When giving opinions, support testimony with the documents and case information that is available. The written material is the foundation upon which testimony will be judged. The expert witness is not an advocate; therefore, the evidence must be defensible.
8. When leaving the stand, assemble material brought along in an easy manner, smile and nod to the jurors, and descend from the stand. If appropriate, shake the hands of both attorneys; then walk confidently to your seat.

The marriage and family therapist is familiar with the systemic approach to understanding context and problems. The legal process, on the other hand, is linear in its search for answers. Therefore, the therapist/witness may find the examination process to be victimizing and withholding. Most family therapists know that the method by which to enter a faulty system consists of joining and engaging. Resistance is merely the method by which the family seeks to remain homeostatic. Armed with this understanding of systemic interaction, the marriage and family therapist can enter the courtroom much as he or she does a family, which can serve to reduce his or her anxiety.

Marriage and family therapists have other very useful therapeutic tools that are applicable to courtroom testimony. Primarily, these tools consist of the communication skills the therapist has mastered through training. An attorney uses the same communicative skills but to a different end. By far, the most difficult problems come from the cross-examining attorney. The opposing counsel will be argumentative and turbulent in an effort to throw the therapist's testimony off track. This behavior is no different than that of a blustery client who attempts to prevent the therapist from uncovering family secrets or weaknesses. The appropriate tactic is to refrain from attacking the lawyer. The therapist should remain calm and friendly and proceed with the testimony. If appropriate, he or she may use reframing techniques to clarify or strengthen the testimony. He or she should continue to point out factual material. When an attorney poses hypothetical questions designed to stop the obvious progress of the testimony, the therapist should respond, "Mr. Anderson, given that set of cir-

cumstances the response to your question would be . . . However, in talking
about the defendant, that hypothesis does not apply because . . ."

Attorneys use nonverbal cues to intimidate witnesses. It is not unusual
for them to glare, scowl, or raise an eyebrow of suspicion while the witness
is testifying. Effective expert witnesses are not distracted by these gestures.
Marriage and family therapists are very used to children squirming and
adults grimacing when questions become difficult or insinuating. Body
language is one of many cues that the accomplished therapist uses for information during the therapeutic interview. When applied in the courtroom, the attorney's nonverbal language provides information regarding
testimony. By checking and rechecking these cues and by attending to the
pattern of the attorney's metalanguage, the expert witness gains assurance
in the cross-examination.

Another very common communication tactic used by attorneys is the
"yes set." Milton Erickson, the seminal hypnotist, used this technique to
lead people into hypnotic trance. In the courtroom, an attorney develops
a line of reasoning that leads the witness into responding with all "yes" or
"no" answers. The questions appear innocuous and banal. Thus, the witness
generally becomes lulled into giving the same response to each in a long
list of questions without thinking about the answer. Then when the witness
is entranced, the lawyer asks a significant question. Unwittingly, the witness
answers in the same manner in which he or she answered the preceding
questions, perhaps appearing stumped and less self-confident.

A typical cross-examination using the "yes set" might go like this:

Attorney: Dr. Edelby, you know Mr. Sachs, don't you?

Dr. Edelby: Yes, Mr. Baker.

Attorney: Dr. Edelby, you have worked with Mr. Sachs for three years?

Dr. Edelby: Yes, Mr. Baker.

Attorney: During that time, you met with Mr. Sachs, his wife, and his
children, right?

Dr. Edelby: Yes, Mr. Baker.

Attorney: When you talked with his wife, she told you that they were
experiencing problems with parenting and communication, correct?

Dr. Edelby: Yes, that's correct, Mr. Baker.

Attorney: Dr. Edelby, it's true that you specialize in family communication and parenting?

Dr. Edelby: Yes, that's true, Mr. Baker.

Attorney: Well then, Dr. Edelby, surely you knew that parenting a
drug-abusing child would stress the marriage?

Dr. Edelby: Certainly, Mr. Baker.

Attorney: Then Dr. Edelby, you knew this marriage had no chance of
enduring?

Dr. Edelby: Yes, . . . er, . . . I mean no. I mean no therapist can—predict . . .
Attorney: That will be all, Dr. Edelby.

As the example shows, the attorney asked what appeared to be innocent questions. The therapist responded courteously and with no elaboration. Then when the therapist appeared entrapped in the "yes set" response mode, the attorney asked the question that revealed the witness as lacking in perception and diagnostic skill. The key to responding well on the stand is active listening to both the verbal statements and the nonverbal cues.

Generally, the opposing attorney's task is to discredit an expert witness in some way. One of the standard techniques involves pointing out that the witness lacks appropriate training or credentials. An attorney might claim that a marriage and family therapist does not receive training in relevant mental health issues, since he or she is neither a psychologist nor psychiatrist. Should such accusations be made, the best response is for the therapist to simply acknowledge the difference in credentials; he or she should not attempt to justify education or training. The attorney will attempt to show that the witness did not perform all necessary clinical interviews and assessments or gather all relevant material to the case. Again, by asserting that the investigation was carried out in a well-established and rational manner, the therapist can dispel such challenges.

The cross-examining attorney may challenge the expert witness' knowledge with citations that present opposing points of view. In responding to the information, the therapist should simply acknowledge the opposing viewpoints, but not attempt to discredit or undercut the attorney. The cross-examining attorney is likely to use his or her own experts whose theoretical framework may be radically different. Some of these practitioners may even criticize their colleague's practice as being "beneath the standard of care." Such statements can inflame and disorient the proceedings. In these instances, the cross-examining attorney may attempt to point out that psychology is an imperfect art and too primitive in its tools of research and analysis to be considered relevant to the issues on trial. The therapist must remember one of the cardinal rules of family therapy: Go with the resistance! The credible witness accepts that there will be challenges to all opinions posed during the trial. No witness can know everything about a specific case or have read all documentation on the subject under investigation. Finally, no case will be totally decided on the merits of the expert witness' testimony.

To summarize, the family therapist who wants to be an expert witness will certainly experience pressure under examination. However, remembering the following rules will help the witness survive cross-examination.

1. Be fully prepared before taking the witness stand.
2. Listen carefully to the questions and narrative of both attorneys. Pay attention to any imprecision or distortion that occurs.
3. Remain calm and confident even when harassed. Do not allow counsel to intimidate.
4. Take time to assess the question. Do not answer until the question is completely understood.
5. Be aware of "yes set" questions.
6. Admit to lack of knowledge when appropriate. Don't appear defeated or distressed if unfamiliar with the reference material that the attorney is posing.
7. Do not argue or disagree with an attorney in court. When appropriate, agree with the attorney.
8. If necessary, ask the judge for assistance when the questioning becomes obscure or difficult.

Liability for Expert Witnesses

Therapists who assume the role of expert witness may have to make negative or adverse comments about patients or clients for whom the court has ordered evaluation and assessment. The court protects witnesses to ensure that the judicial process can function unimpeded by civil liability. In *Kahn v. Burman* (1987), the Michigan court reasoned that if physicians faced potential civil liability for preparing pretrial reports, few would be willing to evaluate malpractice claims in advance of the trial. In *Jordan v. Kelly* (1984), the court affirmed the district court's entry of summary judgment in a case against two psychiatrists who were charged with breach of confidentiality for statements in a child custody case. After the psychiatrists testified at several hearings in which the plaintiff was involved, the plaintiff sued the psychiatrists for unauthorized disclosure of confidential information. In affirming the summary judgment, the court noted that the psychiatrists had testified in several prior hearings, and in none of those hearings did the plaintiff object. Therefore, the court held that the plaintiffs waived their privilege by failing to object (*Jordan* at 2).

The immunity applies to expert testimony where the witness makes comments specific to the case. The immunity is suspended when the witness takes the stand to harm or defame an individual. Judicial immunity refers to material revealed on the witness stand. Information shared with attorneys outside the court is not immune from legal action. Therefore, therapists must proceed with caution when deciding whether to share confidential information within the legal system.

It is comforting that in this time of excessive litigation, protection is extended to expert witnesses. Without freedom from suit, the expert witness would be vulnerable to legal action from those represented, as well as those who seek to harass or defame for whatever reason. Thus, the rule of privilege protects the witness and ensures that the court can obtain professional testimony.

Figuring the Witness Fee

Because being an expert witness is difficult and time consuming, the work deserves honest compensation. Fees are based on whether the expert is a fact or opinion witness. Generally, the opinion witness can set his or her own fee, while the fact witness is entitled to the basic witness fee. If the therapist who is acting as a fact witness is asked to testify on therapeutic opinions, he or she can request more than the basic fee.

It is customary for expert witnesses to compute their fees on an office-hour basis. Included in the fee are the hours spent researching the case, interviewing and assessing the client, reviewing psychological and/or legal documents, attending pretrial conferences, giving deposition testimony, and appearing in court. Fees should be reasonable. Generally, the fact witness can figure the fee at one and a half times the hourly rate. The expert witness fee is usually figured at twice the office hourly rate.

The therapist should arrange with the client and attorney how the bill will be paid and who is responsible for the payment (attorney or client). Some therapists use a formal contract that stipulates fee structure, service, method of payment (e.g., total amount prior to the hearing, installment payments), and contingencies if the case is settled out of court or dismissed. The expert witness who considers all these factors and makes necessary arrangements prior to accepting a case will seldom have trouble with fee collection. In fact, noting how the client and attorney deal with the fee issue will indicate how they will behave during the proceedings.

Being an expert witness can be challenging and rewarding work, but it definitely is not a job for the fainthearted. The work is taxing and very different from marriage and family therapy. Although the skills are the same, the context in which they are employed is very different. Emotions are used to defend and discredit people, body language is employed to intimidate, and words are used to harass. For those who enjoy the challenge of the adversarial process, expert testimony can be enjoyable and rewarding. Those who prefer harmony and congeniality should not expect to find it consulting for the legal system.

CHAPTER FIVE

Family Law
and the Marriage
and Family Therapist

The courts recognize that mental health practitioners are knowledgeable in the treatment and resolution of family-related problems. Indeed, in no other segment of law are mental health professionals regarded as so integral to the legal process as in family law. Attorneys dealing with adoption, severance of parental rights, child custody, and divorce frequently rely on therapists' expertise to assist them in making difficult determinations. As stated in the previous chapter, the marriage and family therapist who wishes to work in the legal system can find many challenges and much satisfaction.

Recent trends in social behavior have challenged existing family law. States are revising their statutes with regard to the definition of marriage, the rights of consenting adults, and the treatment of children. Traditional adversarial procedures, once uniformly accepted as the standard method to deal with civil litigation, are being challenged as inappropriate and even detrimental for certain family problems (i.e., custody, domestic violence, and divorce). New techniques of investigation involve the use of court workers whose specific duties include interviewing the defendant, relatives, friends, and other significant people involved in the legal dispute. These workers then make independent recommendations to the court on the pending litigation. Some jurisdictions even have a panel of mental health experts who may be called as "friends of the court" in especially difficult cases.

Knowledge of family law is essential even for therapists who choose not to serve within the legal system. During the course of therapy, legal issues related to family problems may surface, and the competent therapist must rely on more than a superficial awareness of family laws in his or her state. Simply referring the client to an appropriate attorney or informing the proper legal authorities requires knowledge beyond maintaining therapeutic rapport or facilitating change. Of course, the marriage and family therapist is not expected to give legal advise. Nonetheless, the therapist must consider the legal ramifications of some treatment recommendations and be prepared to discuss these issues within the therapeutic session.

Maintaining a working knowledge of family law is not easy. Family law differs from state to state and is in constant change. When legal questions arise, the therapist should not hesitate to get consultation. If the law is too complex or written in legal jargon, he or she should ask an attorney to interpret it. The therapist should not attempt to give legal advise or clarify law for a client. Such practices leave the therapist open to charges of practicing law without a license. Forming a good consulting relationship with a knowledgeable local attorney is part of good practice.

Family Law

Marriage

The freedom to marry is a personal right recognized in case law Loving v. Virginia (1967) and through the Uniform Marriage and Divorce Act (1970). In Loving v. Virginia, the Supreme Court held that miscegenation statutes designed to prevent marriages between persons of different races violated the Constitution, based on the premise that the right to marry is a basic civil liberty (Loving at 1824). The Court went on to state that the freedom to marry must not be restricted by insidious racial discrimination, as contained in the Fourteenth Amendment, which places the right to marry with the individual and not the state. Even convicted and incarcerated criminals are due the right of marriage (Re Carrafa [1978]).

There are few legal restrictions on marriage. Bigamy, incestuous unions, and in some states, marriage with same-sexed partners remain as specific legal restrictions on marriage. Annulment may be applied to a marriage in which one or both individuals are found mentally unstable. If it can be proven that an individual married as a result of a severe mental illness that was concealed from the other partner, the marriage can be dissolved without legal ramification.

The reasons for marriage are varied. Some individuals marry to declare their affection for each other, others marry to have children, while others seek basic companionship. Regardless of the reason, marriage is changing. Traditional male and female roles are being challenged. Some men are deciding to be househusbands, while some women are selecting careers. Financial and social demands have created dual-career families with no children and middle-income families with nannies to care for the children.

With the diversity in family constellation and purpose and the uncertainty of the continuation of the marriage, couples are entering into prenuptial agreements to guarantee that each individual's property is preserved if they divorce. Some prenuptial agreements specify the rights of parties in the case of divorce or the requirements of the parties during the marriage. Numerous restrictions may be included in a prenuptial agreement. However, whether the contract is written or oral, courts tend to recognize equitable contracts as binding and valid, given that the prenuptial agreement is untainted by fraud and entered into by two competent individuals.

A prenuptial agreement may include the following restrictions:

1. that the primary wage earner provide financial support for the family;
2. that a set amount of child support and/or alimony be paid in the event of a divorce; and
3. that there be a clear agreement as to the custody of the children should there be a divorce (Schwitzgebel & Schwitzgebel, 1980).

The restrictions ensure that the family is guaranteed continued support should the marriage dissolve. Other issues in the prenuptial contract are financial responsibilities, household activities, and other relationships. Couples who are contemplating marriage may find that these contracts take some of the romance and adventure out of marriage. While that may occur, prenuptial agreements assure equitable care and distribution of property. To that end, it is helpful to have two neutral attorneys draw up the agreement to avoid any future claim of unfairness or fraud.

In *Posner* v. *Posner* (1970), the Supreme Court of Florida affirmed the importance of a prenuptial agreement in stating:

> With divorce such a commonplace fact of life, it is fair to assume that many prospective marriage partners whose property and familial situation is such as to generate a valid antenuptial agreement settling their property rights upon the death of either, might want to consider and discuss also—and agree upon, if possible—the disposition of their property and the alimony rights of the wife in the event their marriage, despite their best efforts, should fail (*Posner* at 384).

Prenuptial agreements are becoming the norm for individuals who marry for the second or third time. Generally, these individuals have experienced divorce and loss of property and status. As a result, they are more cautious as they enter into another marriage. Not infrequently, these people seek the assistance of a marriage and family therapist to help them determine the strengths and weaknesses in the relationship and the possible pitfalls that may occur. The marriage and family therapist who works with these remarrying couples must be alert to the complexities of blending families, incomes, and emotional scars.

The prenuptial agreement is often viewed as a preventive tactic to guarantee security and safety from future emotional stress. Certainly, no prenuptial agreement can maintain a marriage or prevent lowered self-esteem. Nonetheless, in working with these individuals, therapists need to underscore the legal importance of the prenuptial agreement and the necessity of building familial harmony through ongoing family therapy and/or attention to developing a successful marital relationship.

Annulment and Divorce

Marriage can be terminated by annulment or divorce. (*Annulment* is defined as the declaration of the court that *for reasons existing at the time of the marriage,* the marriage is invalid.) Reasons cited for annulment include insanity, bigamy, fraud, duress, being under age, and incest. To claim annulment, a person must demonstrate that such a problem existed prior to marriage. Annulment is difficult to prove and therefore not frequently used to terminate a marriage.

By 1989, the divorce rate had exceeded more than one million divorces per year. Certainly, changes in the institution of marriage, financial pressures, the decision to postpone having children, plus the easier means of obtaining a divorce are all factors that add to the increased incidence of divorce.

The move toward no-fault divorce began in California and led to the development of the (Uniform Marriage and Divorce Act (1970), which permits the court to grant a divorce based on the fact that a marriage is irretrievably broken.) The act does add that either party in the action may order a conciliation conference to examine the extent to which the marriage is irretrievably broken. This requirement of conciliation prior to granting the divorce is the court's way of permitting individuals to review their decision to divorce.

Many states provide the opportunity for couples to discuss their thoughts and feelings with a domestic relations counselor. By talking with an objective third party, spouses can reassess their decision and avoid the possibility of making a mistake. In some states, conciliation interviews are conducted by court employees or court-appointed treatment counselors (often marriage and family therapists) in an effort to guarantee that the couple receives unbiased, competent help in sorting out their differences.

The effectiveness of mandatory counseling to assist couples in their decision-making effort is laudable. However, it is questionable whether intervention by a state agency or court order is beneficial. As family therapists know, trying to resolve severe differences when one partner is not amenable is almost impossible. Also, because the conciliation interview is often scheduled late in the separation process, these efforts may be futile. Most laws merely stipulate that an interview be completed by at least one spouse at some time before the divorce becomes final.

Marriage and family therapists working with divorcing couples must be familiar with divorce regulations, property settlements, child custody issues, and spousal maintenance arrangements that invariably follow in any divorce decree. The method by which each of these items is dealt with is specific to the state in which the divorce action is initiated. In states where these issues are not clearly delineated, the Uniform Marriage and Divorce Act is employed.

Legal matters relating to property refer to property acquired *after* marriage. Property held prior to marriage is usually considered separately. States usually define marital property as either *common law* or *community property.* In states where common law is the standard, each spouse owns the property that he or she brought into the marriage, as well as that generated during the marriage, either through personal income, interest or dividends from separate property, inheritance, or personal gifts.

Such distinctions are different in community property states, where anything acquired after the marriage is considered part of the community and therefore must be divided equally in divorce. This division of property applies to savings accounts, pension funds, and financial investments. Since most people have such property, financial matters can become quite complex and difficult to unwind. Therefore, it is strongly recommended that the marriage and family therapist refers couples struggling with property settlement issues to competent accountants, attorneys, or mediators who can assist in making informed decisions.

Spousal maintenance, or alimony, is not as prevalent today as in previous years. Many courts look upon alimony as an assistance to the partner who is either unemployed or underemployed. For this reason, spousal maintenance is usually limited in duration or restricted in some other manner. For example, spousal maintenance may cease when the recipient remarries or cohabitates with a person of the opposite sex. In some states, alimony is granted to help the unemployed or underemployed spouse obtain training or education to become self-sufficient. Upon completion of the learning process and commencement of employment, spousal maintenance ceases. In general, there is a movement to include alimony as part of the property settlement and not a separate factor to be decided upon in the divorce decree.

Child Custody

The emotional trauma and conflict that result in divorce begins long before the final decree is issued. Both parents and children suffer extensive emotional upheaval as a result of the arguing and fighting that typically precede divorce. Litigation, if long and protracted, has its own negative impact on everyone in the family.

The tentacles of divorce reach far beyond the nuclear family to the extended family, friends, teachers, and significant others. Quite often, it is the marriage and family therapist who encounters these dilemmas before any legal action is taken. For instance, the therapist may see a child whose misbehavior in school is symptomatic of fighting parents. The therapist's consultation with the parents may show that they are aware of the problems yet feel that they have exhausted all means of solving them (The therapist who works with the family or the child is keenly aware of the destruction that these troubled marriages and subsequent divorces create.)

Because the pain in troubled marriages affects everyone, the adults and children may experience a feeling of disconnectedness from self and others. This lack of closeness and trust makes it difficult for people to ask for support and love from each other. Consequently, both adults and children continue to drift emotionally.

Although this process is inevitable in divorcing families, it can be arrested. Among more healthy divorcing couples, the recovery from separation and divorce proceeds rather predictably through anger, grief, loneliness, and sadness (not necessarily in that order). During this time, the adults may act out their anxieties over being single, but they do not abandon their responsibility to their children or use them as pawns in battles with one another. For those adults whose marital relationship was stormy and tumultuous, however, divorce is usually a continuation of the same conflicts. Unfortunately, adults in these turbulent relationships often do use the children as a tool or prize on which to center their continued warfare. Musetto (1985) claims that "contested custody arises when parents put personal gain ahead of their children, or when parents, overwhelmed by divorce and family disruption, are so preoccupied with their own problems as to neglect their children" (p. 287).

Court hearings are held in only 10% of all divorce cases in which custody is a primary issue. These battles are often bitter and vicious. People are exposed as unfit or uncaring even when the accusations are unwarranted or unfounded. Children are pitted between competing parents and asked to choose the best custodial parent. Expert witnesses are set against each other in a test of who can present the most convincing argument. Families are deeply harmed. Not surprisingly, attorneys and judges attempt to have spouses resolve their differences through mediation or arbitration rather than ask the courts to do so.

Therapists who work in the field of child custody tend to fall into one of three categories: advocate, impartial evaluator, or mediator. As the name implies, the *advocate* supports one parent over the other. Generally, the advocate is hired by an attorney to represent the interests of the client. Therefore, the advocate's testimony is necessarily biased and circumspect. After all, the attorney and client have hired the advocate to defend the client as the best qualified parent for the child. Unfortunately, the therapist who places himself or herself in this position is only seeing one side of the picture and is not accurately representing the best interests of all parties involved in the divorce. Thus, some marriage and family therapists have justifiably labeled the advocate position as unethical.

The *impartial evaluator* (Gardner, 1986) interviews the parents and children as well as significant others such as stepparents, live-in parental surrogates, prospective stepparents, and others who can add significant information about who would be the *best* parent for the children. This information is garnered through numerous interviews designed to assess the competing adults' assets and liabilities as parents. The goal of the impartial evaluator is to make recommendations regarding everyone's best interest in the case. The examiner must remain neutral in the investigatory process. For this reason, it is strongly suggested that the therapist who performs the custody evaluation be someone other than the therapist who worked with the family prior to the litigation.

The third category of child custody worker is the *mediator*. The mediator is usually a therapist who works with the entire family to resolve the conflict and bring the most beneficial solution for all parties. The mediator uses all the skills of a successful therapist in effecting a resolution to the dispute: redirecting, reframing, clarifying, circular questioning, challenging, and so on. The mediator's role is to bring about cooperation and mutual settlement.

Regardless of which role the therapist takes, the assessment process involves a number of crucial areas. Certainly, the therapist must determine the parents' love and concern for the child. Although individuals may profess love for their children, they may not be able to demonstrate it or even know that it extends beyond physical care and shelter. The therapist must be wary of individuals who come into the investigatory setting with a list of their attributes and good deeds. Far more important than a laundry list is the expressed emotional bond that is demonstrated by the children to the parents and vice versa. Parents must be able to provide their children with direction, education, and socialization skills to live successfully in the adult world. To do this, the parent must be able to provide a stable environment and sufficient time and care to the children so as to nurture their emotional and mental well-being. All of these factors are difficult to assess because they are conclusions that must be based on actual observations. Therefore, (the marriage and family therapist must spend considerable time with the family members to make an accurate assessment.)

A good evaluation consists of interviewing each adult individually for at least one to three hours. If possible, the couple should be interviewed together to determine their degree of willingness to share parenting responsibilities. Each child should be interviewed individually and also with his or her siblings and individual parents. During this time, the therapist should collect background information such as school records and activities, assess emotional health, and determine, if possible, the child's preference for a custodial parent. For the evaluator who is a therapist, it may be difficult to keep the interview from becoming a therapy session. Even though the therapist may be tempted to delve into thoughts and feelings of the various individuals, such issues are tangential to the task of evaluation.

Although some self-report inventories can measure parenting ability, they cannot replace the observations of a well-trained marriage and family therapist who is knowledgeable in childhood development, healthy family interaction, and communication styles. As a guide in evaluating custody, the evaluator may wish to consider Section 402 of the Uniform Marriage and Divorce Act (1970), which sets forth the following items to be considered in custody evaluations:

1. the wishes of the child;
2. the wishes of the parent;
3. the interaction and the interrelationship of the child with his parent or parents, his siblings, and any other persons;
4. the child's adjustment to his home, school, and community; and
5. the mental and physical health of all individuals involved.

(The Uniform Marriage and Divorce Act also states that the court "shall not consider conduct of a proposed custodian that does not affect his relationship to the child")(§ 402). Thus, the court may not arbitrarily deny custody to a parent for sexual preference or religious conviction. By far the most detailed statute defining an environment supporting the best interests for the child comes from Michigan: the Michigan Child Custody Act (1970). It lists these ten factors:

1. the love, affection, and other emotional ties existing between the competing parities and the child;
2. the capacity and disposition of competing parties to give the child love, affection, and guidance and to continue educating and raising the child according to his or her religion or creed, if any;

3. the capacity and disposition of competing parties to provide the child with food, clothing, medical care, or other remedial care;
4. the length of time the child has lived in a satisfactory, stable environment and the desirability of maintaining continuity;
5. the permanence of the existing proposed custodial home as a family unit;
6. the moral fitness of the competing parties;
7. the mental and physical health of the competing parties;
8. the home, school, and community of record of the child;
9. the reasonable preference of the child, if the court deems the child of sufficient age to express preference; and
10. any other factor considered by the court to be relevant to a particular child custody dispute.

(Awarding custody on the basis of the best interest for the child is a difficult task.) Judges still tend to rely upon testimony from an expert witness or a court employee to assist them in determining child custody. Although child custody is generally awarded to one parent with visitation being given to the noncustodial parent on a reasonable and customary arrangement, there are two other schools of thought on the issue. Goldstein, Freud, and Solnit (1973) believe that custody should be awarded to the parent who demonstrates adequate parenting ability, is willing to mediate contact with the noncustodial parent and significant others, and demonstrates maturity and reality in accepting that the divorce resulted from a cadre of problems between the two parents.

A second approach is joint custody, which many states now permit. The presumption is that joint custody permits the child easy access to both parents; moreover, it fosters the relationship between the parents as they both continue to support and care for the child. There is evidence that (joint custody may be effective, but it depends on the parameters of the custody decision and especially on the parents' ability to work together for the benefit of their children.) For example, one type of joint custody arrangement involves moving the child every third day so as to have equal access to both parents. Another places the child in one parent's home for one year and in the other parent's home for the next. The result of such an arrangement may be the child's loss of the sense of continuity and stability, since he or she must literally volley back and forth between the parents' two homes.

(Child custody is one of the most difficult aspects of divorce.) The marriage and family therapist who functions as an evaluator or mediator in these cases will surely experience people at their lowest and highest emotional levels. Thoroughness in completing the necessary work for custody determination does not guarantee that the court will award the case as the evaluator judges. Nor does the court's decision mean the case is closed. Not infrequently, custody cases are reopened for reevaluation of child support, reassignment of custodial rights, and/or review of custodial parent's care and control of the child. Each time the court's decision is reviewed, new evaluations must be conducted and new recommendations made.

Adoption

Marriage and family therapists are a valuable asset to adoption agencies and private attorneys who work in the field of adoption. The procedures for adoption are outlined in the Uniform Adoption Act (1969). Initially, the natural parents must relinquish their legal right to the child. Before signing the legal document to do so, the natural parents must be interviewed by a therapist. The interview should be conducted over a period of time to guarantee that the natural parents understand the significance of their action. If they feel any reluctance, the child may remain with the natural parents, the natural grandparents, or in foster care until a final decision has been reached.

Occasionally, the court may intercede on a child's behalf. This normally occurs if the natural parents abandon the child or are deemed unfit by virtue of severe mental retardation or extreme mental illness. The Illinois Appellate Court upheld a law overturning the need to obtain parental consent to adopt when it was found that a parent was mentally ill for three or more years and was not likely to recover in the near future (re Perez [1973]). The juvenile code of Nebraska (1981) permits termination of parental rights if the parents are unfit because of debauchery, habitual use of intoxicating liquor or narcotic drugs, or repeated lewd and lascivious behavior that the court finds is seriously detrimental to the health, morals, or well-being of the juvenile. This ruling and others similar to it require a formal history of the parent's mental illness, the duration of the problem, and prognosis for recovery before any decisive action can be taken in severing parental rights.

The adoptive parents must also be evaluated on their ability to parent an adoptive child. The adoption counselor working with the family must assess the parents' ability to provide for the physical needs, safety, and general well-being of the child. Most states require an investigation to ensure that the needs of the child will be met and that the adoptive family will receive a child who is not severely mentally or physically handicapped.

In evaluating the prospective adoptive family, the items considered must include the racial and ethnic background, age, physical and mental health of the prospective parents, as well as their religious preference, financial stability, and sincerity. In general, the adoption counselor will attempt to match the prospective parents' interests, social and intellectual background, and racial and religious orientation with that of the natural parents. In cases where the natural parents are unknown, the counselor must rely on personal experience and judgment.

Once the couple is accepted as a prospective family, there is a waiting period. This time may vary, depending on the specific requests of the adoptive parents, (e.g., a female or male child, willingness to accept a child with special problems) and the availability of children.

When a child is placed in the custody of the adoptive home, the counselor must assess and evaluate the placement. The duration of this process varies among the states. If everything is found acceptable, the couple may request a final decree of adoption based on the best interests of the child. The decree is considered final and irrevocable; it is seldom reversed. Some adoptive parents of adolescents who become unmanageable have relinquished parental rights and placed the child with a state agency. Other adoptive parents who find that their child is severely handicapped have also chosen to relinquish their rights and return the child to the adoption agency or attorney who placed the child.

Child Abuse and Neglect

Child abuse and neglect involves serious physical and/or emotional injury to a child resulting from a wide range of harmful actions—from murder, rape, and assault to abandonment and failure to provide for basic needs. The ultimate legal standard for prosecution of the criminal act will be based on the statutory definition of the charged offense. The case may involve civil as well as criminal sanctions by the court. Therefore, the offender may face punishment involving loss of parental rights, imprisonment, and even death.

Because of the helplessness of the child, many states have enacted mandatory reporting laws requiring health care professionals who witness, suspect, or directly learn of child abuse and neglect to report the case to child protective agencies immediately. All states provide anonymity as well as civil and criminal immunity to the reporter who is required to give the information in good faith. Failure to report constitutes a misdemeanor, which can result in a jail term and/or a fine.

Essentially, the therapist is bound to report physical and/or sexual abuse, neglect, and mental or emotional exploitation. Most states require that the therapist, as a reporter, have a reasonable basis for belief or suspicion that the abuse is ongoing or has occurred. Unfortunately, the definitions of *reasonable, neglect,* and *reportable abuse* vary across jurisdictions, which means the marriage and family therapist is responsible for knowing the reporting laws relevant to his or her state.

(Another characteristic of reporting laws is their granting permission for parental freedom in the pursuit of religious beliefs, even if those beliefs may appear to cause harm to their children.) Thus, religious groups that forbid their practitioners to undergo various medical treatments cannot be reported for neglect or abuse in these instances. If the family does not adhere to specific religious convictions, a parent may not deny his or her child medical treatment.

The duty to report child abuse and neglect has met with much criticism. Therapists working with individuals who openly seek treatment for their abusive actions and also those who have sustained only one offense are cited as victims of the mandatory reporting laws. Certainly, this argument can be made, but it is the responsibility of the therapist to inform the client of the mandatory reporting requirements during the initial phase of treatment. Most therapists who have reviewed their legal responsibilities with clients know that clients accept the forewarning as reasonable. Another important point to consider is that most child protective agencies look favorably upon abusing families seeking help for their behavior. As long as the family remains in treatment and shows progress in overcoming their abusive/negligent behavior, the child protective agencies will most likely refrain from prosecution. However, should the family arbitrarily drop out of treatment or continue or escalate the abusive/negligent behavior, the therapist must report the case for further investigation and possible prosecution.

A therapist who testifies in a child abuse case can expect that the proceedings will be directed toward the likelihood that a particular adult committed child abuse and that a particular child has been abused. The battering-parent syndrome (State v. Loebach [1988]) lists a number of traits found in adults who abuse children and is often used to describe the alleged abuser. These characteristics include low self-esteem, quick temper, high blood pressure, strict authoritarian orientation, social isolation, and lack of trust. Certainly, therapists who have worked with abusing adults recognize these traits are not the exclusive domain of the child abuser. Thus, evidence of the battering-parent syndrome, although it may be introduced by the prosecution, does not grant that the defendant is in fact a child abuser. When a mental health professional is called to testify on the characteristics of a child abuser, he or she should note that the literature and research regarding this population is limited and nonconclusive.

When there is question as to whether the injuries sustained by the child are a result of an accident or abuse, testimony may center around the battered-child syndrome (Shuman, 1986). The symptoms associated with this label include unexplained physical injuries, a wariness of contact with adults (including parents), and extremely aggressive or withdrawn behavior. The symptoms found in the child are compared with those noted in the battered-child syndrome; then the symptoms are evaluated as having resulted from abuse or an accident. This evidence is more acceptable to the court than the traits identified in the battering-parent syndrome, since the court considers the sustained physical injuries as *hard evidence,* which is specific and notable as opposed to the *soft evidence* of an individual's emotional make-up.

Another form of testimony involves the use of an expert witness whose work with the child in a therapeutic setting supports the allegation that the child was abused. The expert's opinion drawn from observations in a play-therapy setting may include observable information from the child's symbolic interaction with dolls or other toys. The perplexing problem of using observable behavior as valid testimony makes the noncharacteristic or nonsymptomatic abused child suspect. For this reason, some states choose to prohibit observable data as hearsay.

Mental health practitioners involved in reported child abuse and neglect cases are likely to be asked to evaluate the safety and welfare of the child and the probability of rehabilitating the parent(s). To do this means that the therapist must be able to predict whether further abuse is likely. Such assessment has proven unreliable. More appropriate information for the court might include present research regarding abusive families and possible intervention strategies that might be beneficial in the treatment of specific families. A second alternative includes presenting information that indicates the way another reasonable marriage and family therapist might respond in dealing with the case. The therapist is cautioned not to yield to the court's request for predictive behavior regarding the possibility of future child abuse and neglect.

The marriage and family therapist who works with child abuse and neglect is involved in extremely emotional and mentally taxing work. The therapist must be alert to developing feelings of distance and alienation when working with these cases. Furthermore, the therapist must pay special attention to his or her own inner voice, which may become jaded and suspicious of anyone who appears questionable in relationship to children. Severe child abuse and neglect can cause therapists to ponder their goals and purpose as treatment professionals.

The marriage and family therapist is definitely bound by various legal regulations. To practice ethical and legal therapy requires being mindful of the restrictions of one's jurisdiction. Therapists' knowledge and expertise are valued by their colleagues and clients, but this recognition does not protect them from legal dictates that are part of their daily work. Hence, the dictum "Admit what you don't know!" Rather than venture into work that puts him or her at risk, the therpist should avoid involvement in such cases until he or she has further training, knowledge, and experience with the subject.

Avoiding Malpractice

When an injury befalls an individual because of substandard care by a practitioner, that person may claim that the professional breached his or her legal duty to provide adequate services. Normally, the negligence that the professional exhibited stems from carelessness or inattentiveness. Seldom is the practitioner guilty of deliberate harm to another individual.

In assessing negligence, the courts apply the "average, reasonable man" standard. In other words, how would another marriage and family therapist respond given the same situation? If it is proven that a reasonable individual would have performed differently than the practitioner, the defendant will be found negligent and liable for malpractice.

Certainly, the various laws and legal action cited above reveal the numerous ways in which a practitioner can be liable for malpractice. All clinicians must be fully aware of the potential for malpractice. Even though marriage and family therapists have a low incidence of malpractice suits, they are not immune to civil action. (Unfortunately, malpractice is very real and is a part of today's social awareness.) One should not overreact to the possibility of suit; rather, he or she should let that possibility make him or her a more conscientious and well-informed practitioner.

Because of the serious threat of malpractice, the marriage and family therapist must have adequate insurance. Many liability policies are designed to protect the clinician. However, they vary in content and coverage. Because the most frequent reason for suit is alleged sexual misconduct, some insurance carriers have written an exclusion clause on any claims alleging sexual impropriety on the part of the therapist. The American Association for Counseling and Development Insurance Trust (Thiers, 1987) shows that more than half of the claims filed by counselors and two-thirds of the losses resulted from alleged sexual misconduct. Other allegations included mistreatment, misdiagnosis, failure to report child abuse, and failure to prevent a client from committing suicide. In total, the estimated losses to the insurance provider over the past five years amounts to approximately $3 million.

Most insurance companies select the attorney who will represent the defendant in any litigation. Despite the fact that the insurance company pays the attorney's fees, the law states that the attorney represents the client, not the insurance company. Therefore, the client may dictate what information the attorney may share with the insurance company. Certainly, the attorney must keep the insurance company apprised of the case, but the client has the right to withhold data from the insurance company. Because all insurance companies vary in their policy on settlement, the therapist is advised to consult his or her carrier to determine its policy on expediency of settlement.(Many insurance companies wish to settle cases as quickly as possible.) Therefore, even if the therapist is innocent, it may be cheaper to settle out of court than incur the high cost of a hearing. If the therapist wishes to pursue a court hearing against the discretion of the insurance carrier, the therapist must assume the costs of such actions.

The marriage and family therapist must be alert to the coverage provided by his or her malpractice insurance policy. He or she should read the contents very closely and ask questions of the person selling the policy; if the answers are unclear, he or she should ask again. If the answers are still vague, the therapist should take the policy to an attorney who is knowledgeable in malpractice and who can help decipher the jargon and intent of the policy. The therapist should remember that he or she is the consumer as well as the professional who is vulnerable to malpractice litigation. In considering malpractice protection, *coverage,* not the cost of the policy, should be the deciding point.

(The most important defense to malpractice litigation is prevention.) In other words, avoid suits before they happen. When in doubt, the therapist should consult an attorney in his or her jurisdiction who is an expert in the field of malpractice. (One should not take the word of friends or colleagues regarding law.) Finally, employ the following guidelines to help avoid legal jeopardy.

1. *Most importantly, know national organization's standards of practice and ethical guidelines.* Although legal standards may exceed the limits of the national professional organization, the organizational codes can set a minimum of standard of care for practice. When reviewing the codes, one should make certain that he or she understands the wording. Although the language may be simple, the interpretation of the wording may be different. Ethical codes and laws use words in a precise manner that is not always clear to the reader. When in doubt, consult the national organization's professional practice chair and/or a local attorney.

2. *Do not practice beyond an individual level of expertise.* The therapist must know both the personal and legal limits of his or her ability. In other words, as a nonmedical practitioner, the marriage and family therapist cannot prescribe drugs or attempt to practice medicine in any way. Likewise, the therapist is not an attorney; therefore, he or she cannot render legal opinions or interpret the law. In both of these instances, the therapist should refer the client to the appropriate professional. Moreover, the marriage and family therapist who is unfamiliar with specific treatment techniques or theoretical frameworks should refrain from using such practices until appropriate education, training, and supervision are obtained.

3. *Establish a healthy, working rapport your clients.* The empathy, trust, and concern that a therapist brings to the therapeutic setting is help-

ful in protecting himself or herself against a malpractice suit. Clients feel more benevolent toward their therapist if there is a respectful, attentive atmosphere throughout treatment.

4. *Inform the clients of the standard of care that they can expect.* This can be done at the initial session. During this time, the therapist may present the client with a factsheet, contract, or verbal information about the principles and practice of therapy that he or she will experience. The first session should address (a) fee structure, including charges for missed appointments, third-party payment arrangements, and service charges on unpaid bills; (b) duration of treatment, if possible; (c) methods of treatment that may be used; (d) preliminary goals for treatment; (e) laws to which the therapist must conform; (f) information regarding confidentiality (especially for the systems therapist, who considers the client as the entire family); (g) possible outcomes from the therapy; and (h) information regarding termination. This session is an educative one for both the client and the therapist. By informing the client of what will actually occur in the therapeutic setting, the marriage and family therapist can dispel any faulty expectations the client might have regarding treatment.

5. *Make certain that all individuals working in the practice or employment setting conform to the same established ethical and legal standards of care.* One should not enter into practice or share office space with someone he or she doesn't know or whose practice of therapy is suspect. Any clinician sharing an office with another clinician who is being sued can be sued under a vicarious liability claim. Therefore, it is in everyone's best interest to uphold the highest, most up-to-date standards of care.

6. *The same responsibility applies to individuals under personal supervision.* The therapist must monitor the work of the supervisees very closely, since as the supervisor, he or she is liable for not only the cases that the supervisee staffs with him or her but for all the cases the supervisee treats. If the supervisor has any doubts about the ethical or legal principles of the supervisee, he or she may wish to reconsider the supervisory arrangement with the individual.

7. *Keep well-documented notes of all interactions and other aspects of care regarding clients.* This includes not only casenotes but also any documentation received from other practitioners working with the client. If available, medical histories and documentation of medication being taken at the time of treatment should be included in the record. Any phone contacts, missed appointments, and conversations or letters from significant others in the client's life, as well as reports to governmental agencies (e.g., welfare, disability) requiring periodic updates on the client, should be recorded in the file. Well-organized, clinical records are one of the therapist's best defenses against malpractice litigation.

8. *Maintain strict professional boundaries with the client.* Dual relationships—such as business-client or friend-client—can create confusion and blur boundaries, which may lead the client to have false expectations about the nature of the relationship with the therapist. Even the most innocent of statements made during an informal conversation in the waiting room or at a social event may be used against a therapist should the client decide to sue.

9. *Closely supervise those individual patients who are at high risk of suicide or violent behavior.* Duty to warn is a legal reality that must be fulfilled to the public, significant others, and the client. The therapist must continuously monitor and reevaluate these clients for progress or deterioration.

10. *Know the laws affecting the practice of marriage and family therapy.* Therapists should read the recent legislative and administrative regulations that impact clinical practice, as well as review legal decisions reported in journals and newsletters and by professional organizations.

11. *Consider and reconsider the advisability of taking on clients who have a litigious nature.* These individuals usually complain about other therapists or treatment agents who have not performed to their satisfaction. They also attempt to redirect treatment; convince the therapist of his or her inability to help them in reaching vague, undefined goals; and talk about friends who have been helped or cured more rapidly and at less expense. Not infrequently, these individuals show their unhappiness with nonverbal or passive-aggressive behavior, such as nonpayment of fees and missed appointments. If the therapist senses potential danger for suit from the client, he or she may wish to contract for a specific number of sessions at an agreed upon fee, payable at each session or in advance. Some therapists choose to see potentially litigious individuals only once; then refer them onto another practitioner.

When these individuals fail to pay their bills, the therapist must seriously consider pursuing payment. Most lawyers and insurance companies agree, however, that an attempt to do so invites malpractice action by the litigious client. To avoid the possible suit, the therapist may want to call the individual about the nonpayment. During the course of the conversation, the therapist might wish to inform the client that although services were rendered in good faith, they did not achieve the desired outcome. To that end, the client did not receive the services for which he or she contracted and therefore does *not* have to remit the fee. Although this action may gall the therapist, this concession is minor in the face of the anguish that comes from a malpractice suit.

12. *Finally, hire the best professionals to assist in business operation.* The therapist is an expert in treatment of psychological and emotional problems. Attorneys, accountants, bookkeepers, financial planners,

and bank managers are experts in their respective fields and can give the therapist direction and support in the business end of practice. One should not let the cost of service deter him or her from hiring the best advisors. The therapist's business is his or her livelihood and is characterized by personal identity and self-esteem. Failure to take proper care of oneself is as dangerous to the therapist as is failing to deliver the proper standard of care to the client.

The malpractice crisis has created a furor among treatment agents. Many people question whether any satisfaction and joy can be found in practicing in a profession where everything one owns and stands for can be destroyed by a litigious client. Certainly, suit is a reality, but the possibility of litigation has made therapists more conscientious and responsible on behalf of themselves and the client. Treatment professionals are practicing with more awareness of their impact on the lives of their clients. This heightened consciousness has caused therapists to hone their skills and knowledge through continuing education and supervision. It has also challenged the practitioner to assess his or her professional interactions with clients and colleagues and to assure that those relationships are of the highest quality. Therapy is no longer just talk. It is an active interchange between therapist and client in the discovery and recovery of health and the personal spirit.

CHAPTER SIX

Regulation, Certification, and Licensure

Occupational licensing of professions is not a new idea. Regulation, as we know it today, began approximately one hundred years ago. Credentialing and licensing of physicians, dentists, psychologists, and lawyers has been documented since the early 1900s.

Regulation of professionals involves the establishment of educational standards, the development of curricula, and the certification of training institutions. The authority to regulate professions resides within the power of the individual states, whose licensing and certifying boards work to safeguard the health, welfare, and safety of the general public. Licensing prohibits unqualified persons from practicing designated professions, which range from daycare providers to pharmacists to architects.

Certification and registration laws limit the use of a professional title, such as social worker or psychologist. But this form of control does not prohibit untitled individuals from providing the service; they are only prohibited from using the title of the certified professional. In some states, such laws permit an employer to select the services of an individual who is not certified. But in states where licensing is the rule, an employer must use a licensed individual, regardless of his or her ability to perform the designated job. Since each state delineates the level of autonomy of its licensing board, authority varies from state to state. Some states use a centralized agency for all licensing boards, while other states use autonomous or advisory boards.

To License or Not to License?

In the beginning of this century, licensure was considered advantageous for both the profession and the public. That sentiment changed in the 1960s and 1970s, when a number of federal agencies began to investigate the activities of licensing boards. As a result of these investigations, several criticisms were levied against the boards. Specifically, the studies showed that the boards tended to inhibit competition among members, thus causing the consumer to pay higher fees for services and products. Another charge cited that some people were prohibited from entry into specific fields of work. Finally, because of the restrictive nature of the licensing boards, professionals in the regulated occupations were found to have a higher earning capacity than those who could not obtain licensure or certification (Shimberg, 1980). The boards and their representative professions were accused of monopolistic practices.

These studies led to the initiation of so-called "sunset" laws by elected officials. These laws were designed to abolish those regulatory boards that were shown to be ineffective, punitive, or unnecessary. As the legislators continued their investigations, the media informed the public of the boards' failure to protect the consumer. People began to question the value of using their tax dollars for self-serving boards that did little to inform them of high-quality professional practice or protect them from incompetent practitioners. As a result of legislative, media, and public criticisms, state regulatory boards broadened their activties to include reviewing the credentials of professionals; administering qualifying examinations; and investigating allegations of incompetence, negligence, and unprofessional conduct of their licensees.

Criticisms of the board-regulatory system created a rift among the licensing boards, the public, and the legislature. For example, the boards noted an improvement in the quality of graduates from the professional schools, while the public pointed to the frequency of misconduct by these same professionals. Legislatures claimed that boards were simply guilds designed to promote their own interests in the form of third-party payments. The conflicting issues between these groups necessitates the review of the pros and cons of regulation.

Licensure Ensures Public Safety

Regulatory boards establish minimum academic and training standards and enforce them to assure the public of service by well-trained and legitimate professionals. Unfortunately, the grades an individual receives in academic or other training schools are perhaps more indicative of one's ability to retain and recall information upon formal examination than his or her actual quality of practice. Certainly, standardized curricula do require specific courses and practicum experience. Thus, the knowledge held by regulated professionals is fairly uniform on completion of an academic degree. Research showing that this body of knowledge protects the public from incompetent treatment, however, has not been conducted.

(More important than the actual coursework is use of the knowledge in the presence of a client when professional service is actually delivered.) Practicum and internship requirements stress the development of skills, but students at this level commonly are assigned the less difficult clients. They may also be assigned the so-called chronic cases, who are presumably so dysfunctional that no harm could result from student and intern practice. Consequently, students and interns may not receive training to work with the same challenges they will eventually face in private or public practice.

Incompetence or negligence is not necessarily a result of poor training. Therapists can suffer fatigue, personal stress, and/or mental illness, which may cause them to provide less than adequate service. Senior practitioners may become disillusioned with the profession and fail to attend to client needs. Academic preparation can do little to forestall errors that these individuals may make. Mandating continuing education can help to overcome these problems, but there is no guarantee that the incompetent or negligent therapist will change as a result. The increase in malpractice suits is testimony that licensure and mandated educational requirements do not protect public welfare (Bakker, personal communication, 1988).

Unless a therapist commits a crime, the most severe punishment a regulatory board can stipulate is removal of the certification. However, sanctioned practitioners may thumb their noses at state regulatory boards by merely changing their professional title. Once these people have claimed a new title, they can continue to practice as they had previously. At most, the result of losing certification might consist of these professionals' loss of third-party payment and prohibition from sitting on hospital committees or state advisory boards. Thus, regulating academic standards does not protect the public from faulty practice. In fact, regulation can be circumvented easily by the wry practitioner who chooses to disregard the ethical and legal guidelines of the profession.

Finally, some state regulatory laws cover only the private sector and not those individuals who practice in state agencies, health maintenance organizations, or institutions. The onus for providing competent personnel resides with the employer.

As more innovative methods of health care delivery evolve, there is less opportunity for some state boards to regulate the profession. As one state board administrator said, "A wide range of services are being provided by individuals who would not qualify for licensure or certification if they practiced outside those agencies and institutions" (Lee, personal communication, 1988).

Licensure Defines the Profession

By having the name of the profession written into the state statutes, marriage and family therapy is recognized as a legitimate profession. Because the law delineates the activities of the practitioners, no other body—legislative or judicial, public or private—can interfere with the autonomy of the profession.

Although this may have been the intention of the regulation, standards of care are now being questioned by lawyers representing injured clients, hospital utilization review boards seeking to decrease length of stay, and insurance companies attempting to control the cost of marriage and family therapy. As the price of health care continues to escalate, all mental health coverage comes under scrutiny for efficiency, cost effectiveness, and timeliness. Nonetheless, clinicians and most clients recognize that the problems that brought them to treatment took time to develop and will take time to dissolve. The length of treatment will vary from client to client based on motivation, pathology, and the skill of the therapist.

The capitation (the maximum dollar amount an insuring organization will provide for treatment) on the amount of money or the number of sessions permitted for mental and nervous disorder treatment per insurance package frequently defines duration and form of treatment without taking into consideration the nature of the presenting problem(s). In reality, some benefits programs designate which diagnoses are insurable and which are not. Thus, a therapist dependent on third-party payments may be permitted to treat depression but may be excluded from treating adjustment disorders or marital and family problems.

When treatment direction is mandated by people other than mental health practitioners, the clinician is faced with several interesting dilemmas: Does the therapist treat the financially uncovered mental or nervous disorder and report another diagnosis to the insurance company? Does the therapist refer the client to another practitioner not dependent on third-party payments, or does the clinician treat the client at a reduced fee? These questions have nothing to do with delivering the best service to the client. Rather, they speak to the therapist's ability to understand and cope with the marketplace. When economic and legal decisions come before treatment decisions, the client's welfare may suffer. How then does licensure define the profession in light of these most difficult questions?

Competition for the mental health dollar is strong. The tightening of the economy coupled with the move toward socialization of health care means that professionals must unify their efforts to meet client needs. Instead of insulating themselves against other treatment professionals, marriage and family therapists must work with them to define their profession as an integral part of the mental health delivery system.

Grievance Provisions

State licensing boards provide the public with a legal means to present a grievance against a practitioner. Professionals who violate codes of ethics, commit civil or criminal violations, or practice in an inappropriate manner are subject to investigation and discipline by the board. At first glance, this appears to be a valuable tool for both the public and practitioner. However, some major problems exist with this function.

Most board members are appointed from a list of names given to the governor. Generally, the list is composed of people who have been politically supportive of the governor or who have prestigious positions in local universities or institutions (Height, personal communication, 1988). Sometimes the list is composed of individuals that the state professional organization feels would be valuable board appointees; regardless, the governor may select anyone he or she chooses. Thus, some appointees may not be very interested in the profession, may have vendettas against colleagues, or may simply use the appointment as a stepping stone to another position.

Although associated with the profession, some appointees are affiliated with the theoretical and research end of marriage and family therapy. This contextual difference (i.e., practical systemic family therapy intervention versus exclusively researched-based intervention) creates some pitfalls in assessing the pragmatic problems facing practicing marriage and family therapists. For example, a board member with a theoretical orientation may fail to understand the practicality of treating only those family members who are easily accessible, since the theoretician can demand and get reseach populations of total family units. These significant differences can impact on the way a case is reviewed and finally adjudicated.

Confidentiality and Privileged Communications Provisions

Not all state licensing laws safeguard confidentiality and privileged communications. Although the ethics of the profession do stipulate confidentiality between client and therapist, in those states in which therapist's records can be subpoenaed, the privilege of confidentiality lies with the client. If a client grants permission for the court to hear what went on in therapy, the therapist has no choice but to testify or suffer contempt of court charges. As more states offer licensure, however, the sanctity of client-therapist communication is addressed and often afforded the same privilege as lawyer-client communication.

Regulation of Marriage and Family Therapy

In 1978, the American Association for Marriage and Family Therapy's (AAMFT) Commission on Accreditation for Marriage and Family Therapy Education was initially recognized by the United States Department of Health, Education, and Welfare as an accrediting agency for graduate and postgraduate education and training in marriage and family therapy. Since then, it has also been recognized by the Department of Education. As such, the Commission on Accreditation has actively facilitated the development of numerous accredited university-based and free-standing training institutes in marriage and family therapy. The establishment of specific criteria for programs of study, coupled with recognition of the profession by the United States Department of Defense's Civil Health and Medical Program of the Uniform Services and the Federal Employees Health Benefit Plan, have demonstrated that marriage and family therapy is a distinct form of treatment that requires separate recognition and regulation. States in which marriage and family therapy is regulated are already aware of the uniqueness of the profession. Legislators, family practice lawyers, juvenile and law enforcement personnel, and family physicians recognize that marriage and family therapy offers specific understanding and treatment for the family unit. Why then is it so difficult to obtain licensure for the profession?

Legislators are not interested in supporting legislation that appears self-serving. Because most mental health regulatory bills eventually lead to third-party payment legislation, (legislators view occupational licensing as guild oriented.) Although marriage and family therapists know that licensure/certification defines the profession and provides the public with better trained practitioners, legislators must be convinced that regulation will indeed benefit the public. Therefore, public representatives must be informed and assured that certification is an asset for their constituents.

Regulation does not just happen; it takes committed professionals many years and a lot of funding to pass a regulation bill. It requires clear thinking and strategic planning to engineer a licensing effort. People working toward legislation must be task-oriented individuals who do not mind donating long hours to mobilizing key organizational and legislative personnel to back the bill.

One individual who was responsible for obtaining licensure for marriage and family therapy in two states reports that dealing with legislators is "dirty business." She relates numerous examples of sharp-tongued accusations levied against her while attempting to defend a marriage and family therapy regulation bill to various House and Senate subcommittees. It was only because she believed in the importance of regulating the profession that she endured the verbal assaults and saw the bills through to passage. Another individual responsible for the passage of an omnibus bill says that it took several years and much closed-door negotiation with legislators to get the bill passed. In fact, this marriage and family therapist says that his persistence and unyielding pursuit of the bill guaranteed passage of his state's certification law. These individuals are not unlike other marriage and family therapists who have worked toward licensure for their states.

Numerous factors are involved in the passage of a bill:

1. commitment of several task-oriented people who are dedicated to the profession;
2. a tireless leader who is not afraid of conflict and will press every task force member into action;
3. affiliative relationships with key personnel in the legislature and the community who support the licensure/certification effort;
4. significant money ($100,000–$150,000) to engage a lobbyist or at least $40,000 to pursue the bill without a lobbyist;
5. consistency;
6. patience, persistence, and time spread out over at least three years if the state organization chooses to pursue legislation without a lobbyist;
7. courage, and;
8. follow through with legislators, significant community leaders, and colleagues.

State Regulation Models

Because each state regulates occupations and professions, the regulatory models vary in composition, duties, and reporting standards. For example, Connecticut law does not utilize a board. Instead, a state administrative agency implements and administers the law. According to Connecticut Public Act No. 85-507, Section 20-195b (1985):

> No person shall be certified as a Connecticut certified marital and family therapist on or after January 1, 1986, until such person has passed an examination prescribed by the department (Department of Health Services). The department shall provide for the administration of examinations related to such certification, provide for collec-

tion of an examination fee in the amount of fifty dollars, establish passing scores of such examinations and maintain a registry of persons certified in accordance with the provisions of this act.

Section 3 continues:

The department is authorized to conduct investigations and take disciplinary actions for any of the following reasons: (a) Fraud or material deception in procuring or attempting to procure certification; (b) illegal conduct, incompetence or negligence in carrying out professional functions; (c) any occupationally disabling emotional disorder or mental illness; (d) abuse or excessive use of drugs, including alcohol, narcotics or chemicals; (e) fraud or material deception in the course of professional activities; and (f) willful and significant falsification of entries in any hospital, patient or other record.

Most states have regulatory boards that are composed of professionals and consumers who have no connection to the profession. These boards may direct their own "agency of the state" or operate as the policy- and rule-making body that dictates enforcement to an administrative agency. Such a model is found in California, where administration of the regulatory code is handled by the Department of Consumer Affairs.

There are also autonomous boards and so-called umbrella boards. Autonomous boards are free-standing boards that are responsible for promulgating the rules and regulations related to the profession. Such a board exists in Nevada, where Chapter 374, Statutes of Nevada (1973), mandates the licensing and regulation of individuals engaged in marriage and family counseling. As the law states:

An act regulating marriage and family counselors; declaring the policy of the state; establishing a board of examiners; requiring certification of marriage counselors; creating disciplinary and hearing procedures; establishing a fee schedule; defining the scope of regulatory activities; providing penalties and remedies; and providing other matters properly relating thereto.

Omnibus boards—like those found in Florida, Tennessee, and Arizona—are composed of several allied professions, such as social work, marriage and family therapy, and counseling. This type of board has a financial advantage over the autonomous board in that it can generate larger volumes of application fees, examination fees, and other revenues that finance operation either directly or indirectly. These boards use the various professional representatives to set standards and establish regulations for the practice of all the allied groups designated in the bill. In other words, social workers and counselors may work together to develop and/or adjudicate marriage and family therapy issues. However, some composite boards—such as the Georgia Composite Board of Professional Counselors, Social Workers, and Marriage and Family Therapists—endeavor to keep the professions separate on topics specific to the individual disciplines. To that end, the law established subboards to ensure that each profession would be represented in the decision-making process specific to issues of the designated occupation. As Section 43-7A-6(a) (1985) states:

> Those members of the board from the professional counseling specialty, the social work specialty, and the marriage and family therapy specialty shall constitute a separate standards committee for their respective specialty. Each standards committee by majority vote shall approve or disapprove the granting of all licenses in that specialty, approve the examination required of applicants for licensure in that committee's specialty and provide for the grading of that examination, and provide for other matters relating to licensure in that specialty.

Alabama and Virginia are among the states that regulate marriage and family therapy as a subspecialty of another profession. This model assumes that marriage and family therapy is a specialized application of a general discipline such as professional counseling. In other words, this model does not recognize marriage and family therapy as a distinct discipline, which is by far the least acceptable to the profession of marriage and family therapy.

Regulatory statutes are complex documents that stipulate title, practice, duties, and board design. Therefore, the reader must pay close attention to the wording and definition of terms used when reviewing the statutes (i.e., *licensure, certification, registration*). Practitioners should note the section entitled "Prohibited Acts," which designates what the clinician can and cannot do legally and ethically. Anyone who is confused or baffled by the state rules and regulations should call the state regulatory board or the attorney general's office for further assistance.

Tom Clark (personal communication, 1988), chair of the Association of Marital and Family Therapy Regulatory Boards, recognizes that regulation of marriage and family therapy is essentially paradoxical in that the benefits and detriments of regulation go hand in hand. As he states, "I choose to emphasize the benefits and believe many of the detriments are best reduced by carefully drafting the initial statutes and by timely revision of them as circumstances within society, the profession, the field and the designated regulatory agency evolve."

Regulation and the Future
of Marriage and Family Therapy

The threat of so-called "sunset" legislation is always looming. Not long ago, the Florida law was "sunsetted" (dissolved). It was only through diligent work on the part of the professionals in Florida that the sunset ruling was overturned.

However, more detrimental than sunset legislation is the opposition that marriage and family therapy experiences from other professions. Certainly, every recognized mental health profession is concerned about cost-containment measures in the health care delivery system. Since competition for mental health dollars is fierce, posturing for recognition by third-party payers will inevitably continue. Furthermore, as health maintenance organizations and preferred provider organizations continue to dictate standards of practice and hire a diversity of uncertified service delivery personnel, the quality of acceptable treatment will diminish.

As Robert Lee (personal communication, 1988), chair of the Michigan Marriage Counseling Board, states:

> I see two possible outcomes as contemporary health care delivery
> proceeds: (a) marital and family therapy will become "something
> else" that various professions do or (b) because individuals using
> their mental health benefit primarily want it, and it is an economical
> treatment modality, the service-providing agencies will see the merit
> to hiring individuals formally trained and identified as marital and
> family therapists.

In order for state regulation to continue, marriage and family therapy boards must operate in a reasonable and responsible manner, both for the consumer and the profession. Public education through newspaper and magazine articles, radio and television talk shows, community service announcements, and local consumer-awareness talks sponsored by civic and hospital organizations are all methods by which to promote the profession and educate the public regarding the value of marriage and family therapy. By representing marriage and family therapy as a distinct discipline within the health care delivery system, marriage and family therapists can promote the tenets of the profession to the public and other professionals.

CHAPTER SEVEN

Clinical Practice

The clinical practice of marriage and family therapy can take place in many environments: businesses, public agencies, the military, and private practice. Although the skills needed to facilitate change are the same regardless of the milieu, the personality, goals, and needs of the therapist may vary considerably. For example, therapists working within a military context may enjoy a structured work environment, guaranteed income, and medical benefits, while the private practitioner may prefer a more autonomous setting in which he or she can define the work hours, income level, and clinical population. Because marriage and family therapy can be practiced in so many diverse settings, the clinician has the option to change work environments as needs vary and evolve. Thus, marriage and family therapy is a profession in which one has numerous opportunities to explore theoretical frameworks and various racial, religious, and cultural differences, as well as meet interesting and at times challenging people and work in different employment settings.

Private Practice in Marriage and Family Therapy

Building and managing a successful private practice requires skill, knowledge, and patience. No clinician has entered the business world of private practice without error or trepidation. After all, graduate school in the social sciences does not usually prepare the clinician for the entrepreneurial world of debits and credits. In fact, most therapists are more concerned with the delivery of service than filing tax reports and business plans and monitoring office supplies.

Private practice is a business that, if it is to succeed, needs careful attention and ongoing revision. Without constant assessment of and attention to all the necessary elements of any business, the organizational demands become unwieldy and ultimately destructive to the practice.

Private practice is not for everyone. Successful private practice requires a pragmatic view of reality, an entrepreneurial spirit, and boundless energy. The clinician in private practice must know marketing, public speaking, and business and personnel management techniques. The concept of unconditional positive regard is valid for the therapeutic relationship but is counterproductive in the development and operation of a private practice. There are clients who don't pay their bills, insurance companies that demand excessive paperwork before paying claims, and attorneys who threaten litigation. Sound business practices, along with well-developed clinical skills, are needed in order for one to cope with these pressures and succeed in private practice.

The Business of Private Practice

Private practice is a service delivery business similar in operation to accounting, law, and medicine. In these professions, the goal is to bring assistance, help, or protection to people. This goal defines the objectives on which the practice must be developed and monitored. Goals are the backbone of any organization. Regardless of the function of the business, without goals, there is no known purpose or rationale for direction and decision making. By identifying the goals of the practice, the clinician can direct attention to those areas of knowledge that are both interesting and challenging.

New private practitioners frequently fail to establish their practice goals, which leads to accepting all types of cases simply to earn a living. Although economic survival is essential, a "shotgun" method for the establishment of a practice causes the clinician to spend exorbitant time researching and facilitating treatment plans. It simply is not a good use of time.

Instead, the clinician should be marketing programs and therapy to potential referral sources such as hospitals, employee assistance programs, physicians, attorneys, and public service agencies. Public speaking and effective marketing strategies draw clientele faster than the indiscriminate acceptance of clients who present problems for which the clinician has minimal or no training. Besides, treating unfamiliar psychological problems can create legal liability, since the likelihood of making mistakes is enhanced.

Planning an effective and successful practice requires an action plan that specifies the method by that the goals and objectives of the practice will be met. To implement the plan, the therapist must set a timeline by which to meet the stated goals, as well as advance financing to assure proper execution. Such knowledge requires networking with other clinicians who have experience in establishing a private practice. The new private practitioner can learn from senior therapists who have already made mistakes and learned from them.

Private practice also involves researching various practice newsletters that specify fees for services, income from direct client payments, and third-party payment information. These articles are not often found in journals. Therefore, the private practitioner needs to talk with other private practitioners and accountants who have worked with service delivery businesses to find out which newsletters and documents are particularly useful. Clinical supervisors may also be a good source of information for these particular questions.

If private practice is the sole form of income, the clinician must address the topics of insurance for the practice, the physical plant in which the practice is located, and his or her family. There are numerous forms of insurance: disability insurance, overhead insurance, medical insurance, malpractice insurance, life insurance, and property insurance. Each provides protection from various problems that may occur during the operation of the business. For example, if a clinician becomes gravely ill and cannot return to work for several months, he or she must guarantee that the bills for the operation of the practice will continue to be paid.

The correct insurance package can offer protection in these instances. Therapists should check with an insurance broker or professional national organization to find out the forms of insurance offered, what they cost, and what actual benefits they provide. All insurance packages are legal documents that can be complex and obtuse. If the verbiage is too difficult to understand, one should hire an insurance attorney or neutral broker to interpret the language and to render an opinion on the various offerings. (Insurance is too important to treat haphazardly.) For this reason, it should not be purchased based solely on cost. Hopefully, the clinician will not have to use the insurance, but it is better to be prepared than face financial ruin because of lack of it.

(Control is essential for a successful practice.) The therapist in private practice must pay close attention to the material that comes into and leaves the office. Loss of documents and information can create problems in client rapport and business affiliations. Disorganization leads to confusion and hard feelings, which affect the office atmosphere and staff rapport. Misplaced files, reports, and billing statements create an unprofessional climate, which can cause clients uneasiness and distrust. Because the therapist is a model for the client, he or she is expected to demonstrate healthy, organized behavior. (An out-of-control office is a silent message that can unwittingly undo hours of fine therapy.)

Control also involves effective personnel management. Job descriptions, employee policies, and performance standards for all employees must be established. By knowing what is expected and how well the tasks are to be done, employees can measure performance against accepted standards. This delineation of work expectations is nothing more than boundary setting in an office environment. Rules and limits are essential to guarantee safety and the development of trust in an employment setting, as in a family setting. The successful private practitioner is direct and consistent in the application of policies for all staff. Staff meetings, as well as performance reviews, underscore professional office practice and serve as reinforcement for a healthy work climate.

Loss of control can influence numerous parts of a practice. The following case illustrates how failure to maintain effective control can devastate a private practice.

Case One

Financial Management

Five marriage and family therapists formed a loose partnership. Their services consisted of marriage and family therapy, custody evaluations, and testimony. The clinicians hired a secretary/bookkeeper, who they trusted without question. The employee learned that the therapists knew little about the finances of the office, so she developed her own method of tracking the money. The partners noted that they were working particularly hard but realizing few dollars for their work. Although they talked to the bookkeeper and she described the problems, they did not listen to her. Nor did they ask an accountant to review their books for the possible money leak.

By the end of the fiscal year, the partnership was having difficulty meeting its financial responsibilities. The clinicians decided that something needed to be done; therefore, an accountant was called in for consultation. Upon reviewing the books, the accountant noted several entry errors on all the therapists' accounts. There also appeared to be an interesting dilemma in the way the money was being allotted to the various clinicians. The bookkeeper did not always credit the client payments to the correct therapist. Therefore, some clients were not billed, while others were charged for sessions they did not receive. Furthermore, insurance collections had not been filed for four months. Outstanding insurance was not rebilled, and new insurance clients never filled out the necessary forms to permit the office to file on the accounts.

When the bookkeeper was asked about the errors, she was dumbfounded. She felt that the therapists had given her full license to operate the accounting procedures as she saw fit. Therefore, when the therapists found no problem with her work, she continued as usual. She added that insurance filing was in arrears because the office work was too heavy for one person; she had filed insurance claims only when she had the time.

The clinicians were amazed with the bookkeeper's response. They did not realize that the office was out of control because they were working too hard. They acknowledged that the bookkeeper was overwhelmed only after they solicited information from her. They also became aware of the importance of monitoring their individual accounts to be certain that clients and insurance companies paid their bills. Finally, they realized that one of them had to supervise the secretary/bookkeeper.

This case reveals the necessity of keeping control in a private practice office. Therapists who are concerned with delivering high-quality treatment frequently abdicate the operation of the office to others. Thus, essential tasks may not get done. Despite the competencies of office workers, the therapist is ultimately responsible for everything related to the office. As the business owner, the clinician should be invested in all aspects of the practice. Failure to actively participate in the operation of the business may create problems similar to the ones described in the previous case.

Being a therapist can be helpful in dealing with the inevitable personal conflicts encountered in running a business. Generally, conflicts occur when dealing with personnel issues. Marriage and family therapists know the importance of timing strategies and interventions. Laying the proper groundwork is essential for a successful therapeutic move. However, business does not always afford the clinician the same standards. The following case demonstrates how blurring the boundaries of employer and therapist can have negative results.

Case Two

Tara Kendig

Tara Kendig worked for John Douglas for three years. She was an extremely conscientious secretary who frequently put in numerous hours of overtime. John appreciated Tara and reinforced her superior performance with raises and small verbal comments of recognition.

In Tara's fourth year of employment, she became very ill. Although there was no apparent cause for Tara's problems, she continued to call in sick and leave her job early. John spoke with Tara about her absences. He referred her to another physician and even offered to pay for the second opinion. The second doctor confirmed the first doctor's results and suggested that Tara might be suffering from job stress. Therefore, John counseled Tara about stress and gave her a week off to recuperate. Nothing changed. As the year progressed, Tara's absences increased. When she worked, her performance was excellent. John began to hire temporary secretaries to fill in for Tara. The cost of Tara's salary plus the fee for temporary help began to impact John's income. He began to wonder if Tara would ever recover.

By the end of the year, John was feeling the effects of Tara's erratic work. He was resentful and hopeless. Each morning, he approached the office with trepidation. Would Tara call in sick again? John spoke with colleagues about the dilemma. His friends told John to terminate Tara. John felt absolutely terrible. How could he fire a good friend? Yet as the resentment built, John knew he had to make a decision. He confronted Tara about her work. She cried and promised to do better if John would keep her. Reluctantly, he consented. However, her attendance remained sporadic and unexplainable. Finally, after 18 months, John terminated Tara. He suffered emotionally and financially because of her problems, yet he felt that he had to be fair and give her the opportunity to change before he could let her go.

John Douglas allowed the problems to continue far too long. He lost his boundaries with Tara because he regarded her as a friend rather than an employee. Had he responded to her as an employer rather than an understanding and caring therapist, his business and his mental health would not have taken such a heavy toll. Some business decisions are very cut and dried: Do I purchase a new computer or live with the old one? Others are more conflictual because they require the therapist to suspend clinical skills and invoke the pragmatic skills of a business manager.

When making decisions, the effective private practitioner should consider the following points:

1. the goals and objectives of the clinical practice;
2. the priorities of the clinical practice;
3. a clear understanding of the identified problem as it impacts the practice;
4. the number of alternative solutions to the identified problem;
5. the importance of making the decision;
6. personal blind spots in the areas of business;
7. personal strengths in the operation of a business; and
8. personal and professional resources who can aid in the decision-making process (e.g., attorneys, accountants, colleagues).

Decision making is the conscious selection of an alternative from two or more possible solutions to a problem. Treatment people pose decision-making questions to their clients daily. Sometimes the decision is illusive because of denial or disinterest. The same situation occurs for the private practitioner when faced with issues and dilemmas that are either unfamiliar or monotonous. To let disinterest or apathy infect a private practice is to invite disaster.

The Future of Private Practice

Legislators in 27 states have enacted laws mandating care for mental health coverage. Fourteen of these states require insurers to pay for mental health care in specific types of policies, while the remaining 13 states have laws that mandate that a mental health coverage option be made available for an extra cost in premiums.

However, this trend toward mandated mental health care is diminishing because lawmakers fear that the demand for mental health treatment is far greater than was first anticipated. For this reason, four states—Georgia, Nevada, Virginia, and Tennessee—have passed bills to measure the impact of mental health legislation. Some states have even established commissions to study the cost of mental health coverage to state employees and insurers. The result is that the trend toward passage of mandated mental health coverage is decreasing.

In an effort to supply mandated mental health coverage at a reduced fee, some states with mandated health laws have included health maintenance organizations (HMOs) as mental health service providers. These companies must provide outpatient service at a set fee for a limited number of visits per designated time period (usually one year). Other states with mandated coverage have amended their laws to require more control over the delivery of service. In other words, some states require clients to obtain preauthorization before they can obtain treatment, while other states are ordering peer review of all treating clinicians and utilization review of all treatment plans during various stages of treatment. Such requirements make the therapist accountable to the insurer and place the treatment direction in the hands of the third-party payer. In such instances, costs may be cut, and the client may receive less than adequate treatment.

These cost-saving measures are becoming the standard of mental health care. Managed care is big business, which has led to the rise of health care consulting firms, major insurance conglomerates, nationwide HMOs, and preferred provider organizations. The purpose of these businesses is to cut the cost of mental health treatment to the minimum, although these companies also claim to be interested in quality treatment. Managed-care companies are concerned with locating treatment personnel who will provide short-term, symptom-oriented treatment. Essentially, managed-care organizations are interested in resolving the behavioral difficulties that prohibit the client from functioning in daily activities. There is less concern with the resolution of core issues creating the present symptomatology. Managed health care organizations pay more attention to the number of clinician-generated treatment plan extensions and referrals for added assessment and treatment. Thus, if a private practitioner wishes to contract with managed-care organizations, he or she will have to conform to the standards of that organization. Failure to do so will result in a dissolution of the contract with the managed-care organization.

Cost-saving treatment measures are only short lived. Without resolution of the actual dilemmas producing client symptomatology, somatization of mental and nervous disorders continues, creating more medical costs and continuing the frequent return of clients to therapy.

The added costs of paperwork and telephone time to the managed-care gatekeepers requires attention to overhead expenses, probable increases in office personnel, and possible decreases in direct client hours. The only way to avoid these business problems is to refuse to participate in managed health care programs or to refuse to accept third-party-payment clients. Therapists who choose this route are limiting their caseload to those individuals who can pay full fee or are accepting clients at reduced fees. Both these options are workable but have some limitations.

Clients who pay full fee tend to be from specific economic, racial, and age groups. Reduced-fee or sliding-scale clients are more varied in these characteristics. However, because the therapist is working at a reduced rate, he or she may have to exceed a 40-hour work week to earn an adequate living. Thus, private practitioners must be mindful of the goals for their practice and the types of clientele that they wish to serve. Proper attention to these requirements will allow the clinician to decide whether to contract as a provider for managed health care or to pursue private practice that generates its income from other sources.

Advantages and Disadvantages
of Private Practice

The seasoned clinician knows the freedom that private practice can bring. Yet that same practitioner knows that the freedom of private practice is earned after many years of intense work in developing a referral network and building a strong client caseload. The advantages of private practice are numerous.

1. *Autonomy*—The private practitioner can decide upon his or her office hours, vacation times, sick leave, and pay schedule.

2. *Client care follow through*—The private practitioner can serve the client throughout the treatment process. Unlike hospital or public agency treatment personnel, who are regulated by utilization review committees, the private practitioner can handle a complete case, from beginning to end.

3. *Caseload control*—Private practice permits the practitioner to design the practice to his or her specifications. The private practitioner can determine the type of clientele he or she wishes to serve and the method by which he or she wishes to deliver treatment. This freedom gives the therapist an outlet for creative program design and a sense of accomplishment.

There are also some disadvantages that the clinician considering private practice should explore.

1. *Fluctuating income*—Although private practice does promise more income than public practice, the early years are often marked by slim income and financial frustration. Income will vary until a referral network is in place and a caseload is established. Generally, after the practice matures, the income becomes more stable.

2. *Isolation*—Private practice can be lonely. In public practice, the therapist may be in contact with a number of other treatment people. The private practitioner who has no office support may spend the entire day conversing with clients. Challenge from colleagues, as well as relaxed conversation, is necessary to avoid burnout.

3. *Multiple responsibilities*—Private practice requires full responsibilities to clients and creditors. The private practitioner must shoulder the responsibilities for either hiring an effective office support person or managing the office personally. Furthermore, the therapist must be fully aware of client needs and be available for coverage even when not in the office.

Private practice is a service business in which therapy is the product. Success requires knowledge of effective business practices and decision-making skills. A business is a form of family that has rules and slogans by which it identifies itself. Like most families, business has both constructive and destructive models of behavior. It can be autocratic and rigid or codependent and enmeshed. Any given business is the reflection of its founder and therefore takes on his or her characteristics. If left unchecked, it can be stifling and destructive, but with proper attention and nurturance, business can be alive, invigorating, and challenging. Although private practice may seem overwhelming at first, it permits the clinician the freedom to design an environment in which therapy can be delivered without the encumbrances of external structures or dictates. Such independence, if managed effectively, allows the clinician to be innovative and powerful in the therapeutic session.

Public Practice in Marriage and Family Therapy

The public practice of marriage and family therapy involves conducting marriage and family therapy in a publicly supported agency or institution. Generally, these organizations tend to be funded by governmental sources, public contribution, or grants. However, there is a new form of public practice that does not fit this definition. It involves the delivery of human services to medical insurance subscribers in health maintenance organizations. The mental health practitioners who work in these public settings are salaried individuals who must adhere to bureaucratic regulations while delivering quality treatment.

Regardless of the arena, the public practice of marriage and family therapy is a challenging and exciting area in which to work. The clinician encounters numerous types of people, assorted treatment issues, and complex biopsychosocial problems that are not as frequently seen in any other treatment milieu.

Public Practice Options

The Public Agency Public practice involves providing treatment in an agency or setting that is financially supported by public funding. In a public practice environment, clinicians are usually salaried employees who carry a caseload, provide emergency or crisis coverage, participate in staffings and bureaucratic meetings, and prepare statistical reports on client-related hours. The size of the caseload varies depending upon the setting. Frequently, the agency requires a set number of client contact hours and a specific number of professional hours during which the therapist is expected to do paperwork, attend meetings, and obtain continuing education or supervision.

Working for an agency is rigorous. Caseloads at public agencies may range from 25 to 32 hours of client contact per week. Coverage both during the evenings and weekends is standard procedure. Paperwork, especially in federally funded programs, can be extensive and repetitive. After all, the paperwork justifies the agency's activities and positions it for further funding. Without the paperwork, the agency may cease to exist.

Agencies must deliver services specified in the grants or face losing revenue. For example, some agencies provide services to Hispanics who live in the barrios, while other agencies deliver services to victims of rape or sexual abuse. Generally, because the agencies are publicly funded, the clients tend to come from low- to lower-middle-income families. These individuals frequently are struggling with financial, psychological, and physical problems, which compound the marriage and family therapist's task of rehabilitation. Combined with these already difficult issues, the agency funding contract may specify that the treatment must be administered in a brief therapy format. Given these varied challenges, the therapist must be knowledgeable in community services, teamwork, and short-term therapy.

It is not surprising that this setting can produce maximum stress and discouragement on the part of the marriage and family therapist. In fact, burnout is commonplace in these settings because so much must be accomplished in so little time. Because of the pressure, ethical problems may inadvertently occur. For instance, a family that is struggling with a schizophrenic child may not be eligible for sufficient treatment to handle this complex problem. Yet the family may be unable to afford treatment in the private sector or to obtain adequate services for the child through the school psychologist. What can the marriage and family therapist do? Referral is not an option because of finances; education is limited since classes on parenting are generic and written material is generally not available to the public on this problem. Perhaps the family can be referred to a support group. Eventually, the family may suffer a crisis and be ineligible to obtain further agency assistance because they have used their maximum number of treatment hours for the year. The ethical marriage and family therapist does not abandon or neglect clients in treatment; yet agency policy may conflict with ethical dictates in some cases.

Governmental Agencies State and county governmental agencies provide services for the indigent, working-poor, disabled, and criminal populations. Therapists working in these settings frequently find it difficult to operate with a systems perspective, since the governmental agencies generally view the client as a single individual with specific needs. Therefore, marriage and family therapists in these positions may experience frustration in attempting to employ good family therapy procedures.

For example, a marriage and family therapist who works in a state or county hospital may be assigned to a patient who has been hospitalized for emotional problems. After interviewing the individual, the therapist may realize that the client is merely the symptom bearer of the family system. Since good clinical practice dictates working with the entire system, the clinician may wish to interview the family. In this situation, the clinician may be permitted to interview the family in service to the patient;

however, the therapist's mandated responsibility is to the patient. Thus, the therapist may be unable to continue family treatment.

This situation presents an interesting dilemma to the marriage and family therapist. Ethically, the clinician is dedicated to maintaining high standards of professional competence. Yet this situation prohibits the practitioner from delivering the best possible treatment. Codes also require the clinician to remain accountable to the standards of the profession and to carry out activities that advance the goals of the profession. Unfortunately, the organization's regulations are different from those of the systemic family therapist. What does the marriage and family therapist do in this situation? How does the clinician justify his or her treatment when it is below the highest standards of the profession?

These settings generally supply the clinician with a substantial caseload, which may require various levels of clinical involvement. Some clients may be seen only once or twice a year, while others, especially those affiliated with the criminal justice system, may be interviewed weekly or monthly. Each state or county agency defines its service-delivery expectations. In other words, some state and county agencies may require the marriage and family therapist to do therapy with the patient or the patient and his or her family, while other agencies may simply require the therapist to interview the patient for data-gathering purposes. The regulations vary from agency to agency; therefore, the clinician who wishes to work for governmental programs should investigate the areas in which he or she is interested.

Because most state and county agencies do not require their practitioners to be licensed or certified, many people can fill therapist positions without having appropriate credentials. Not infrequently, these noncredentialed individuals supervise credentialed therapists. If the supervision is purely administrative, the clinician is generally free to pursue treatment directions as he or she sees fit. However, if the supervisor is in charge of clinical supervision, the marriage and family therapist may encounter both professional practice and ethical dilemmas in delivering the prescribed treatment direction. Should such a problem occur, the clinician must speak with the supervisor and explain the dilemma as clearly as possible. If the client is at risk and the supervisor is unyielding, the marriage and family therapist must seek direction from the supervisor's superior. The therapist should definitely document the discussions and the rationale for treatment direction. If talking with the superior is unsatisfactory, it may be necessary to get advice from the personnel department. It is unwise to let one's clinical judgment be compromised simply to avoid confrontation with a supervisor.

Still another issue may develop in government agency programs. Individuals seeking treatment may exceed their defined duration of treatment but may need ongoing assistance because they are highly dangerous to themselves or others. In such situations, the marriage and family therapist has a duty to warn the identified victim, the agency administrators, and the police. Denying care to such an individual simply because length of treatment has been exceeded puts the therapist, the agency, the community, and the identified victim(s) at risk. Despite the agency regulations, the clinician is legally bound to report this individual.

Military Assignments The military offers unique ethical and legal dilemmas for the marriage and family therapist. As an officer in the armed services, the practitioner's first responsibility is to the government; therefore, the therapist working in this system may encounter unique problems associated with confidentiality, privacy, and recordkeeping. The military retains the right to know if anyone with whom the clinician is working is a physical threat to the safety of equipment, the base, or the country. As such, the marriage and family therapist is bound to report any valid information regarding potentially dangerous military personnel.

Despite these difficulties, the military has made definite inroads to guarantee that personnel who experience difficulty with alcohol, licit and illicit drugs, and family trauma receive immediate help. This treatment is generally administered through military supported in- and outpatient programs. One such program is the Army Family Advocacy Program, composed of an interdisciplinary team that is specially trained to deal with physical and sexual abuse. The program is designed to address two distinct problems: child abuse and spousal abuse. The child-abuse team acts as an advocate for the child and works in conjunction with state agencies to protect the child's welfare; the spousal-abuse team is treatment oriented and is designed to intervene in the family system.

The marriage and family therapist who works in these programs has the opportunity to facilitate healthy familial change. The thorny side to this work is the military's right to subpoena any person working with the children or the adults in these cases. Upon subpoena, the clinician must testify and must reveal the case record. Generally, the military will not intervene if the family is motivated to work through their difficulties. However, if the family is unable to change and there is probable cause to fear for the safety of the family or base personnel, the military is free to investigate and file charges. In fact, the clinician in the case is permitted to contact the base commander and have the male in the home ordered to live in the barracks until safety can be ensured.

Another difference for the military therapist occurs when working with people with special security clearance. Because people in these positions can be blackmailed, the military reserves the right to remove a person from his or her position during the investigation and the treatment process if damaging information about him or her is uncovered (e.g., allegations of child molestation). Depending on the person's rank and impact on the lives of others, the military may curtail his or her career. The marriage and family therapist in this position must accept the fact that he or she is employed by the armed services and is legally bound to inform them of detrimental material uncovered in the course of therapy.

/ **Health Maintenance Organizations (HMOs)**   Therapists working for HMOs are faced with similar problems. They may have caseloads of from 32 to 40 client hours per week and are expected to take coverage for weeknights and weekends. Paperwork and meetings are also a part of their job requirements. Because HMOs sell their coverage to numerous employers, the population using these services may differ from those clients at public agencies. Generally, HMOs limit the number of treatment sessions to between 15 and 25 sessions per year. The therapeutic hour varies from 30 to 50 minutes.

There are often other limitations on treatment in these organizations. Some HMOs do not permit inpatient chemical dependency treatment, while others specify diagnostic categories that are not treatable through their insurance plan. These categories are not generally known to the subscriber. Thus, a family with a bulimic daughter may not be able to obtain services through an HMO that does not recognize eating disorders as a psychological problem. Again, the ethical marriage and family therapist is faced with a dilemma: Treat the family problem but label it with an acceptable diagnosis, or refer the family to a private practitioner? Remember, the insurance will not pay for treatment from anyone other than an HMO provider.

Managed health care organizations are neither public practice nor private practice. These facilities pay therapists a salary, provide benefits, and make demands upon their employees similarly to the public agencies. Burnout is as high in these settings as in the public sector. The primary difference is the socioeconomic level of the client and the varied number of professionals in the treatment team. There is no question that the public and HMO sectors provide marriage and family therapists with a great deal of challenge and professional collegiality.

Public versus Private Practice

Borenzweig (1981) studied licensed social workers practicing in California and identified three groups: those in private practice ($n = 50$), those employed in an agency and engaged in part-time private practice ($n = 33$), and those employed exclusively by an agency ($n = 51$). He found that the lifestyles of private and public practitioners were more similar than different. As expected, the clients of private practitioners came from middle- and upper-class families, while those clients of agency practitioners were lower in socioeconomic status. Public agency clients tended to be more mixed racially and ethnically. Agency clients were more likely labeled psychotic then private practice clients. Also, more children were seen in agencies, and more young adults were seen in private practice. Private practitioners spent about 15% more of their work time seeing clients, and agency practitioners devoted more time to paperwork and bureaucratic business.

Generalizing these findings to all public practices is unwise, but the information does support the idea that public and private practices differ. Each has advantages and disadvantages. Public practitioners may earn less, but their benefits are usually fairly good. Private practitioners typically earn more, but their work environment is less secure. Private practitioners may be able to express their creative abilities more easily through the development of their practice, but they risk being overwhelmed by the diversity of tasks (e.g., bookkeeping, office management, billing). Public practice is a demanding yet important sector of employment for marriage and family therapists. It offers a wide variety of settings, clientele, and treatment issues. It is a wonderful training ground in which to learn about client problems and treatment methodology. Finally, the public sector tests the therapist's diagnostic and treatment skills, while offering a unique learning experience.

Business Practice in Marriage and Family Therapy

Business practice in marriage and family therapy refers to practicing therapy in a business environment. Providing therapy services to businesses was once a turf relegated to the psychiatrist and psychologist. Within the last 10 years, however, opportunities have increased for marriage and family therapists to serve the needs of businesses and their employees.

Today's marriage and family therapists are integrating themselves into the business and industrial environments and finding that the workplace is similar to the family system. Most of the theoretical constructs that the marriage and family therapist uses in resolving difficulties are applicable to the work setting. There are "grandparents" in the form of administrators, "parents" who are equivalent to the direct supervisors, and "children" who are the employees providing direct service, technical application, or maintenance on the product. The business environment also provides different socioeconomic strata, cultural differences, age variations, and political pressures found in the family system. Therefore, the marriage and family therapist need not feel unfamiliar in this new marketplace.

The Business Environment

Mental Health Issues The employment setting is fraught with stressors. Budget crises, layoffs, cutbacks, problem employees, and poor management skills contribute to decreased morale, excessive absenteeism, and reduced productivity. As a result, business and industry are searching for methods to preserve and maximize human resources. Managers are highly aware of the costs involved in maintaining troubled employees with poor work habits. Benefits personnel recognize that 12% to 19% of the employees constitute 65% of all the medical insurance claims. Statistics abound on the effects of drug usage, alcohol abuse, and mental illness on productivity and workman's compensation claims.

The cost of these human problems is ultimately passed on to the consumer as increased prices, higher insurance rates, and poor-quality products. Thus, the troubled employee impacts not only his or her family but also fellow workers, the employer, and the public.

History of Mental Health Intervention in the Workplace Personal problems extend beyond the home environment to the workplace. Employees must get along with co-workers and management regardless of personal differences. Stress resulting from time constraints, lack of resources, and poor management techniques adds another level of personal unrest for many workers. Thus, the individual with unsuccessful life-coping skills is at greater risk for developing further emotional problems. Frequently, these people respond with erratic behavior, drunkenness, tardiness, and/or prolonged absenteeism from work. In the past, management overlooked these problems. Only when the behavioral difficulties became too great did management suspend or terminate the employee. Unfortunately, these disciplinary efforts did little to change or correct employee behavior. In fact, termination of well-trained employees proved too costly. Thus, a new method of dealing with problem employees had to be developed.

Initially, employers hired occupational health specialists to perform health screening and employee physicals. These examinations indicated which potential employees were likely to suffer from medical problems that might influence work performance. Often the medical director or the occupational health nurse conducted weight control clinics, eye examinations, and onsite training on topics such as smoking cessation, cardiopulmonary resuscitation (CPR), and safety practices. Many of these early industrial medical health interventions dealt with alcoholism and alcohol-related problems, as well as issues associated with job stress and daily living. As occupational medicine departments grew in popularity, so did the range of their functions.

By the 1970s, another occupational specialty appeared and was known as occupational alcoholism programs. These programs were designed to inform employers that 95% of the alcoholics were not derelicts but *functional alcoholics,* many of whom were in the workforce. Consequently, employee-oriented alcoholism programs were revised to intervene in the alcoholic system before it progressed to the more debilitating stages. Research from these early programs showed that emotional problems were the principle reason for employee absenteeism in 61% of the companies (Phillips, 1961) and that 80% to 90% of all industrial accidents and 80% of firings were related to personal problems (Manuso, 1979).

Today's statistics continue to bear out the early research. U.S. business and industry loses an estimated $102.3 billion per year as a result of personal problems that impinge on employee job performance. Of this total amount, $54.7 billion is directly caused by alcoholism and alcohol-related incidents; $26 billion is caused by drug-related problems; and $21.6 billion is the result of mental illness (Assistance Programs, 1988). These costs underscore the strong need for the development and implementation of occupational health and employee assistance programs.

Employee Assistance Programs (EAPs) EAPs are an accepted benefit among both large and small companies in both the public and private sectors. The enthusiasm and acceptance of these programs as an integral part of human resource centers is a tribute to staff professionalism and concern for the welfare of both the employee and the organization. Of course, each organization has specific demands that the EAP must address: the size of the workforce, philosophy of the organization regarding employee problems, supervisory experience with human relations issues, security, and confidentiality.

Marriage and family therapists trained in systems theory will recognize that a large, hierarchical organization is very similar to an extended family. Transgenerational issues, triangulation, systemic dysfunction, problems in communication, secrets, and hidden agendas are as prevalent and significant in industry as they are in families. Industry merely replicates family dynamics on a larger scale. Therefore, the theories and facilitation skills utilized in rebuilding dysfunctional marriages and families are equally employable in solving employee relations difficulties in the work environment.

Because EAPs are considered an employee benefit, management expects that the program will contribute favorably to productivity. Although EAPs do not produce "hard" dollars, an effective program will generate so-called "soft" dollar gains such as decreased usage of health care benefits and increased morale by applying effective intervention strategies in the early stages of identification of a troubled employee. To assure early detection and treatment, the EAP coordinator must be well known and trusted, and the program must be thoroughly publicized through inhouse documents and inservice training programs. Posters identifying the program and phone number must be strategically placed in all work areas and lunchrooms. Finally, employees must trust that confidentiality will be strictly guarded unless they have waived that right.

EAPs are one of the most rapidly growing segments of the mental health marketplace. One half of the *Fortune* 500 companies have operating EAPs. Between 1972 and 1978, approximately 2,000 EAPs were established within U.S. businesses (Gomez-Mejia & Balkin, 1980). An estimated 10% of the total number of employees use services offered by EAPs. In fact, EAPs now outnumber community mental health centers, and it is likely that many more such programs will be created in the near future.

The purpose of many EAPs is to provide general assistance to employees in areas such as chemical dependency, psychological services, legal assistance, financial counseling, chronic physical health problems, job performance, and career/retirement planning. Typically, the EAPs based in larger companies offer more of these services than programs in smaller companies. However, the determining factor in the type of services offered is the human resources philosophy of the organization.

A survey of 1,000 organizations' counseling/clinical services indicated the following areas are most frequently incorporated within EAPs (Ford & McLaughlin, 1981):

Type of Service	EAPs Offering the Service
Alcohol rehabilitation	100%
Emotional therapy	94%
Marital/family therapy	91%
Financial counseling	87%
Legal counseling	79%
Career planning	70%

There are two major EAP formats: (1) externally based service centers or programs and (2) internally based programs. Internal programs are made up of employees in the organization who are identified as the EAP program. The program functions as a point of referral to community resources or internal counseling resources. Internal programs provide various types of services: (1) assessment and referral; (2) assessment, referral, and counseling; and (3) internally based program services with an offsite location for assessment, referral, and/or counseling services.

Some internal programs are administered through the employer's occupational health department. In these programs, the occupational health nurse or EAP coordinator assists employees in obtaining appropriate referral resources. Some smaller companies that do not have an EAP coordinator have contracts with social service agencies to provide therapy. In these instances, the agencies generally accept payments based on recommendations by the employees' insurance coordinator, who is usually a trained therapist with expertise in diagnosis and referral. These programs act as screening agents for the employees. The coordinator assesses the employee, makes the referral, and then follows up. Generally, if the referral is acceptable to the employee, the coordinator has no further involvement with the case. A coordinator stays involved with an employee only when a supervisor makes a referral that is directly related to employee job performance.

Another more elaborate model involves the establishment of an inhouse counseling center staffed by therapists on contract or employed by the company. This format permits employees to obtain a set number of office visits during the working hours. Although convenient for the employee, these programs are costly for the company, since they necessitate hiring or contracting with therapists and paying for treatment during working hours.

Staff qualifications within internal programs will vary according to program approach. Clearly, programs providing counseling within the organization require staff with formal counselor training, credentials, and experience. Those programs that only provide referral services usually require staff that have only basic clinincal training. In the past, a recovering executive was often put into this referral role. Today, companies are more likely to hire professionally trained staff to conduct referral services.

The alternative EAP format is the service center program, an externally based model in which the business contracts with an independent EAP service supplier in the community. The service center conducts assessment and may provide short-term counseling. This program design emphasizes assessment and referral exclusively, precluding the need to hire and supervise any mental health staff for either referral or treatment.

In some companies, an inhouse EAP refers employees to a service center that provides assistance on a contractual basis. Generally, a social service agency or mental health center is designated as the vendor for these services. The company either sends employees to the agency for treatment at no cost or contracts with the agency to provide services for a set fee. This is the type of EAP found in many rural areas because the local community mental health center is the only place where adequate services are available. Some large unions provide EAP services at the union office or hiring hall. Union coordinators at the worksite refer employees to the service, which acts as a referral source.

A more recent innovation is the hiring of a consulting employee assistance firm that has a network of therapists contracted for service at a reduced fee. These programs generally provide an established number of therapy sessions (6–10 sessions is typical) for which the company pays a reduced fee. If therapy extends beyond this number of sessions, the employee uses his or her insurance to pay for continued treatment. This model is becoming more prevalent and is evolving into an effective method of delivering managed health care to business and industry.

From the models of EAP programs described above, it is clear that assessment and referral are the services most commonly found in today's EAPs. The advantages of an internal program include good program control by management, good communication within the organization, ownership of the program, increased credibility with some supervisors, and onsite problem-assessment capability. The disadvantages are confidentiality problems and the need for a larger financial base to afford qualified personnel to staff the EAP.

In the near future and as the financing for mental health services changes, larger companies may hire staff to provide treatment services at the worksite. Marriage and family therapists are likely to be hired as staff for these onsite treatment centers.

All of these models exist. Some are more beneficial than others. Basically, the EAP of the eighties is a method of delivering high-quality mental health benefits while controlling costs. The future and organizational direction of the EAP in the nineties is less clear. Both HMOs and Preferred Provider Organizations (PPOs), another form of managed care, are competing with EAPs for the mental health dollars derived from the workplace. HMOs are employing occupational health nurses and social workers to provide direct service to employees seeking mental health treatment. To stay viable, some EAPs are moving into the gatekeeper position for managed-care organizations. These EAPs are providing precertification and utilization review for the major payers.

Such a move takes the EAP out of the treatment end of mental health coverage and puts it into the administrative end of the industry. Thus, many EAP employees must develop new business and management skills necessary to act as the middlemen in this era of managed health care. Some EAP directors are wondering if the EAP will survive this recent upheaval in the insurance industry. Whether the EAP changes in format, survives intact, or becomes obsolete remains to be seen. The reality is that managed health care is changing the face of mental health care and service delivery, and the employee assistance program is feeling that change. The marriage and family therapist interested in pursuing a career in employee assistance programs must be alert to the uncertainty of this marketplace and must follow the evolution of the industry to know which career paths remain vital.

Ethical Issues
in Employee Assistance Programs

(Psychotherapy practiced in a business environment can create ethical problems for the marriage and family therapist.) For instance, confidentiality is more vulnerable in an occupational setting than in a mental health clinic. Managers who are concerned about employee productivity and profit margins may be more interested in the total organization than in one individual. Thus, a troubled employee's confidentiality may be less important than the overall goal of a department or work area. Additionally, a supervisor who lacks adequate managerial training or who is experiencing personal conflicts may not always have the best interests of the employee in mind. In such instances, the supervisor may attempt to pressure a troubled employee into sharing confidences or force the EAP counselor to reveal confidential material. In fact, some managers who learn of employees' using EAPs may prohibit the employee from advancement or transfer to another work area. Although marriage and family therapists recognize that seeking help with personal and family difficulties is a way to solve problems and enhance productivity, not everyone is as enlightened. Some employers feel that anyone seeking help for psychological problems is weak and probably incompetent. Thus, (confidentiality must be strongly guarded in the work environment.)

In those programs where supervisory referrals to the EAP are an adjunct to disciplinary measures, the employee's right to confidentiality is maintained unless an illegal act is uncovered (e.g., embezzlement). With supervisory referrals, the supervisor is informed if the employee has attended the counseling session and is willing to accept the recommendations of the EAP counselor. In most organizations, an employee's refusal to accept a disciplinary referral is grounds for probation or termination.

(The important component of an effective EAP is the supervisory referral system.) Supervisory referral assures that supervisors are well trained in identifying but not diagnosing. By referring the employee to the EAP coordinator, the supervisor guarantees that the employee will be confronted regarding his or her reduced performance and will be offered the opportunity to obtain help. Thus, the supervisor does not need to counsel the employee. The employee is also given a chance to gain professional assistance in rectifying his or her personal problems.

Usually, an EAP offers assistance with marital problems, child management, stress, substance abuse, and legal and financial difficulties. The average cost to a company varies, depending on the model adopted. Thus, program costs have a wide range: $4 to $87 per employee per year with average costs amounting to $28 per employee per year. Mental health treatment is a real bargain compared with medical treatment: The average cost of medical claims per employee per year is between $110 and $175. Since effective therapeutic intervention reduces medical claims, an active EAP can offer a company significant savings on its benefits package. Recent statistics on EAPs show that for every $1 invested in the EAP, a business can expect to save $3 as a result of increased productivity and morale and decreased tardiness and absenteeism.

Marriage and family therapists can act as EAP coordinators or consultants to EAP networks. These programs offer the therapist an interesting population with diverse issues. Although the individuals come from an employment setting, they generally present problems similar to those found in either an agency or private practice setting. The primary difference may be in the presentation of job-related problems that are specific to an industry, department, or manufacturing process. Therefore, the marriage and family therapist must keep the following concepts in mind when working for or consulting with an employee assistance program.

1. View the case systemically.
2. Pay careful attention to the organizational politics involved.
3. Assess the ability and sensitivity of the employee to initiate the strategies necessary to resolve the problems.
4. Point out the alternative responses the employee has available.
5. Create a decision-making environment in which the employee selects and implements an effective response.
6. Keep high-quality records to document work with the employee.

The Future of Business Practice

Private employee assistance programs are expanding their scope of coverage to include managed health care. This is a new generation of EAPs designed to reduce mental health costs by as much as 20%. In the recent past, insurance plans have increased rates by as much as 30% per year. These increases continue even with effective utilization of review teams and restructured benefits plans.

In the new generation of EAPs, the coordinator is viewed as a gatekeeper whose task is to design and implement a structured, closed referral network of therapists who will deliver services at an agreed upon reduced rate for a guaranteed amount of clients. In this design, the gatekeeper assesses patient needs, determines diagnosis, refers, monitors, and assesses the quality of treatment. The gatekeeper is employed by the EAP and is a clinician with expertise in mental health and substance abuse. The referral network is composed of physicians, doctoral-level clinicians, social workers, marriage and family therapists, chemical dependency workers, and treatment facilities. The gatekeeper continuously monitors and audits the treatment of the contracted professionals. All financial arrangements are approved by the gatekeeper and are not negotiable. In fact, referral sources grant the EAP or provider network a 12% to 20% discount on treatment fees for the opportunity to be part of the referral system.

The case-managed delivery system appears to be proliferating. Whether it is effective has yet to be determined. It is still in its infancy, and many problems exist. Paperwork is exorbitant, and payment turnaround is at least 30 to 45 days. Regardless of client need, treatment is limited to a set number of visits per year, after which the client is financially responsible for further treatment. Clerks administering payment for service are not always knowledgeable about the details of the plan and therefore are not always accurate in the information they share with the practitioner. Consequently, payment for service may be inaccurate or forestalled because of poor auditing techniques.

Provider networks are not created equally. Although they can be a boon to a clinician's practice, they can also be a bust when turnaround time for payment exceeds three months, as it sometimes can. The marriage and family therapist who wishes to join a provider network should research the efficiency and quality of the referrals, clerical support, and financial remuneration of the organization before accepting assignment.

The occupational environment is recognized as an appropriate setting for the early identification of a number of psychological problems. This awareness has created a number of employee assistance programs and provider networks to serve people with alcohol, chemical dependency, and family-related problems. The marriage and family therapist interested in working in this area will find the clients challenging and often eager to overcome their difficulties, since these individuals wish to maintain their jobs and enhance their work performance. When considering program models in which to work, the clinician must review the program objectives, the known level of operational and organizational dysfunction within the program model, the method of achieving the objectives, whether treatment objectives can be obtained, and the measure by which to evaluate service delivery. Not all therapists will be comfortable working in a business setting where the dominant goal of the organization is profit for the owners. Therefore, the marriage and family therapist considering this environment must honestly assess his or her personal values and respond accordingly. Not to do so may result in personal dissatisfaction, which can interfere with effective therapeutic treatment.

Conclusion

The numerous clinical settings in which marriage and family therapy is practiced give the profession a variety and richness not always found in other careers. Mental health treatment is no longer a minor part of the medical treatment realm. Marriage and family therapy is an integral part of the mental health delivery system and bears the same recognition and scrutiny of its fellow mental health care providers. Such a dubious honor permits the profession to share in the competition for the mental health dollar with other more established mental health professions. Thus, while developing, honing, and implementing therapeutic techniques, ethical codes, certification, and licensing, marriage and family therapy must develop marketing stategies, build provider networks, and wrestle with the options of participating actively or passively within the managed-care system.

CHAPTER EIGHT

Educational Practice

Although marriage and family therapists are trained as clinicians, some individuals choose to practice as educators. These people utilize their training and knowledge in group dynamics and human communication to facilitate learning and meaningful interaction in hospitals, churches, mental health centers, community agencies, physicians offices, conciliation courts, public and private schools, universities, and free-standing institutes. Generally, therapists working in these arenas tend to cover a diverse range of topics, which can include parent education, sex education, family communication, chemical dependency awareness and recognition, values and morals, conflict resolution and problem solving, dating-skills training, marriage, and divorce recovery. Because marriage and family therapists working as educators disseminate a vast array of information, they are able to reach a varied population who might never seek therapy as a method to enhance or rehabilitate their family system. Thus, the therapist/educator is less restricted in the marketplace than the clinician.

The Marriage and Family Therapist/Educator

The discussion in this chapter is not meant as an exhaustive review of the numerous arenas in which the marriage and family therapist/educator can deliver service. Marriage and family therapist/educators who are interested in pursuing the instructional or training aspects in marriage and family therapy are encouraged to interview professionals in the field for assistance and direction in developing career paths and new audiences.

The University-Based Therapist/Educator

Educational practitioners—also known as academicians, academics, academy members, professors, and instructors—teach, do research, write, and supervise the practice of students in master's and doctoral programs. The academicians with supervisory and/or clinical affiliation in various national organizations, such as the American Association for Marriage and Family Therapy (AAMFT) and the American Psychological Association (APA), may also provide supervision in postdegree institutes to individuals seeking clinical or supervisory membership in those organizations.

Academicians experience both extreme pressure and flexibility, since the career requires them to contribute to the base of professional knowledge through research and teaching. In other words, the professor has the task of developing and learning new material in the field while providing timely information and clinical expertise to students, clinicians with degrees, and colleagues. This stress creates a milieu that demands proficiency and creativity. Certainly, the rigors of this environment can lead to ethical and legal dilemmas in delivering relevant coursework and valid, well-substantiated research that protects its subjects. Also, academicians must interact with students, supervisees, and employees in an ethical fashion. Thus, the university-based therapist/educator must be vigilant in his or her pursuit of knowledge and delivery of information while carefully monitoring relationship boundaries to avoid dual relationships.

Research Careers

The lifestyle attached to research positions is not an easy one. People in these positions must teach at least one or two courses per semester, sit on various doctoral committees, engage in research programs, publish, perform community service, participate in the governance of their academic department, attend conferences, and take on leadership in professional associations. Should the academic experience difficulties in mastering these professional milestones, tenure may not be granted. It is not surprising that individuals facing these stressors may encounter personal dilemmas that may make them question their career objectives.

Those individuals who decide to continue in academia face more challenges and demands as they climb the academic career ladder. A faculty member is expected to develop a research program that will generate funding outside the university (e.g., government agencies such as the National Institute of Mental Health, private foundations, and large corporations). Emphasis is placed on outside funding because it indicates the quality of the research program and the strength of the investigator's ideas. Since family research money tends to finance the topics of immediate social concern, researchers typically tailor their attention to those matters that are of interest to grantors. Unfortunately, what is favored at one time may not be favored a few years later. Such pressure to produce accurate, viable research can create an environment that may tax the professor, test the acumen of the investigative staff, and stress the department. Therefore, the researcher must acknowledge and adjust to the changing initiatives of funding agencies and the stringent demands of the research institution.

Researchers are constantly faced with the challenge of developing ethically based investigations that respect the dignity of the participants. The 1988 AAMFT ethical code is not as detailed on ethical research practices as is that of the APA. Nonetheless, in planning a research project, the marriage and family therapist/educator has the responsibility to carefully evaluate both the legal (e.g., duty to protect, informed consent) and ethical (e.g., confidentiality) ramifications of the study and to present the protocol to the institutional review board for approval. Students who conduct research that is supervised by faculty must be informed of their ethical responsibilities to the subjects, school, and profession.

The researcher must safeguard both the subjects and the research assistants. Generally, universities have detailed procedures for monitoring faculty and student research so that it will not harm subjects. In those projects that require concealment of technique, the investigator must reveal the rationale for the experimentation in a logical, understandable manner so as to allay physical or mental discomfort or harm to the participants. In experimental research, participants must be informed of what will happen to them and the possible harm they might incur as a result of the experimentation. Certainly, a research procedure must not be used if it is likely to cause damage to the participants. In studies that require the researcher to change a protocol to collect information generally unavailable by accepted investigative technique (e.g., extended unstructured interviewing), the researcher may be creating a "special relationship," as defined by the *Tarasoff* case. Should such a relationship uncover threats to another, the researcher may be bound to protect the potential victim (Appelbaum & Rosenbaum, 1989). Finally, the investigator must provide the participants with documentation about the nature of the study so as to remove any misconceptions about the research. Above all, the investigators and participants must be protected from any negative consequences of the procedure.

Thus, the researcher functions in a multirole capacity: investigator, educator, ethicist, and publicist. This multifaceted position is certainly intriguing and dynamic, as it permits the academic the freedom to design a project, see it through, publish it, and possibly revise it for further benefit to the field.

Teaching Careers

By implication, a teaching career is more focused on instruction than research. A career in teaching is typically available at the universities and colleges that offer the master's degree as the terminal degree in marriage and family therapy.

The career ladder and timing of promotions is the same for teaching and research positions. However, the criteria for promotion differs. At teaching institutions, faculty teach three or four courses each semester, approximately double that at research universities. Consequently, tenure and promotion decisions weight the quality of teaching more heavily than research. Nonetheless, the tenure criteria for teaching faculty often includes publishing, the development of new courses, and advising undergraduate and graduate students.

Teaching family science or marriage and family therapy presents unique ethical issues. The content of many courses is on family structure, interfamilial problems, and sexuality. The educator delivering this material must be clear and direct. Some students may be fascinated by the data, while others may be surprised or even disconcerted about information that differs from their subjective awareness. When these situations arise, the student may become inquisitive, passive, or argumentative about the subject matter. The ethical educator takes time to listen to him or her and help the student understand the material in a helpful and healthy context.

For example, a student who has grown up in a family that never expressed feelings may find it difficult to acknowledge that healthy families express both positive and negative emotions openly. In fact, the unexpressive graduate student in marriage and family therapy may find it difficult to permit his or her client to display emotion or verbalize intense feelings. The educator must gently support and direct such students to explore their own feelings, as well as those of the student practicum's client. Assisting students in overcoming these personal obstacles is part of the training experienced by students in most degree and postgraduate programs.

Perhaps one of the most difficult ethical dilemmas a therapist/educator faces is confronting and counseling a student who does not have the personal or interpersonal skills to function effectively as a therapist. At times, individuals pursue marriage and family therapy training for personal discovery and problem resolution. These individuals bring their unique emotional problems to the academic setting. While some of these students may be able to overcome their personal problems through individual therapy and awareness created by learning about their family of origin, others may be unable to do so.

A common reaction when therapist/educators attempt to discuss these problem areas with students who cannot adjust is outrage, recrimination, and threat of litigation against the professor and/or the school. Certainly, anyone faced with this reaction may be forced to reconsider. However, the skills commonly applied to the therapy setting are helpful in the educational context and can be used to counsel these individuals out of the marriage and family therapy profession. Faculty is responsible for addressing these problems, and failure to do so can jeopardize both the public and the profession.

Free-Standing Institutes

Free-standing institutes provide continuing education for degreed professionals who may not have obtained their credentials from approved marriage and family therapy programs or programs that emphasized marriage and family therapy treatment. These institutes are aimed at educating the professional who is actively practicing marriage and family therapy. In general, these institutes are run by clinicians who provide realistic strategies for practitioners dealing with difficult treatment dilemmas, ethical problems, and professional practice issues. The institutes give classes that are graded by level of clinician competency and knowledge. Because the institutes deliver training that is tailored to student needs, the curriculum is varied yet specific to the individual's professional maturity. Thus, the free-standing institute is a forum for all levels of clinicians to meet, discuss, build, and challenge their knowledge in marriage and family therapy.

Unlike the university-based therapist/educator, the clinician/educator does not have to meet the rigorous demands of a research-based institution. However, free-standing institutes still experience the same pressure to provide ethical instruction and accurate, state-of-the-art courses. Even though these institutes do not grade students, student exploitation is still possibile, since some of these institutes provide approved supervision for entrance into national organizations or registries.

Free-standing institutes attract a number of experienced practitioners who must obtain continuing education credit in order to maintain their membership, certification, or licensure in national organizations and/or states granting licensure. These individuals may be older, more experienced, and well recognized in the field. Therefore, it may be easy for them to intimidate or distract the instructor. When such incidents occur, the marriage and family therapist/educator must acknowledge the individual's information while continuing to deliver quality instruction to the others in the class. To let the more verbal clinician disrupt the lecture or demonstration is a violation of other students' right to quality education. Thus, free-standing institutes must adhere to the same codes of ethics and legal principles that universities follow.

Therapist/Educator Practice Options

Besides the teaching and research positions in academia and free-standing institutes, several other options exist for the marriage and family therapist who is primarily interested in educational practice. For example, employers and employee assistance program coordinators solicit prevention education for stress management, alcoholism and chemical dependency, interpersonal communication, and conflict resolution. Marriage and family therapist/educators are frequently hired to deliver this information on a consulting basis because of their direct experience with these subjects. These training arenas are generally filled with employees who are interested in obtaining information that will help them perform their work assignments and handle interpersonal interactions better. Therefore, the therapist/educator who delivers this type of training must be dynamic, well versed in the subject matter, and have training in teaching the adult learner. Frequently, these programs include both didactic and interactional or experiential material to facilitate learning. Because these programs are delivered in a business setting, the marriage and family therapist/educator must adhere to the protocol and regulations of such an environment. Not to do so could create a situation in which the adult learner would resist the trainer and the information. Furthermore, it could jeopardize the therapist/educator's chances of obtaining further training contracts within the business community.

Many public schools now require sex education for students. Marriage and family therapists are the logical ones to provide this instruction. Community mental health centers and other community agencies need access to parent education classes, marital and family enrichment classes, and other psychoeducational resources. As health costs escalate, health care providers and third-party payers seek help from those professionals who can design and implement effective educational programs.

Some of these programs are preventive in nature, some are rehabilitative, and some are both. Many family court systems, for example, require parents convicted of child abuse to take parent education courses as a stipulation of sentence. The judge's objective for these clients is to correct parenting deficiencies and to prevent future abuse. Conciliation courts offer instructional programs to individuals and couples dealing with the problems of single parenthood, stepparenting, stepgrandparenting, blending families, and triangulation within stepfamilies.

All these programs are extensions of the work done in the therapy setting. Each course requires preparation of content and instructional material and a dynamic presentation. Because the court system is a legal entity, information must be delivered that speaks to the laws of the specific state (e.g., custody laws, community property statutes). The therapist/educator who presents this material must be fully versed in the significant laws pertaining to the subject matter. The material must be presented in an unbiased manner that is comprehensible to the participants regardless of their intelligence and academic background.

Finally, the therapist/educator who works with or for the court system must be credible and approachable, since people in these classes tend to be experiencing family stress, which can be emotionally disturbing and distressful. Not to relay the information in such a manner can lead to unethical practice, since marriage and family therapists know that they have the ability to influence and alter the lives of others. Therefore, the therapist/educator must exercise caution when making teaching recommendations. (The unapproachable therapist/educator can intimidate the attendees and cause them to dismiss, misuse, or misunderstand the information.)

Marital enrichment is an example of the same treatment serving the purposes of rehabilitation and prevention. Emerging out of the human potential movement during the late 1960s and early 1970s, (marital enrichment programs are patterned experiences designed to teach specific skills required for marital success.) The primary objective of some programs is to heighten feelings of attachment and affection between spouses. Some programs achieve both intimacy and increased skills, depending on the intent of the program designer.

Whichever is emphasized, the consumers of these programs were originally only those wanting to improve already satisfying relationships. As research mounted showing the effectiveness of these programs, several studies found the programs were helpful to couples experiencing high marital stress (Brock & Joanning, 1983). These results have tended to help therapists view educational interventions as an important component of their practices.

Over time, more of what we call therapy is becoming educational. Fifteen years ago, training couples in communication skills would probably not have made up a portion of their therapy. Such training is common today. The same change has come about for training in parenting skills. It is now incorporated into therapy and not relegated to only a separate experience for clients. Even the research on family therapy treatment for schizophrenia shows that psychoeducational methods are more effective than traditional therapy.

This integration of educational practice with traditional mental health practice has several influences on professionals. First, as noted above, traditional therapy is becoming more educational. As a result, therapy itself—and good therapy, in particular—is more readily identified than in the past. The well-trained marriage and family therapist educates the family on the process of treatment. In so doing, the therapist earmarks the significant process levels of treatment, thereby teaching clients what stage of therapy they are in, how long that stage will last, and how long therapy itself will last.

Second, (more responsibility for the effectiveness of therapy is being attributed to the therapist) As in the college classroom, students take some responsibility for what they learn, but by and large, the instructor is held responsible for students' progress. As therapy becomes more educational, the expectations for therapists change. In other words, the therapist becomes both a facilitator and teacher. For example, parents need to be taught how to manage incorrigible children, stepparents need to learn how to blend families, and children need to be instructed on methods to control their impulsive behavior. Eventually, as the body of knowledge about helping families becomes as extensive as that about what schoolchildren need to learn, what is now called therapy will become known as training and psychoeducation.

Third, a newly defined career track has emerged for educational practitioners, that of Family Life Educator (FLE). In 1981, the National Council on Family Relations established a certification program for FLEs. The criteria consist of coursework in family theory and dynamics, human development, sexuality, interpersonal relations, family resource management, parent education, public policy, ethics, and family life education methods. In addition, a one-course practicum experience is required prior to receiving either the bachelor's or master's degree and 1,000 hours of direct service afterward. While the certification is not well known, it does provide employers with some guidance on the level of training they might ask for when attempting to hire a professional who will deliver high-quality educational services to families. More information about this certification is available from the National Council on Family Relations, whose national office is in Minneapolis, Minnesota.

Whether a marriage and family therapist seeks certification as a family life educator or not, educational practice is a fast-growing area for treatment and prevention and one capable of being practiced in a number of settings. As prevention becomes a greater thrust within the health care system, educational practice will be the primary means of carrying out that initiative. The future is bright for educational practitioners.

Marriage and Family Therapy Supervision

The field of marriage and family therapy specifies two aspects of training: instruction in theory and supervised practice. Though some students may receive their training in an academic setting, others may be practicing clinicians who have chosen to develop or hone their skills. The practicing clinicians frequently are from other mental health disciplines in which marriage and family therapy was not stressed or taught. These students present different supervisory needs from those of academic students. Thus, the supervisor must be attuned to the needs of the various theoretical and clinical levels of individuals seeking supervision. Simply applying the same form of supervision to all student populations is inappropriate and belies sound ethical practice.

Ethical Supervision

The goal of supervision is to model a healthy, helping relationship while imparting fundamental therapeutic knowledge. Supervision is not therapy. It is a dynamic relationship between supervisee and supervisor in which information, skills, and professionalism are nourished and promoted. In this interaction, the supervisor designs and facilitates an open environment that is conducive to learning and questioning. The primary concern is that the values of the profession be imparted and demonstrated throughout the supervision process.

Because supervision is a hierarchical relationship, there is the potential for exploitation. Therefore, the supervisor must be vigilant as to his or her impact on the supervisee's development as an effective clinician. In order to avoid any adverse results from the supervisory interaction, the supervisor must clearly define the relationship verbally and, where appropriate, contractually. The purpose of the contract is to define the specifics of the relationship and to protect the rights of the supervisee. An effective supervisory contract dictates the time, place, frequency, and length of the sessions. It also states the expectations in the areas of confidentiality, self-directedness, decision making, treatment facilitation, and contract revision. By creating an environment that facilitates feedback, the supervisor promotes the growth of the supervisee and the profession.

Supervisor's Legal Liability

Under the law, a supervising marriage and family therapist has a professional responsibility to provide the accepted and usual standard of care specific to supervision. For example, the supervising therapist must assess the clinician's ability, noting his or her strengths and weaknesses; monitor the treatment he or she delivers; and forbid him or her to practice beyond the scope of his or her capabilities. The supervisor is in fact responsible and accountable for the supervisee's behavior and facilitation of treatment with the client and therefore must pay close attention to the ethical and legal actions of the supervisee. Failure to do so may create liability for the supervisor.

This culpability may vary, depending on the nature of the supervision. In working with academic students, the supervisor must make certain that the supervisee assigned to the client is competent enough to diagnose and treat the case, given appropriate supervision. The supervisor must review the treatment plan, make certain it is correct, and assure that it is carried out effectively. This may involve group supervision with peers, direct supervision after completion of the session, being in the room while the treatment is being delivered, observing the supervisee through a one-way mirror, and/or reviewing and critiquing audio- and videotapes. Each supervisor has his or her own technique. Sometimes it is predicated on the supervision that the supervisor received in his or her training, while at other times it involves a composite of various supervision frameworks. There is currently no universal method or technique for supervision.

Since marriage and family therapy has its own set of theoretical constructs, the experienced clinician seeking supervision may not be aware of the difference between the practice of individual or group therapy and that of marriage and family therapy. The supervisor must impart this information to the trainee and determine the extent of the supervisee's grasp of the information. The supervisor in this situation must also clarify the exact nature of the relationship to the supervisee: consultant supervisor, employer supervisor, or training supervisor. Each of these positions has the same ethical implications, although there are slightly different legal consequences, depending on the supervisor's role.

The _consulting_ position requires a clearly defined explanation of the supervisor's responsibilities. Generally, a consulting supervisor sees the supervisee and the supervisee's client jointly for a limited time period. Occasionally, the referring supervisee may choose to send the client to the supervisor for an impartial assessment. Although it may be argued that the client is technically in a clinical relationship with the supervisee, the supervisor usually receives reimbursement for the supervision and/or supervisory consultation. Therefore, should the supervisor provide negligent assessment, he or she could be held as accountable as if he or she had delivered negligent treatment.

The _employer_ supervisor may also be liable under the doctrine of _respondeat superior_ ("let the master respond"). As was mentioned in Chapter 3, this theory holds the employer liable for the acts of his or her employees within the scope of their employment. Even if the employer did not provide the treatment, the court can find him or her liable for the conduct of employees. In Arizona, for example, a psychiatrist who employed a psychologist at his institute was found liable for a percentage of the settlement with a client with whom the psychologist had sexual relations. Although the court recognized that the psychologist was the perpetrator of the action, the court said that the psychiatrist should bear at least a minimum amount of the responsibility for his employee's misconduct (_Hall_ v. _Stich, Ph.D., and the Schulte Institute for Psychotherapy and Human Sexuality, Inc., Schulte, M.D., and Schulte_).

Training supervisors (e.g., agency employees supervising students or trainees as part of the employee's job requirements, field instructors) bear the same responsibility as supervisors of academic students. In fact, some field instructors supervise academic students. Therefore, the supervisor is accountable to the supervisee and the client for responsible treatment. In other words, the supervisor must meet regularly with the supervisee, assess his or her competency, review the client record to determine the appropriateness of the treatment, ascertain the adequacy of the treatment, make treatment corrections when indicated, and continually review the treatment plan to note client progress. All this is necessary to make certain that the supervisee does not practice beyond the scope of his or her competency.

Because of the liability considerations, supervisors must understand the ethical and legal guidelines of the profession. A supervisor accepts both the responsibility for treatment delivery and the actual control of the treatment plan when he or she accepts a student as a supervisee. Should a lawsuit ensue as a result of a supervisee's actions, the court will make the decision as to the degree of the supervisor's culpability. Certainly, the employer supervisor is at greater risk than the consulting supervisor, whose sole responsibility is to use due care and demonstrate professional competence.

Good-quality supervision is the product of experience, both in the consulting room and as a supervisor. When included in the context of other forms of marriage and family therapy practice, supervising trainees is a rewarding experience that forces the supervisor to become clearer about what he or she believes about marriage and family therapy. In many ways, the rewards and the frustrations of supervising are similar to those of rearing children: In attempting to pass on something of what one knows to the next generation, he or she comes to know it for the first time.

Ethical Issues in Educational Practice

Whether the marriage and family therapist conducts educational practice as a researcher, teacher, or family life educator, the roles of supervisor and teacher are vulnerable to several ethical problems. At the basis of these problems is the dual relationship. By definition, when a supervisor occupies a dual role with a student, some aspects of the roles must conflict.

For example, when a supervisor who is responsible for evaluating a supervisee's progress also provides therapy to that supervisee, the evaluation aspect of the supervisor's role may conflict with the therapist role. The conflict may result in any of several possible outcomes. Either the supervisor's evaluation or the therapeutic acceptance may suffer because the supervisor/therapist may permit information from working with the student as a supervisee to impact on working with the student as a client. The supervisor/therapist may realize that the student/client's uncovering of significant personal therapeutic material has impaired the student's immediate ability to be objective in working with a specific family. Thus, the supervisor/therapist may excuse the student's failure to assist that client family in overcoming a therapeutic impasse while the student is working on personal core family-of-origin issues. Although the practice of providing therapy in the context of supervision is no longer accepted by the AAMFT Commission on Marriage and Family Therapy Supervision, students still encounter and seek such dual relationships because they feel safe with their training professors (Brock & Sibbald, 1988).

Another commonly accepted dual relationship involves the barter exchange of supervision for services of some kind (e.g., carpentry services, exchange of research services, cleaning services). The complicating factor in these arrangements is that the supervisor must monitor the quality of work done by the student. If the work is unsatisfactory, the quality of the supervision may be influenced by either the student or the supervisor. Educators experience dual-relationship problems with highly responsive students who are eager to engage their mentors in challenging discussion regarding the profession during off hours. These lengthy talks, although seemingly innocent, may draw the professor away from personal and family responsibilities and may inadvertently build student-teacher affiliations that extend far beyond the accepted relationship limits. When this occurs, it can taint the instructor's ability to assess the student's performance accurately. Another pitfall of this type of dual relationship is that the student-teacher connection can be misperceived or misunderstood as being intimate or seductive. Certainly, when this perception problem occurs, the relationship becomes distorted, imbalanced, and potentially exploitive. Thus, the student and the educator must be wary of the danger of such dual relationships and make every effort to avoid them.

In the context of educational practice, dual roles with supervisees and students must be entered into with care. Is attending a social event with students appropriate for a supervisor? Most supervisors do attend such events but only on a limited basis so as to avoid potential problems that could bias their evaluation of the student. Can or should a spouse provide supervision to a partner? Should a spouse take a course from a partner? Generally, the answer to these questions is no because aspects of the dual roles may conflict, and the person in the least powerful position may suffer. Consequently, in all dual relationships, it is the responsibility of the more powerful role-player to recognize the potential for harm and take steps to protect the less powerful person. In most instances and for all types of marriage and family therapy supervision, that responsibility belongs to the supervisor.

Finally, there are other ethical dilemmas that the therapist/educator may encounter. Although these problems are not specifically dual relationships, they are just as difficult to solve. Professors are well aware that working with marriage and family issues requires knowledge of the social structure of the family, as well as the cultural, religious, and political philosophies of family members. Knowing the language of the client may be critical, as well. Students from foreign cultures who pursue degrees in marriage and family therapy may not always understand these subtleties. In fact, these students may be struggling with language or disenfranchisement issues that may interfere with their ability to work in depth with some of their practicum families.

Supervisors of these students must be very patient and gentle in guiding them toward building language skills and exploring cultural differences while learning the constructs of marriage and family therapy. Because these students are facing their own issues of family disconnectedness, language difficulty, and homesickness, the supervisor must point out the importance of staying focused on treatment issues while staying aware of personal factors that may incorrectly influence treatment decisions.

Conclusion

Supervision is essential to effective marriage and family therapy practice. Competent supervision is necessary in the transmission of the profession's values and standards. In particular, supervision should cover the concepts of professional liability, client confidentiality, appropriate intervention skills, theoretical constructs, consultation with and referral to adjunctive specialists, informed consent, privileged communications, guidelines for facilitation of treatment, and methods for appropriate treatment termination. Although much of today's supervision may be defensive because of the litigious nature of our society, supervision should cover the importance of the ethical issues of the appropriate delivery of marriage and family therapy. By offering high-quality supervision, marriage and family therapy educators safeguard the profession, provide for the protection of clients' rights, and ensure therapists' personal and professional protection.

CHAPTER NINE

The Future of Marriage and Family Therapy

Until 1970, most psychotherapists were taught specific theoretical constructs that were applied equally to all forms of psychological distress. These philosophies were based on particular theories of pathology, inquiry, facilitation techniques, and treatment. As researchers began developing new methods of psychological inquiry and treatment techniques, more therapeutic models evolved. Investigation into these various theoretical paradigms revealed that various treatment schools worked equally well across the spectrum of clients; therefore, therapists adopted a more eclectic orientation that combined more than one philosophy and technique. Concepts such as the healing effects of a positive therapeutic relationship, the revivification of childhood traumas, and practicing new behaviors became identified with good therapeutic treatment.

Systemic family therapy is a relatively new approach to the treatment of marital and family problems. For the most part, other treatment models use an individually oriented, linear method of understanding human problems. Although most disciplines recognize that family problems impact individuals, their families, and communities, few embrace the systemic treatment model.

Not all marriage and family therapists are systemically oriented. Some are reassessing systems theory and questioning it as the central organizing framework for treatment. In fact, some marriage and family therapists find the systemic orientation too provincial because they believe it does not consider gender differences, childhood experiences, addictions, adulthood events, sociopolitical ideologies, and religious orientations. Their criticism of systems theory is particularly forceful on the issue of family violence. With such divisions in the discipline, systemic marriage and family therapists find themselves misunderstood, ignored, or even sabotaged by some treatment professionals, institutions, and insurance companies.

Despite these obstacles, marriage and family therapy continues to thrive. It is quite healthy for a profession and its members to question theory and operation. Without constant assessment and evaluation, the profession can become stagnant and antiquated. There is little chance of that happening to marriage and family therapy in the near future.

The Outlook for Marriage and Family Therapy

The entire health care delivery system is in flux. Many medical and mental health practitioners are questioning their future and for good reason. The nature of the economy, threats of malpractice, the direction of individual rights, the definition of *family,* the transitory nature of the population, and the cost of health care impact the profession more strongly than in previous decades. Forecasters proclaim the decline of individualized health care and the rise of managed care. Other predictors indicate that cost-containment measures are creating rather than solving problems. Yet other soothsayers predict another generation of health care that has not yet been defined. The result is that no one truly knows the future of either health care delivery or marriage and family therapy. The only certainty is that people will continue to have both medical and psychological needs that will require assistance from professional treatment personnel.

At one time, family therapists practiced in isolation and obscurity for fear of criticism by their colleagues. Today, marriage and family therapy is routinely practiced in nearly every mental health setting:

conciliation courts;
foster and residential care facilities;
social service agencies;
mental health centers;
divorce mediation organizations;
correctional institutions;
hospitals; and
private medical and mental health practices.

The marriage and family therapist may function as a treatment provider, as well as an administrator in most of these settings. Training in systems theory permits the individual to assess the environment, the various interactions within the environment, and the strategies needed to correct dysfunction. Thus, it is not surprising to find that marriage and family therapists are at ease as consultants in companies requiring organizational development. The same skills they use in the consulting room apply in the boardroom. (Marriage and family therapists are change agents who effectively assist people to redesign relationships, sociopolitical structures, and ineffectual behavior)

As people struggle to obtain a better quality of life, they seek professionally trained individuals to assist them in sorting out viable alternatives to their present lifestyle. Whether a client is requesting help with adoption or coping with aged, infirm parents, the marriage and family therapist has the skills and knowledge to lead him or her into making an acceptable decision. As previous chapters have illustrated, marriage and family therapists face difficult questions of ethical and legal dilemmas and professional practice issues. (The theory, research, and practice of marriage and family therapy as a distinct discipline has given it a credibility and a foundation on which to grow and develop.)

As the discipline of marriage and family therapy continues to develop, it gains an identity among both practitioners and the public. The validation of licensure and certification assures that marriage and family therapy is a recognized discipline with an established field of study and a code of ethical principles that guides treatment and safe practice for the public. Laws concerning confidentiality, informed consent, privileged communication, recordkeeping, and professional conduct bind treatment professionals to uniform delivery of a standard of care that is measured against existing practices. Such underpinnings serve to strengthen the professional identity and solidify the profession as one of the major mental health professions.

(Just as the design of the family is in transition, so too is that of the profession that treats the family.) Marriage and family therapy is an active discipline, one that evolves in relationship to the individuals it treats. Various schools of thought exist and are employed to aid the family in its quest for a more healthy existence. Along the path, some treatment methodologies will be modified, others will rise to full acceptance, and others will fall into oblivion. For a particular treatment method to be successful over time, it must embody the ethical components of integrity and professional responsibility. Treatment procedures and adherence to professional standards are not isolated aspects of professional life. Ignoring the relationship among treatment, theory, and professional standards leaves the profession without structure and the therapist without power to help families change. The life of the profession is as active as those who facilitate and use it.

Conclusion

The best interests of families are served when the profession can challenge its theoretical frameworks, evolve professional standards, and provide ethical and legal guidelines by which the membership and the public can be assured quality and effective treatment. Ignoring the fundamental principles of professional practice or permitting colleagues to do so diminishes both the practice and the profession of marriage and family therapy. The purpose of this book has been to bolster both by enhancing the practitioner's understanding of the ethics, legalities, and issues common to professional practice.

APPENDIX A

Ethical Practices in Marriage and Family Therapy: A Research Study

In 1988, Gregory Brock and Jeanette Coufal, at the University of Kentucky, conducted the first nationwide study of marriage and family therapists practice behavior related to ethics and the *American Association for Marriage and Family Therapy (AAMFT) Code of Ethical Principles.* To identify the standards of professional practice among marriage and family therapists, Brock and Coufal surveyed 1,000 randomly selected AAMFT clinical members; 540 responded. The questionnaire asked whether and how often respondents engaged in 104 clinical behaviors mostly related to ethical practice. The findings of the study likely generalize to the entire AAMFT membership because the sample was randomly selected, the return rate was high (54%), and the demographic make-up of the sample closely matched that of the AAMFT membership.

Not all the results are reported here, only those related to the topics addressed in a 1989 issue of *Family Therapy Networker* (Brock & Coufal, 1989) and a few pertaining to important issues faced in practice today. The complete results can be found in the professional journals and the *AAMFT Ethics Case Book* (scheduled for publication in 1991). Completing the questionnaire is an effective way to learn all portions of the AAMFT ethical code. It is especially useful as a teaching tool. To inquire about the questionnaire, contact Gregory W. Brock (see address on page 159).

Items from The Ethical Behavior Index for Marriage and Family Therapy are excerpted from "Ethics and Pratice," an article that first appeared in the *Family Therapy Networker.* It is reprinted here with permission. To order back copies or a subscription ($20), call (301) 589-6536.

Confidentiality

Confidentiality is an important characteristic of all psychotherapeutic relationships, and its significance is recognized in the *AAMFT Code of Ethical
Principles.* Yet the study revealed a number of concerns. For example,
therapists rarely discuss clients by name with friends, but 35% discuss
clients anonymously with friends sometimes or frequently. Likewise, nearly
half of those surveyed only sometimes obtain client permission to tape
sessions or permit observation.

Surprisingly and despite the risk of triangulation, 69% of therapists
sometimes or more frequently are willing to keep one spouse's secrets
from the other. If the secret is an affair, therapists are very willing to keep it
hidden: 96% rarely or never reveal an affair to the other spouse.

Surveyed items pertaining to confidentiality (all numbers are per-
centages):

Limit case notes to name, date and fee.

Never	Rarely	Sometimes	Often	Always
52.3	22.9	13.3	8.4	3.0

Store client records in unsecured area or cabinet.

Never	Rarely	Sometimes	Often	Always
55.3	22.4	10.5	5.8	6.0

See a minor client without parental consent.

Never	Rarely	Sometimes	Often	Always
49.9	29.9	16.3	3.4	.6

Tell child about parent's disclosure to you.

Never	Rarely	Sometimes	Often	Always
46.1	37.0	15.2	1.5	.2

Tell parents about child's disclosure to you.

Never	Rarely	Sometimes	Often	Always
23.5	49.5	22.9	3.8	.4

Inform intended victim of client's threat to harm.

Never	Rarely	Sometimes	Often	Always
9.5	15.6	16.0	10.3	48.7

Break confidentiality to report child abuse.

Never	Rarely	Sometimes	Often	Always
6.2	10.8	16.8	12.3	54.0

Report client's crime disclosed in therapy.

Never	Rarely	Sometimes	Often	Always
46.7	36.2	13.0	1.5	2.5

Get client consent to tape session or have observer.

Never	Rarely	Sometimes	Often	Always
3.8	13.4	30.0	14.5	38.3

Discuss clients (without names) with friends.

Never	Rarely	Sometimes	Often	Always
25.3	40.2	31.1	2.8	.6

Discuss a client (by name) with friends.

Never	Rarely	Sometimes	Often	Always
93.8	5.0	.7	.2	.2

Inadvertently disclose confidential information.

Never	Rarely	Sometimes	Often	Always
29.0	63.7	7.3	0	0

Report non-compliance to parole officer when court referred client shows no progress.

Never	Rarely	Sometimes	Often	Always
17.6	15.8	23.3	18.1	25.2

Keep one spouse's secret(s) from the other.

Never	Rarely	Sometimes	Often	Always
7.5	30.7	30.7	12.3	18.9

Reveal spouse's affair to other spouse.

Never	Rarely	Sometimes	Often	Always
83.7	12.3	3.2	.2	.6

Obtain clinical information w/o client consent.

Never	Rarely	Sometimes	Often	Always
69.7	24.7	5.2	.4	0

Termination

About 40% of therapists are likely (sometimes or more often) to terminate on the basis of no progress or if clients cannot pay for their sessions. Very few end therapy for the sole purpose of initiating a sexual relationship with a client. Only a small percentage abruptly end therapy without referring.

Terminate therapy if clients cannot pay.

Never	Rarely	Sometimes	Often	Always
29.9	30.1	25.9	11.3	2.8

Abruptly terminate a client without referring.

Never	Rarely	Sometimes	Often	Always
81.2	15.4	2.1	.6	.8

Terminate therapy just to have sexual relationship.

Never	Rarely	Sometimes	Often	Always
95.7	3.0	.4	.9	0

Continue therapy when little or no progress occurs.

Never	Rarely	Sometimes	Often	Always
9.6	48.1	38.2	3.6	.6

Deception (Strategies)

No portion of the AAMFT code prohibits prescription of life-threatening symptoms, and it is rarely used in therapy. At least sometimes, however, 53% prescribe exaggeration of a symptom. Siding with one family member against another is frequently practiced, and therapists frequently refuse therapy when one spouse does not attend (no-shows).

Side with one partner/family member against another.

Never	Rarely	Sometimes	Often	Always
24.5	38.5	33.3	3.7	0

Prescribe exaggeration of a symptom.

Never	Rarely	Sometimes	Often	Always
25.6	21.8	43.0	8.8	.8

Prescribe a life threatening symptom.

Never	Rarely	Sometimes	Often	Always
92.0	6.4	1.4	.2	0

Refuse therapy session when one spouse no-shows.

Never	Rarely	Sometimes	Often	Always
28.3	36.0	28.5	5.3	1.9

Context (Role Definition)

Therapists tend not to accept expensive gifts from clients, loan them money, or ask favors. Hugging clients is practiced by most therapists. Only 12% at least sometimes give clients a peck on the cheek. Over 40% at least sometimes attend clients' special events, such as weddings or parties.

Kiss a client (peck on cheek).

Never	Rarely	Sometimes	Often	Always
61.3	26.9	11.4	.4	0

Hug a client.

Never	Rarely	Sometimes	Often	Always
4.3	32.9	45.5	16.4	.9

Tell client, I'm sexually attracted to you.

Never	Rarely	Sometimes	Often	Always
79.1	17.0	3.7	.2	0

Accept client's gift worth at least $50.

Never	Rarely	Sometimes	Often	Always
69.3	24.3	6.0	.4	0

Raise fees during the course of therapy.

Never	Rarely	Sometimes	Often	Always
37.4	27.4	31.0	3.0	1.1

State possible negative side effects of therapy.

Never	Rarely	Sometimes	Often	Always
2.7	12.7	42.0	29.7	12.9

Ask favors from clients.

Never	Rarely	Sometimes	Often	Always
61.8	34.3	3.9	0	0

Accept client's decision to commit suicide.

Never	Rarely	Sometimes	Often	Always
76.0	20.2	2.6	.6	.6

Lend money to clients.

Never	Rarely	Sometimes	Often	Always
83.4	15.3	1.3	0	0

Avoid certain clients for fear of being sued.

Never	Rarely	Sometimes	Often	Always
32.4	39.9	22.4	3.8	1.5

Charge clients no fee for therapy.

Never	Rarely	Sometimes	Often	Always
28.4	43.8	22.2	4.3	1.3

Give a gift to a client.

Never	Rarely	Sometimes	Often	Always
47.5	35.3	16.3	.9	0

Go to a client's special event (wedding or party).

Never	Rarely	Sometimes	Often	Always
15.6	42.3	38.2	3.5	.4

Accept services in lieu of therapy fee.

Never	Rarely	Sometimes	Often	Always
53.5	32.8	12.0	1.1	.6

Accept a gift worth less than $5 from a client.

Never	Rarely	Sometimes	Often	Always
13.3	26.9	41.7	11.8	6.4

Issues

The findings reflect several issues currently under debate within the field. For example, no consensus was found on whether a therapist should consider one client's positive diagnosis of Human Immuno-deficiency Virus (HIV) infection as lethal, therefore obligating the therapist to report that fact to the client's partner. Ethics committees responsible for making changes in ethical codes have discussed this issue without resolution. The findings of this study indicate the need for guidance.

Tell client that partner is HIV (AIDS) positive.

Never	Rarely	Sometimes	Often	Always
44.3	14.2	14.4	9.1	17.9

Effective January 1, 1989, the AAMFT changed the code that prohibited sexual involvement between therapist and client within one year of termination; the one-year term was changed to two years. The findings of the study indicated this change in the code will demand adjustment in therapist behavior.

Become sexually involved with a former client within one year of termination.

Never	Rarely	Sometimes	Often	Always
92.5	6.2	.7	.2	.4

Become sexually involved with a former client within two years of termination.

Never	Rarely	Sometimes	Often	Always
84.2	12.0	3.2	.2	.4

Some time ago, the American Psychiatric Association (APA) redefined *homosexuality* as nonpathological by removing it from *DSM-III* as a diagnostic category. This change was a strong signal to mental health professionals, and most marriage and family therapists concurred. Some have not.

Treat homosexuality as pathological.

Never	Rarely	Sometimes	Often	Always
62.4	17.1	13.3	3.7	3.5

Standards of Behavior in Clinical Practice

What most therapists do or don't do in the context of working with clients serves to define the practice of marriage and family therapy. Using 90% agreement among therapists as a criterion to identify a standard, the following items qualify as standards of practice:

Do not refuse clients based on race, religion, or gender
Do not employ sexual surrogates in therapy
Do not conduct a custody evaluation without consulting with children
Do not conduct psychological testing
Do not hit, strike, or otherwise assault clients
Do not claim a practice specialty without training

Do not become sexually involved with clients within one year of termination

Do not engage in sex with a supervisee

Do not get paid to refer clients

Do not engage in petting or kissing with clients

Do not borrow money from clients

Do not discuss a client by name with friends

Do not sign for hours a supervisee has not earned

Do not encourage spouses to engage in illegal sexual practices

Do not practice under the influence of drugs or alcohol

Do not exaggerate or distort research findings

Do not claim clinical membership in AAMFT while associate or student

Do not terminate therapy just to have sex

Do not prescribe life-threatening symptoms

Do not claim authorship beyond actual contributions

Do not engage in sexual behavior with employees

Do not falsely state credentials

The results of this study revealed that not all therapists adhere to the AAMFT ethical code. Such findings should not be surprising; not every one obeys the law either.

The findings are most useful in giving the field feedback on itself and in helping bring consensus on what one should do in marriage and family therapy practice. If one's opinions and actions on some of the items making up the survey were out of the mainstream, he or she should review the foundation of those beliefs and discuss them with a supervisor or colleague.

For more information about The Ethical Behavior Index for Marriage and Family Therapy, contact Gregory W. Brock, Ph.D., 315 Funkhouser Building, University of Kentucky, Lexington, KY 40506–0054.

APPENDIX B

Forms for
Clinical Practice

Note: Consult an attorney regarding legal implications before using any of the following forms.

- **Face Sheet**
- **Insurance Information**
- **Authorization to Release Information**
- **Request and Consent for the Release of Confidential Information**
- **Therapist Disclosures**
- **Patient-Therapist Agreement**

Face Sheet

Your cooperation in completing this questionnaire will be helpful in planning our services for you. Please answer each item carefully or ask your therapist for clarification if you do not understand an item.

Name_____ Today's Date_____

Birthdate_____ Driver's License # _____

Address_____ City_____

State_____ Zip_____ Home Phone_____

Social Security Number_____ Marital Status_____

Marriage Date_____ Divorce Date_____

Spouse's Name_____ Spouse's Age_____

Children's Names   Birthdates   School

_____

_____

_____

Employer_____ Work Phone_____

Occupation_____

Physician_____ Phone Number_____

Medications taken presently_____

Major health problems?_____

Problems with alcohol?_____ Drugs?_____ Eating?_____

Have you been in treatment before?_____ When?_____

With whom?_____

Please describe your reason for seeking treatment at this time_____

_____

Notify in case of emergency_____

Relationship?_____ Phone Number_____

Who may we thank for referring you to us?_____

Insurance Information

Client Name

Insured Person's Full Name   Birthdate

Social Security   Relationship to Client   Work Phone
Number

Primary Insurance   Group or Union Name   Group or Local
Company   I.D. Number

Insurance Company Address   Insurance Company
                                              Phone Number

Employer's Name

Employer's Full Address

Benefits Office Phone Number
for Verification Purposes

How much is your deductible?   How much have you satisfied?

If you use a managed health care plan, how much is your co-pay?

Authorization to Release Information

Date_____

I, _____ ,

authorize _____ to
release the following circled information. Note any limitations.

A. Psychological evaluations and assessments

B. Records of outpatient treatment

C. Records of any inpatient treatment

D. Records of marital and family outpatient therapy

E. Records obtained during any court-appointed evaluations

I understand that I have the right to review and copy any information that I have authorized for release. I also know that I can revoke the consent at any time. This consent may be used [ ] once or [ ] may be used as a continuing consent (note your preference). I understand that by signing this release, I am waiving the privilege of privacy.

Please forward the information to:

Name_____

Address_____   _____

_____

Signature_____

Date_____

Witness_____

Request and Consent for the
Release of Confidential Information

Date_____

I, _____ .
       Client Name

_____
       Address

authorize_____
                Name of Discloser of Information

to release the following information _____

_____
       Nature of Information

to _____
       Name of Receiver of Information

_____
       Address

I hereby give my consent for any and all of the above requested information
to be released for one time only [   ] or as a continuing consent [   ] (note your
preference).

_____
Signature of Client or Person
Authorized to Consent for the Client

_____
Date

Therapist Disclosures

Supervision: Some insurance companies require master's-level therapists to be supervised by a certified clinical psychologist or psychiatrist. Therefore, to utilize your insurance coverage, my treatment for you is being supervised by _____. This does not guarantee insurance payment, however.

Duty to Warn: Arizona law requires that a therapist must inform child protective services if child abuse is suspected or revealed. Therefore, any information regarding this issue will be reported to the Child Protective Service Agency.

Arizona law also requires a therapist to inform an individual and/or the proper authorities when a life-threatening accusation is made about another individual. Should such a statement be made, the therapist must inform the threatened individual.

Confidentiality: Therapists are bound by their code of ethics to keep all information shared in the therapy session confidential. This rule can be broken only if the duty to warn is enforced by the therapist.

Minor children's right to confidentiality will be discussed both with the parents of the child(ren) and the child(ren). Decisions regarding child confidentiality will be made on a client-by-client basis. Please discuss this matter thoroughly with the therapists.

Records: The therapist will retain client records for three years following termination of treatment. After three years, the records will be destroyed unless there have been further transactions, therapy, or claims between the client and therapist.

Conduct of Therapy: The therapist shall adhere to the code of ethics of his or her respective profession and to the laws of Arizona as they pertain to client-therapist relationships.

_____   _____
Date   *Patient's Signature (or Responsible Party)*

_____   _____
Date   *Therapist's Signature*

Patient-Therapist Agreement

Fees are an important issue to anyone receiving professional services. This sheet was prepared to clarify fee policies.

Fee Rate: The basic fee is _____ per _____-minute session. Longer or shorter sessions are prorated from this basic fee. Fees for psychological testing are based in time spent with the client plus time required for scoring and interpreting test data. Diagnostic/psychological testing reports will **not** be issued until you have made full payment for these reports.

Phone Consultation: Our standard prorated fee will be charged for telephone time.

Payment Method: Payment is required at the time services are rendered. Payment may be made by check, cash, or credit card. Should an account remain unpaid due to unforeseen circumstances, after thirty (30) days, a 1-1/2% (18% per annum) **rebilling and interest charge** shall be added beginning the 31st day until the charges are paid in full. Office visits will not be rescheduled until new payment arrangements are made. Defaulted accounts shall be sent to collection, and if a lawyer is hired to collect the outstanding balance and occurring charges, patient agrees to pay all cost and a reasonable attorney's fee incurred.

Missed Appointment: If you are unable to keep an appointment, please notify the office immediately. If an appointment is cancelled or missed without 24 hours' prior notice, you will be billed for the session.

Insurance and Third-Party Payments: As a general policy, we do not accept insurance assignments and request payments at time of service. If you wish to file with your insurance carrier, the receptionist will give you a superbill to send to the insurance company for reimbursement. There are a few exceptions to this policy (e.g., CHAMPUS, PPO, etc.). In these particular cases, the patient shall pay all nonallowable, co-payment, and deductible charges when services are rendered, and a written change will be added to this agreement.

Responsibility: The patient (or referring parent, in the case of minors) is considered responsible for payment of the professional fees. If we reach a written agreement to bill a third party, such as a divorced spouse, relative, or insurance company, and that third party fails to make timely payments, the therapist shall notify the client in writing that he/she is responsible for payment and the therapist will provide a bill for services. Payment of the past-due balance and current amount shall be made by the patient or referring parent within thirty (30) days of the date of that bill according to the terms set forth above.

By signing this agreement, the patient agrees he or she has read it carefully and has received a copy of both this agreement and the page titled "Therapist Disclosures." The client agrees to being any and all questions or concerns that may arise regarding these fee policies to the therapist at the beginning of the session.

_____   _____
Date   *Patient's Signature (or Responsible Party)*

_____   _____
Date   *Therapist's Signature*

APPENDIX C

AAMFT Code
of Ethical Principles
for Marriage
and Family Therapists

Note: The AAMFT Code of Ethical Principles for Marriage and Family Therapists *is reprinted here by permission of the American Association for Marriage and Family Therapy. This revised version of the* Code *went into effect on August 1, 1988. The AAMFT can make further revisions of the* Code *at any time, as it deems necessary.*

The Board of Directors of the American Association for Marriage and Family Therapy (AAMFT) hereby promulgates, pursuant to Article II, Section (1)(C) of the Association's Bylaws, the Revised AAMFT Code of Ethical Principles for Marriage and Family Therapists, effective August 1, 1988.

The AAMFT Code of Ethical Principles for Marriage and Family Therapists is binding on all Members of AAMFT (Clinical, Student, and Associate) and on all AAMFT Approved Supervisors.

If an AAMFT Member or an AAMFT Approved Supervisor resigns in anticipation of or during the course of an ethics investigation, the Ethics Committee will complete its investigation. Any publication of action taken by the Association will include the fact that the Member attempted to resign during the investigation.

Marriage and family therapists are encouraged to report alleged unethical behavior of colleagues to appropriate professional associations and state regulatory bodies.

1. Responsibility to Clients
Marriage and family therapists are dedicated to advancing the welfare of families and individuals, including respecting the rights of those persons seeking their assistance, and making reasonable efforts to ensure that their services are used appropriately.

1.1 Marriage and family therapists do not discriminate against or refuse professional service to anyone on the basis of race, sex, religion, or national origin.

1.2   Marriage and family therapists are cognizant of their potentially influential position with respect to clients, and they avoid exploiting the trust and dependency of such persons. Marriage and family therapists therefore make every effort to avoid dual relationships with clients that could impair their professional judgement or increase the risk of exploitation. Examples of such dual relationships include, but are not limited to, business or close personal relationships with clients. Sexual intimacy with clients is prohibited. Sexual intimacy with former clients for two years following the termination of therapy is prohibited.

1.3   Marriage and family therapists do not use their professional relationship with clients to further their own interests.

1.4   Marriage and family therapists respect the right of clients to make decisions and help them to understand the consequences of these decisions. Marriage and family therapists clearly advise a client that a decision on marital status is the responsibility of the client.

1.5   Marriage and family therapists continue therapeutic relationships only so long as it is reasonably clear that clients are benefiting from the relationship.

1.6   Marriage and family therapists assist persons in obtaining other therapeutic services if a marriage and family therapist is unable or unwilling, for appropriate reasons, to see a person who has requested professional help.

1.7   Marriage and family therapists do not abandon or neglect clients in treatment without making reasonable arrangements for the continuation of such treatment.

1.8   Marriage and family therapists obtain informed consent of clients before taping, recording, or permitting third party observation of their activities.

2. Confidentiality
Marriage and family therapists have unique confidentiality problems because the "client" in a therapeutic relationship may be more than one person. The overriding principle is that marriage and family therapists respect the confidences of their client(s).

2.1   Marriage and family therapists cannot disclose client confidences to anyone, except: (1) as mandated by law; (2) to prevent a clear and immediate danger to a person or persons; (3) where the marriage and family therapist is a defendant in a civil, criminal or disciplinary action arising from the therapy (in which case client confidences may only be disclosed in the course of that action); or (4) if there is a waiver previously obtained in writing, and then such information may only be revealed in accordance with the terms of the waiver.   In circumstances where more than one person in a family is receiving therapy, each such family member who is legally competent to execute a waiver must agree to the waiver required by subparagraph (4). Absent such a waiver from each family member legally competent to execute a waiver, a marriage and family therapist cannot disclose information received from any family member.

2.2   Marriage and family therapists use client and/or clinical materials in teaching, writing, and public presentations only if a written waiver has been received in accordance with subprinciple 2.1(4), or when appropriate steps have been taken to protect client identity.

2.3   Marriage and family therapists store or dispose of client records in ways that maintain confidentiality.

3. Professional Competence and Integrity
Marriage and family therapists are dedicated to maintaining high standards of professional competence and integrity.

3.1   Marriage and family therapists who (a) are convicted of felonies, (b) are convicted of misdemeanors (related to their qualifications or functions), (c) engage in conduct which could lead to conviction of felonies, or misdemeanors related to their qualifications or functions, (d) are expelled from other professional organizations, (e) have their licenses or certificates suspended or revoked, (f) are no longer competent to practice marriage and family therapy because they are impaired due to physical or mental causes or the abuse of alcohol or other substances, or (g) fail to cooperate with the Association at any stage of an investigation of an ethical complaint of his/her conduct by the AAMFT Ethics Committee or Judicial Council, are subject to termination of membership or other appropriate action.

3.2   Marriage and family therapists seek appropriate professional assistance for their own personal problems or conflicts that are likely to impair their work performance and their clinical judgement.

3.3   Marriage and family therapists, as teachers, are dedicated to maintaining high standards of scholarship and presenting information that is accurate.

3.4   Marriage and family therapists seek to remain abreast of new developments in family therapy knowledge and practice through both educational activities and clinical experiences.

3.5   Marriage and family therapists do not engage in sexual or other harassment or exploitation of clients, students, trainees, employees, colleagues, research subjects, or actual or potential witnesses or complainants in ethical proceedings.

3.6   Marriage and family therapists do not attempt to diagnose, treat, or advise on problems outside the recognized boundaries of their competence.

3.7   Marriage and family therapists attempt to prevent the distortion or misuse of their clinical and research findings.

3.8   Marriage and family therapists are aware that, because of their ability to influence and alter the lives of others, they must exercise special care when making public their professional recommendations and opinions through testimony or other public statements.

4. Responsibility to Students, Employees, and Supervisees
Marriage and family therapists do not exploit the trust and dependency of students, employees, and supervisees.

4.1   Marriage and family therapists are cognizant of their potentially influential position with respect to students, employees, and supervisees, and they avoid exploiting the trust and dependency of such persons. Marriage and family therapists, therefore, make every effort to avoid dual relationships that could impair their professional judgement or increase the risk of exploitation. Examples of such dual relationships include, but are not limited to, provision of therapy to students, employees, or supervisees, and business or close personal relationships with students, employees, or supervisees. Sexual intimacy with students or supervisees is prohibited.

4.2   Marriage and family therapists do not permit students, employees, or supervisees to perform or to hold themselves out as competent to perform professional services beyond their training, level of experience, and competence.

5. Responsibility to the Profession
Marriage and family therapists respect the rights and responsibilities of professional colleagues; carry out research in an ethical manner; and participate in activities which advance the goals of the profession.

5.1 Marriage and family therapists remain accountable to the standards of the profession when acting as members or employees of organizations.

5.2 Marriage and family therapists assign publication credit to those who have contributed to a publication in proportion to their contributions and in accordance with customary professional publication practices.

5.3 Marriage and family therapists who are the authors of books or other materials that are published or distributed should cite appropriately persons to whom credit for original ideas is due.

5.4 Marriage and family therapists who are the authors of books or other materials published or distributed by an organization take reasonable precautions to ensure that the organization promotes and advertises the materials accurately and factually.

5.5 Marriage and family therapists, as researchers, must be adequately informed of and abide by relevant laws and regulations regarding the conduct of research with human participants.

5.6 Marriage and family therapists recognize a responsibility to participate in activities that contribute to a better community and society, including devoting a portion of their professional activity to services for which there is little or no financial return.

5.7 Marriage and family therapists are concerned with developing laws and regulations pertaining to marriage and family therapy that serve the public interest, and with altering such laws and regulations that are not in the public interest.

5.8 Marriage and family therapists encourage public participation in the designing and delivery of services and in the regulation of practitioners.

6. Financial Arrangements

Marriage and family therapists make financial arrangements with clients and third party payors that conform to accepted professional practices and that are reasonably understandable.

6.1 Marriage and family therapists do not offer or accept payment for referrals.

6.2 Marriage and family therapists do not charge excessive fees for services.

6.3 Marriage and family therapists disclose their fee structure to clients at the onset of treatment.

6.4 Marriage and family therapists are careful to represent facts truthfully to clients and third party payors regarding services rendered.

7. Advertising

Marriage and family therapists engage in appropriate informational activities, including those that enable laypersons to choose marriage and family services on an informed bzsis.

7.1 Marriage and family therapists accurately represent their competence, education, training, and experience relevant to their practice of marriage and family therapy.

7.2 Marriage and family therapists claim as evidence of educational qualifications in conjunction with their AAMFT membership only those degrees (a) from regionally-accredited institutions or (b) from institutions recognized by states which license or certify marriage and family therapists, but only if such regulation is accepted by AAMFT.

7.3 Marriage and family therapists assure that advertisements and publications, whether in directories, announcement cards, newspapers, or on radio or television, are formulated to convey information that is necessary for the public to make an appropriate selection. Information could include: (1) office information, such as name, address, telephone number, credit card acceptability, fee structure, languages spoken, and office hours; (2) appropriate degrees, state licensure and/or certification, and AAMFT Clinical Member status; and (3) description of practice.

7.4   Marriage and family therapists do not use a name which could mislead the public concerning the identity, responsibility, source, and status of those practicing under that name and do not hold themselves out as being partners or associates of a firm if they are not.

7.5   Marriage and family therapists do not use any professional identification (such as a professional card, office sign, letterhead, or telephone or association directory listing) if it includes a statement or claim that is false, fraudulent, misleading, or deceptive. A statement is false, fraudulent, misleading, or deceptive if it (a) contains a material misrepresentation of fact; (b) fails to state any material fact necessary to make the statement, in light of all circumstances, not misleading; or (c) is intended to or is likely to create an unjustified expectation.

7.6   Marriage and family therapists correct, wherever possible, false, misleading, or inaccurate information and representations made by others concerning the marriage and family therapist's qualifications, services, or products.

7.7   Marriage and family therapists make certain that the qualifications of persons in their employ are represented in a manner that is not false, misleading, or deceptive.

7.8   Marriage and family therapists may represent themselves as specializing within a limited area of marriage and family therapy, but may not hold themselves out as specialists without being able to provide evidence of training, education, and supervised experience in settings which meet recognized professional standards.

7.9   Only marriage and family therapist Clinical Members, Approved Supervisors, and Fellows—**not** Associate Members, Student Members, or organizations—may identify these AAMFT designations in public information or advertising materials.

7.10   Marriage and family therapists may not use the initials AAMFT following their name in the manner of an academic degree.

7.11   Marriage and family therapists may not use the AAMFT name, logo, and the abbreviated initials AAMFT. The Association (which is the sole owner of its name, logo, and the abbreviated initials AAMFT) and its committees and regional divisions, operating as such, may use the name, logo, and the abbreviated initials AAMFT. A regional division of AAMFT may use the AAMFT insignia to list its individual Clinical Members as a group (e.g., in the Yellow Pages); when all Clinical Members practicing within a directory district have been invited to list themselves in the directory, any one or more members may do so.

7.12   Marriage and family therapists use their membership in AAMFT only in connection with their clinical and professional activities.

Violations of this Code should be brought in writing to the attention of the AAMFT Committee on Ethics and Professional Practices at the central office of AAMFT, 1717 K Street, N.W., Suite 407, Washington, DC 20006.

Effective August 1, 1988

AAMFT Policies and Procedures
Regarding Advertising and Ethics

The AAMFT Ethics Committee regularly receives requests from members for AAMFT policy and procedures regarding AAMFT-related advertising.

The general policy of AAMFT regarding advertising and ethics is the AAMFT Code of Ethical Principles for Marriage and Family Therapists, specifically Principle 7, Advertising, and Subprinciples 7.1 through 7.12, reprinted on [pages 172-173].

However, these policies regarding advertising and ethics are further amplified in procedures established by the Association with approval by the Board of Directors on March 6, 1988, which include the following:

    I. Advertisement by Clinical Members
    II. Advertisement by Approved Supervisors and Fellows
    III. Advertisement by Accredited Programs
    IV. Advertisement by Non-Accredited Programs

I. Advertisement by Clinical Members

Yellow Pages Advertisement

Subprinciple 7.11 of the AAMFT Ethical Code [see p. 173] states the requirements for Yellow Pages Advertisement. Accordingly, the following guidelines should be followed if members wish to start a Yellow Pages listing utilizing the AAMFT name, logo, and/or abbreviated initials, AAMFT.

A listing may be initiated by (a) a division officer or someone designated by the division—this is the preferred method—or (b) a Clinical Member who is interested in being listed. (Hereafter in these guidelines the initiating party—be it a division-designated or an interested Clinical Member—is referred to as the "sponsor.") In either case, an individual desiring to list in Yellow Pages Advertisement may not use the AAMFT name, logo, or abbreviated letters unless the guidelines, below, are followed:

1. According to the Code, it will be necessary for the sponsor to contact every AAMFT Clinical Member in the specific telephone service area to give each the opportunity to list. Contact the AAMFT Central Office or the Division Office for a list of members in the community (a printout of names and addresses can be given by zip code). The more people who list, the less it costs: the charges can then be pro-rated among all listers.

2. It will not be possible to determine how much it will cost each listing member until there is a firm commitment from all interested individuals. After this commitment and determination of individual costs, it is recommended that each person be required to send a check for his or her listing for the entire year in advance to the sponsor. Yellow Pages companies typically put the cost of the listing on the personal bill of the sponsor, and they expect the sponsor to be responsible for collecting the appropriate share from each person listed.

3. If these procedures are followed, what may be listed before the alphabetical listing of Clinical Members is any of the following:
   - The AAMFT logo
   - The name of the Association—The American Association for Marriage and Family Therapy
   - The initials AAMFT

4. Although the logo may be used by divisions, the name of the division should be used in the display advertisement if it is sponsored by the division. Using the Texas Division as an example, the advertisement should read in one of these two ways:
- Texas Association for Marriage and Family Therapy
- AAMFT—Texas Division

5. For a print of the logo, the sponsor should contact the AAMFT Central Office for a camera-ready copy for the Yellow Pages. Requests should be made to the Ethics Committee, AAMFT, 1717 K Street, NW, Suite 407, Washington, DC 20006, (202) 429-1825.

6. Adjacent to the logo, before the alphabetical listing of Clinical Members, the Yellow Pages may print, under "The American Association for Marriage and Family Therapy," a phrase in italics such as:

American Association for
Marriage and Family Therapy
Texas Division
*Since 1942, the professional association
of marriage and family therapists*

(List of Local Clinical Members)

Other phrases that could be used include:
- *Partial Listing of Clinical Members*
- *Subscribing to a professional code of ethics*

7. If possible, the headings of the listing should be "AAMFT—American Association for Marriage and Family Therapy" or "AAMFT—Texas Division." This will insure an alphabetical placement under "aa," rather than "am."

8. For the listing of participating Clinical Members, the following can be listed: the person's name, degree, name of business, address, telephone number. If a business is listed, it must follow, not precede, the Clinical Member's name.

9. Listings that utilize the AAMFT name, logo, and/or abbreviated letters must be made up solely of Clinical Members, *not* businesses (although the member's business may follow his or her name and degree), nor accredited programs, or Associate or Student members.

10. Listings that utilize the AAMFT name, logo, and/or abbreviated letters may *not* include members' specializations. While the AAMFT Ethical Code (Subprinciple 7.8) allows members to represent themselves as specializing within a limited area of marriage and family therapy if they can provide evidence of training, education, and supervised experience which meet recognized professional standards, such a listing under the AAMFT name, logo, and/or abbreviated letters would imply that this specialization has been verified by AAMFT.

11. Please give the Yellow Pages representative the AAMFT Central or Divisional office number for validation of clinical membership in AAMFT for those wishing to list under the AAMFT name or logo.

12. Individual Clinical Members may identify their membership in AAMFT in individual advertisements they take out in Yellow Pages. What may be listed is described in #8, above. The ad may state, for example, "Clinical Member of the American Association for Marriage and Family Therapy."

If you have any questions regarding this professional listing, contact the Ethics Committee, AAMFT, 1717 K Street, NW, Suite 407, Washington, DC 20006, (202) 429-1825.

Stationery, Business Cards, etc.

1. Clinical Members, *not* Associate or Student members, may identify their membership in AAMFT on their stationery, business cards, etc. However, they may not use the AAMFT logo on such printed materials, or use the name of the Association or the initials AAMFT in a manner which would imply they officially represent the Association. A sample card:

Jane Doe, Ph.D.
Center for Family Therapy
999 Whitaker Avenue
Columbia, IL   88818

*A Clinical Member of the American
Association for Marriage and Family Therapy*

II. Advertisement by Approved Supervisors and Fellows

1. Approved Supervisors and Fellows may advertise these designations in Yellow Page listings of Clinical Members, on business cards, stationery, etc. Appropriate listings areas follows:
- Fellow, American Association for Marriage and Family Therapy (or AAMFT Fellow).
- Approved Supervisor, American Association for Marriage and Family Therapy (or AAMFT Approved Supervisor).

2. They may also list these designations in appropriate professional contexts such as program listings, clinical and research journals and newsletters.

III. Advertisement by Accredited Programs

The following are the policy and guidelines approved by the AAMFT Commission on Accreditation for Marriage and Family Therapy Education:

1. Accredited programs may not use the AAMFT name, logo, or initials in their advertisement.

2. Instead, they may have printed on their stationery and other appropriate materials a statement such as, "The (name of program) of the (name of institution) is accredited by the AAMFT Commission on Accreditation for Marriage and Family Therapy Education."

IV. Advertisement by Non-Accredited Programs

Programs which are not accredited by the AAMFT Commission on Accreditation for Marriage and Family Therapy Education must take care in printed program materials, program advertisement, and in student advisement, not to state that their courses and training opportunities are accepted by AAMFT for meeting AAMFT membership requirements.

Note: The Principles of the AAMFT Ethical Code Regarding Advertising are reprinted in the first part of this appendix, Section 7, pages 172–173.

AAMFT Procedures for Handling Ethical Matters

Note: The AAMFT Procedures for Handling Ethical Matters *are reprinted here by permission of the American Association for Marriage and Family Therapy. This revised version of the* Procedures *went into effect on August 1, 1988. The AAMFT can make further revisions of the* Procedures *at any time, as it deems necessary.*

The Board of Directors of the American Association for Marriage and Family Therapy, pursuant to Article II, Section (1)(C) of the Association's *Bylaws* (hereafter, the *Bylaws*), promulgates the revised *AAMFT Procedures for Handling Ethical Matters* (hereafter, the *Procedures*), effective June 10, 1990.

I. The Role of AAMFT Divisions.

1.00 Role of Divisions. It is the policy of AAMFT that the primary role of divisions in regard to ethics is to educate AAMFT members and the public about the *AAMFT Code of Ethical Principles for Marriage and Family Therapists* (hereafter, the *Ethical Code*) and about the procedures for filing complaints.

    1.01 General Public. In regard to the general public, this role includes answering inquiries from the press about the *Ethical Code.*

    1.02 Complaints. Divisional officers may facilitate, educate, and inform persons about how to follow the procedures for filing an ethical complaint. When a person makes an initial complaint or discusses a potential complaint with a division officer, staff person, or member, he or she should be referred to the AAMFT Ethics Committee, 1717 K Street, NW, Suite 407, Washington, DC, 20006, 202/429-1825.

    1.03 AAMFT Members. The divisional ethics role includes disseminating copies of the *Ethical Code* and the *Procedures,* providing workshops on the *Ethical Code* and the *Procedures,* and periodically disseminating information prepared by the AAMFT Ethics Committee to AAMFT members in the division (for example, Third Party Payor Policy, Confidentiality of Ethics Cases Policy, Appropriate Advertising in Conformity with the *Ethical Code* policies, and so forth).

2.00 Confidentiality. All information concerning ethical complaints made against AAMFT members should be treated in a strictly confidential manner by division officers, staff persons, and members. Insuring that confidentiality is maintained is important in order to protect the rights of the individual members who are the subject of complaints, and to protect AAMFT and its divisions because of improper disclosure of information. Under the terms of these *Procedures,* all information regarding complaints shall be treated in a strictly confidential manner.

2.01 Publication or Dissemination of Information. It is clearly inappropriate for members to disseminate any information regarding a complaint (including the existence of a complaint) to any member of the public or to any AAMFT member who is not directly involved in the processing of the particular complaint under consideration. The *Procedures* allow the AAMFT Ethics Committee or the AAMFT Judicial Council, at their discretion, to publish to AAMFT members information regarding the final disposition of an ethics complaint. The dissemination of information regarding the outcome of complaints is to be made by the AAMFT Ethics Committee, and/or the AAMFT Judicial Council, and not by anyone else, including divisional ethics committees or divisional officers or members.

2.02 Materials. All written materials and all copies of materials regarding ethics complaints received in divisional offices should be sent immediately to the AAMFT Ethics Committee in Washington, DC.

2.03 Correspondence. Correspondence concerning ethical complaints received by divisions should be mailed as "personal and confidential" to the AAMFT Ethics Committee, and where appropriate, restricted to delivery to the intended recipient.

2.04 Discussion of Complaints. Any necessary discussion of cases by division officers, staff, or members should take place where conversations cannot be inadvertently overheard by other members of an office, or members of the public.

2.05 Divisional Staff. Secretaries and paid and volunteer divisional staff who receive information about complaints should be instructed on the confidential nature of the information. Consideration could be given to asking officers and staff to sign pledges to uphold the confidentiality of any ethical case they may have referred to the AAMFT Ethics Committee.

2.06 Division as a Complainant or Subject of a Complaint. A division (represented by its board) may, on occasion, be a complainant or charged with a violation in an ethical case. But in these situations, the board as an entity is treated as a complainant or a charged group. Confidentiality should be strictly maintained in such situations.

2.07 Questions about Disclosure. When division officers, staff, and members have questions about whether information may properly be disclosed, these should be referred to the AAMFT Ethics Committee.

3.00 Advisory Ethical Opinions. It is the policy of AAMFT that its Ethics Committee may on occasion choose to give advisory opinions about ethical issues raised by a member of the Association (see section II, #6.00). It remains the policy of AAMFT that divisions, division officers, and divisions ethics chairs and committees do not give advisory opinions.

II. The AAMFT Ethics Committee.

1.00 Basis and Scope of Authority of the Ethics Committee.

1.01 Jurisdiction over Individuals.

1.011 Jurisdiction over Members and AAMFT Approved Supervisors. The *Bylaws* (Article III, Section 1) provide for two classes of membership, as follows:

Section 1. The membership shall be divided into two (2) classes:

A. Voting Members. The voting membership shall be composed of clinical members and fellows. Clinical members and fellows shall be considered clinical members.

B. Non-Voting Members. The non-voting membership shall be composed of student members and associate members. Student and associate members shall be considered non-clinical members.

The Association has authority over these members and AAMFT Approved Supervisors. This authority is derived from Article III, Section 7 of the *Bylaws*, which require that:

Members in all membership statuses shall be governed by and abide by the *Bylaws* of the Association and all rules and orders lawfully made thereunder.

1.012 Jurisdiction over Applicants. The Association also has jurisdiction over applicants for membership and the Approved Supervisor designation in relation to matters pertaining to the decision whether to grant membership in the Association and/or the Approved Supervisor designation.

1.013 Jurisdiction over Resigned Members. The Association also has jurisdiction over resigned members and Approved Supervisors in relation to complaints of ethical violations which occurred during the period of membership or the Approved Supervisor designation (provided the complaint is received within one year of the date of resignation).

1.02 Responsibilities of the Ethics Committee. The Bylaws of the Association (Article VI, Section 6) further authorize the Ethics Committee to:

Review the *AAMFT Code of Ethical Principals for Marriage and Family Therapists* and interpret it to the membership and to the public, and shall consider allegations of ethical standards made against members. It shall be the specific responsibility of the Committee to conduct investigations of alleged violations of the *AAMFT Code of Ethical Principles for Marriage and Family Therapists*, and to resolve such allegations by mutual agreement with the member, or to make a recommendation of disciplinary action to be taken against the member and, if the case is heard by the Judicial Council, to prosecute the charges against the member.

2.00 Membership and Meetings of the Committee.

2.01 Membership. The Committee shall consist of four Clinical Members of the Association and two persons not members of the Association who shall act as public members of the Committee, all of whom shall be appointed by the President and with the approval of the Board of Directors. The President shall receive suggestions for membership from the Chair of the Committee.

2.011 Term of Members. Each member of the Committee shall serve for a three-year appointment period, except that any person chosen to fill a vacancy shall be appointed for the unexpired term for the member whom he or she shall succeed.

2.012 Number of Terms. No Committee member who is a member of AAMFT shall serve for more than two consecutive terms.

2.013 Appointment of the Chair. The President shall appoint the Chair of the Committee from one of the four Association members who are currently members of the Committee.

2.014 Resignation from the Committee. Any member who misses two consecutive Committee meetings shall be deemed to have resigned from Committee membership unless the member can demonstrate good cause to the satisfaction of the Committee.

2.02 Voting. All Committee members, including public members, shall have full voting privileges.

2.03 Action by Majority. All actions by the Committee shall be made by a majority of those Committee members present and voting. No Committee member shall vote on any particular case in which he or she has a conflict of interest, whether because of personal knowledge of the charged member, or for any other reason.

2.04 Schedule of Meetings. The Ethics Committee ordinarily meets three (3) times each year at approximately four-month intervals.

3.00 Procedures for Handling Ethical Complaints.

3.01 Role of Committee. One role of the Ethics Committee is to investigate complaints of violations of the *Ethical Code* and, if violations are found, to take action by mutual agreement with the member involved, or to recommend disciplinary action.

3.02 Committee Constraints. In carrying out its responsibilities, the Ethics Committee shall act in accordance with the articles of incorporation and *Bylaws,* with the *Ethical Code,* and with these *Procedures.* AAMFT adjudication proceedings are not formal legal proceedings.

3.03 Subject's Use of Legal Counsel. The subject under investigation (whether an AAMFT member, an applicant for membership, an Approved Supervisor or an applicant for the Approved Supervisor designation; hereafter referred to as the member) may consult with his or her legal counsel at any time, but the member himself or herself is to be an active participant in these proceedings. The member must respond to the charges himself or herself.

3.04 Initiation and Withdrawal of Complaints.

3.041 Written Complaints by Members and Non-Members. The Ethics Committee shall receive written complaints from both members of the Association and non-members. The complainant must have personal knowledge of the alleged behavior complained about or be in a position to supply relevant, reliable testimony or other evidence on the subject. Any AAMFT member who knows of a violation of the *Ethical Code* should bring this fact to the attention of the Committee in the form of a complaint. Complaints must be in writing. Complaints must be signed and accompanied by the complainant's address.

3.042 Anonymous Complaints. Anonymous complaints shall not be recognized as a basis for action.

3.043 Initiation of a Complaint by the Committee. The Ethics Committee may proceed on its own initiative when it has been presented with sufficient allegations which, if proven factual, would constitute a violation of the *Ethical Code.* For example, the Committee could proceed on information received from another professional organization or from public sources. If the Committee decides to proceed on its own initiative, it shall prepare a written statement concerning factual allegations of an *Ethical Code* violation or violations.

3.044 Time Limitations. The Ethics Committee may determine, at its discretion, that a complaint cannot be investigated because the events complained about occurred too far in the past.

3.045 Complaints Regarding Resigned Members. A complaint will be considered by the Ethics Committee within one year from the date of resignation of membership or termination of membership for non-payment of dues, provided the alleged violation occurred during the period of the person's membership.

3.046 Withdrawal of Complaints. If the complainant wishes to withdraw the complaint after the member has been charged, the Ethics Committee must obtain the member's permission before terminating the inquiry. If permission is withheld, the inquiry must be completed.

3.0461 Proceeding with the Case on the Ethics Committee's Own Initiative. In such instances, however, the Ethics Committee may decide to proceed with the case pursuant to Section II, #3.043 of these *Procedures*.

3.047 Time Requirements for the Adjudication. AAMFT shall make its best efforts to adhere strictly to the time requirements specified in these *Procedures*. However, failure to do so will not prohibit final adjudication unless the person under investigation can show that such failure was willful or unfairly prejudicial.

3.05 Initial Action by Executive Director.

3.051 Determination of AAMFT Membership. Upon receipt of a complaint, the Executive Director or his or her designee (hereafter Executive Director) shall determine whether the person about whom the complaint has been made is a member or applicant for membership in the Association.

3.0511 Non-Member. If the person is not a member, a recently resigned or terminated member, or an applicant for membership in the Association or for the Approved Supervisor designation, the Executive Director shall so inform the complainant, shall explain that the Association has no authority to proceed against the person, and may refer the complainant to another agency or association with proper jurisdiction.

3.0512 Recently Resigned Member. If the person is a recently resigned or terminated member, the complaint shall be referred immediately to the Chair of the Ethics Committee who will determine whether the alleged violation occurred during the period of the person's membership (provided the complaint is received within one year from the date of resignation). If it is determined that the Ethics Committee has jurisdiction, the investigation will proceed pursuant to Section II, #3.06 ff of these *Procedures*.

3.0513 Applicant for Membership or the Approved Supervisor Designation. If the person is an applicant for membership in the Association or an applicant for the Approved Supervisor designation, the complaint shall be referred immediately to the Chair of the Ethics Committee. The Ethics Committee will conduct an investigation of the complaint, pursuant to Section II, #3.06 ff of the *Procedures*.

3.05131 Outcome of the Investigation. Upon completion of the investigation, the Ethics Committee will take two actions:

3.051311 Ethical Matter. If the investigation results in charges of alleged ethical violations against the applicant, the Committee may find no violation of the *Ethical Code* and close the matter, or it may find a violation(s) of the *Ethical Code* with recommended actions to be taken against the applicant, including whether the application shall proceed or be terminated, pursuant to Section II, #3.08 ff of these *Procedures*.

3.051312 Application for Membership or the Approved Supervisor Designation. Upon completion of the investigation, the Ethics Committee will make a factual report to the Membership Committee (in the case of applicants for membership) or to the Commission on Supervision (in the case of applicants for the Approved Supervisor designation). If no violation of the *Ethical Code* is found, the decision whether to proceed with the application is made by the Membership Committee (in the case of an application for membership) or by the Commission on Supervision (in the case of an application for the Approved Supervisor designation).

3.052 Investigation of Applicants for Membership and the Approved Supervisor Designation Regarding Professional Ethics and Conduct.

3.0521 Statement of Professional Ethics and Conduct. All applicants for AAMFT and for the AAMFT Approved Supervisor designation are required to complete a *Statement of Professional Ethics and Conduct* and to agree to abide by the *AAMFT Code of Ethical Principles for Marriage and Family Therapists*. The *Statement* is a questionnaire, asking applicants whether any of the following actions have been taken against them:

3.05211 Actions by Other Professional Associations. A finding of a violation of the AAMFT Ethical Code or the code of any other professional association or currently under investigation by AAMFT or any other professional association.

3.05212 Actions by Regulatory Bodies. Suspension, revocation, restriction, denial, or any other disciplinary action regarding the applicant's registration, certification, or license to practice therapy by federal or state regulatory bodies or foreign jurisdiction, or presently under investigation by any regulatory body.

3.05213 Actions on Privileges. Suspension, restriction, or any other disciplinary action regarding privileges to practice therapy in a hospital, HMO, and so forth.

3.05214 Convictions. Conviction of a felony, or a misdemeanor related to the practice of therapy.

3.05215 Claims of Unethical Behavior. Claims made for alleged unethical behavior made in civil suits or any other forum in the last ten years clearly alleging unethical behavior.

3.05216 Actions In Lieu of or to Avoid Formal Action. Voluntarily given up privileges, registration, certification, or license to practice therapy, or agreed to restrict practice in lieu of or to avoid formal action.

3.0522 Investigation. When the applicant identifies one of these actions, or if an applicant falsely claims AAMFT membership, the information shall be referred immediately to the Chair of the Ethics Committee. The Ethics Committee will conduct an investigation of the matter, pursuant to Section II, #3.06 ff of these *Procedures*.

3.0523 Outcome of the Investigation. Upon completion of the investigation, the Ethics Committee will take two actions:

3.05231 Ethical Matter. If the investigation results in charges of alleged ethical violations against the applicant, the Committee may find no violation of the *Ethical Code* and close the matter, or a violation(s) of the *Ethical Code* with recommended actions to be taken against the applicant, including whether the application shall proceed of be terminated, pursuant to Section II, #3.08 ff of these *Procedures*.

3.05231 Application for Membership/Supervision Designation. Upon completion of the investigation, the Ethics Committee will make a factual report to the Membership Committee (in the case of applicants for membership) or to the Commission on Supervision (in the case of applicants for the Approved Supervisor designation). If no violation of the *Ethical Code* is found, the decision whether to proceed with the application is made by the Membership Committee (in the case of an application for membership) or by the Commission on Supervision (in the case of an application for the Approved Supervisor designation).

3.053 AAMFT Member. If the person is a member of the Association or an Approved Supervisor, the Executive Director shall forward a copy of the complaint to the Chair of the Ethics Committee.

3.06 Preliminary Determination by Chair of Ethics Committee with the Advice of Legal Counsel for the Association.

3.061 Determination if Grounds for a Complaint. The Chair of the Ethics Committee or his or her designee (hereafter, Chair), with the advice of the Executive Director and the legal counsel for the Association, shall review the complaint and shall determine whether it states allegations which, if proven factual, would constitute (a) violation(s) of the *Ethical Code*. In the event the Chair, in consultation with the Executive Director and legal counsel for the Association, cannot decide on such action or on any other action required of them under these rules, the matter shall be referred to the full Ethics Committee for decision.

3.0611 Insufficient Grounds. If the complaint does not state factual allegations which constitute (a) violation(s) of the *Ethical Code,* the Chair shall so notify the complainant in writing. Notification to the complainant shall explain why the allegations do not warrant further action by the Ethics Committee and shall enclose a copy of the *Ethical Code*. All members of the Committee shall be informed of this decision.

3.0612 Sufficient Grounds. If the complaint states allegations which, if proven factual, would constitute (a) violation(s) of the *Ethical Code,* the Chair shall so notify the complainant in writing and shall request the complainant's permission to use his or her name, disclose his or her name, and provide a copy of the complaint (or a summary) to the member in the Ethics Committee's investigation. The Chair shall also request that the complainant agree in writing to waive any relevant client/therapist privilege available to him or her so that the Ethics Committee may obtain information from the member and others. All correspondence to the complainant shall be marked "personal and confidential" and sent by certified mail, return receipt requested to the complainant only.

3.062 Complainant Refusal of Permissions. If the complainant refuses permission for the use or disclosure of his or her name, the Chair of the Ethics Committee may refer the matter to the full Committee or, with the advice of legal counsel, shall decide whether it may proceed with the complaint with an investigation on the Committee's own initiative pursuant to #3.043 of these *Ethics Committee Procedures*.

3.07 Preliminary Investigation by Chair of the Ethics Committee or Investigating Subcommittee.

3.071 Notification of the Member. After the Chair of the Ethics Committee receives permission for the use of the complainant's name, or after a decision to proceed on the Committee's own initiative is made, the Chair of the Ethics Committee shall notify the member of the complaint. The notice to the member:

(a) shall be sent by certified mail, return receipt requested (or when necessary and appropriate, other written, secure, and confidential means), shall be marked "personal and confidential" and shall be deliverable to the member only;

(b) shall state the portions of the *Ethical Code* relevant to the allegations of the complaint;

(c) if the complainant has granted permission for the use of his or her name, shall enclose a copy or a summary of the complaint, or if the Ethics Committee is proceeding on its own initiative, shall state the Committee's basis for statement of the complaint;

(d) shall enclose a copy of the *Ethical Code* and a copy of these *Procedures*;

(e) shall direct that the member respond to the allegations, in writing, within thirty (30) days from receipt of the notification;

(f) shall inform the member that failure to respond in writing within thirty (30) days may result in termination of his or her membership in the Association.

3.0711 No Response by Member. If no response is received by the member within thirty (30) days, the matter shall be submitted to the full Ethics Committee. If a charged member does not respond to the charges, or to each specific allegation, the Ethics Committee may take the lack of response as an admission of the facts contained in the allegation.

3.0712 Response by Member. If a response is received from the member within thirty (30) days, or before the matter has been referred to the full Ethics Committee, the Chair of the Ethics Committee with the advice of legal counsel for the Association shall either (a) close the case and notify the complainant, the member, and all members of the Ethics Committee; (b) impanel an investigating subcommittee, if additional facts are needed before the submission to the full Ethics Committee; (c) seek needed additional information; or (d) submit the case to the full Ethics Committee at its next meeting.

3.0713 Resignation by Member. If a charged member resigns from membership of the Association at any stage of the Committee's investigation of the complaint, the Committee will nonetheless complete its investigation, and may publicize a proven violation in accordance with #3.086 of these *Ethics Committee Procedures*.

3.072 Preliminary Investigation by the Chair. The Chair of the Ethics Committee, assisted by Legal Counsel and the Executive Director, has the authority to gather sufficient information so that the Committee may review the complaint. For example, the Chair may deem it necessary to write the member or the complainant for further information, or contact state regulatory bodies or other professional associations.

3.073 Investigating Subcommittee.

3.0731 Membership of Subcommittee. The Chair, at his or her discretion, may appoint an investigating subcommittee. If an investigating subcommittee is impaneled, it shall be composed of at least two persons, one of whom will be appointed as chair of the subcommittee. At least one member of the subcommittee must be a member of the Ethics Committee. The Chair may also appoint former members of the Ethics Committee to serve on such subcommittee; in such instances, the Chair shall appoint a current Committee member as chair of the subcommittee.

3.0732 Instructions for the Subcommittee. The Ethics Committee or the Chair shall prepare, with advice of legal counsel to the Association, instructions specifying the scope of the subcommittee's investigation, including: (i) the names of the persons who should be contacted; and (ii) the areas of inquiry which should be pursued.

3.0733 Authority of the Subcommittee. The subcommittee shall investigate the allegations of the complaint in accordance with its instructions. The subcommittee shall have the authority to pursue its investigation by corresponding with or by interviewing, personally or by telephone. the persons named in the instructions.

3.0734 Appearance by the Member before the Subcommittee. The subcommittee shall give the charged member the opportunity to appear before the subcommittee or the full Ethics Committee to make a statement, at the member's expense. In any such appearance, the charged member shall have the right to be assisted by counsel, but must be an active participant himself or herself at the appearance. The member may ask to have a tape recording made of the appearance and shall pay for the expense thereof, including providing a copy of the recording to the subcommittee or the full Ethics Committee.

3.0735 Report by the Subcommittee. After completing its investigation. the subcommittee shall make a full report to the Ethics Committee, detailing the subcommittee's findings of facts and shall include records of its investigation.

3.074 Submission to the Full Ethics Committee. If the Chair of the Ethics Committee in consultation with legal counsel for the Association decides to submit the case to the full Ethics Committee, he or she shall:

(a) forward to each member of the Ethics Committee a copy of the complaint, or his or her statement of the complaint; a copy of his or her letter to the member; a copy of the member's response, if one was received, or if no response was received, a statement to that effect; and a copy of the report of the investigating subcommittee, if one was impaneled;

(b) present the case to the full Committee at its next meeting;

(c) notify the member and the complainant that the case has been submitted to the full Ethics Committee.

3.08 Action by the Full Ethics Committee.

3.081 Action during Litigation. Civil or criminal litigation pending against members shall be no bar to the consideration of complaints by AAMFT. It shall be within the discretion of the Ethics Committee whether to proceed during the course of litigation or to wait until its completion.

3.082 Findings of Other Professional Associations, Regulatory Bodies, and Courts as the Basis for a Finding of a Violation of Subprinciple 3.1. According to Subprinciple 3.1 of the *AAMFT Code of Ethical Principles for Marriage and Family Therapists,* it is incumbent for members to maintain their good standing with other professional associations to which they belong and with regulatory boards which have jurisdiction over their professional practice, as well as to avoid conduct which could lead to conviction of felonies, or misdemeanors related to their qualifications or functions. When a member has been disciplined by another professional association or regulatory board, or convicted of a felony, or a misdemeanor related to his or her qualifications or functions by a court, it is the policy of the AAMFT Ethics Committee that the Committee will presume that such findings are correct and appropriate.

3.0821   Member's Demonstration of Evidence to Overcome Presumption.
In order to overcome this presumption, the member must prove to the
Committee's satisfaction one or both of the following:
   3.08211   A Flawed Process. That the process was so flawed that the
   finding of the association or board is not entitled to a presumption of
   correctness (for example, demonstrated bias of one of the decision
   makers, failure of the body to allow the member to be heard, etc.).
   3.08212   Action Too Severe. That in the case of a disciplinary action by
   an association or board, the action was far in excess of the member's
   conduct (for example, having one's membership terminated for an
   inadvertent advertising error).
3.0822   Absent Evidence, the Committee's Recommended Action. Absent compelling evidence of one or both of the above, the AAMFT Ethics
Committee will not question or go behind the finding of the association,
board, or court, and will move on to its decision about what disciplinary action it will recommend.
3.0823   Other Charges Based on Actions by Disciplinary Bodies. On occasion, when a member is charged by the Ethics Committee with an alleged
violation of Subprinciple 3.1 on the basis of the action by another association, board, or court, the Committee also decides to charge the member
with additional alleged violations of the AAMFT *Ethical Code* growing out
of facts related to the charge of violation of Subprinciple 3.1.
   3.08231   Clear Evidence. If the evidence is clear concerning these
   other alleged Ethical Code violations, the Committee may make a finding of violations.
   3.08232   Disputed Evidence. However, if there is a dispute concerning
   the facts of these other alleged *Ethical Code* violations, the Committee
   at its own discretion may decide to drop the other alleged *Ethical Code*
   violations and rely solely on the finding of the violation of Subprinciple
   3.1. Since the Committee must carefully allocate its limited resources to
   conduct investigations, it is appropriate for the Committee to limit its investigations to cases where there is serious factual dispute but no allegation of violation of Subprinciple 3.1.
3.083   Settlement by Mutual Agreement. After review of the complaint, response of the member, and report of the investigating subcommittee, if one
was impaneled, the Ethics Committee may attempt to settle the case by mutual agreement with the member.
   3.0831   Possible Actions in Mutual Agreements. In making such a settlement, the Committee may recommend to the member that he or she
   agree to the Committee's request that the member cease and desist; accept censure; be placed on probation and/or rehabilitation; be given supervision, education, and/or therapy; perform community service; agree to
   suspension (holding membership in abeyance for a specific purpose, for
   example, rehabilitation) or termination of membership (a permanent bar to
   readmission) with or without publication; suspension or termination of the
   Approved Supervisor designation; publication of the terms of the settlement by mutual agreement under the conditions specified in #3.086; or
   any other action which the Committee deems appropriate. The Ethics
   Committee may appropriately impose more stringent requirements upon
   individuals previously found to have violated the *Ethical Code* or any other
   relevant professional or state regulatory code of professional conduct.

3.0832 Written Agreement. The mutual agreement shall be reduced to writing and shall detail the facts upon which it is based and the manner in which it is to be instituted and/or supervised.

3.0833 Supervision of the Agreement. The agreement shall be instituted and/or supervised by the Ethics Committee and/or any member of the Association so designated in the agreement.

3.0834 Finalization of the Agreement. The agreement shall become final as soon as it is reduced to writing and agreed to by the member and the Ethics Committee or at any other time designated in the agreement. The agreement shall be filed in the membership file of the member.

3.0835 Failure to Meet the Terms of the Agreement. If at anytime the member fails to fully meet the terms of the agreement, the matter shall be returned to the Ethics Committee for further action, and may serve as grounds for recommending termination of membership.

3.084 Other Action. If the Ethics Committee does not attempt settling by mutual agreement or if an offer of a settlement by mutual agreement is not accepted by the member, it will either drop the charges and close the case, or make a formal recommendation to the Judicial Council that action should be taken.

If the Committee recommends formal action it shall:

(a) recommend action to be taken, including an order to cease and desist; censure, probation, supervision, therapy, education, or rehabilitation; performing community service; suspension (holding membership in abeyance for a specific purpose. for example, rehabilitation) or termination of membership (a permanent bar to readmission); suspension or termination of the Approved Supervisor designation; or any other action which the Association is authorized to take against a member;

(b) recommend the manner in which the action will be instituted and/or supervised;

(c) notify the member of the recommendation;

(d) send the member a copy of the findings and recommendations of the Ethics Committee; and

(e) inform the member by certified mail, return receipt requested (or when necessary and appropriate, other written, secure, and confidential means), that he or she has a right to a hearing before the Judicial Council of the Association, and that if he or she does not request a hearing before the Judicial Council within thirty (30) days from the receipt of notification, no hearing will be held, and the Ethics Committee recommendation for action will become final.

The Ethics Committee may appropriately impose more stringent sanctions upon individuals previously found to have violated the *AAMFT Code of Ethical Principles of Marriage and Family Therapists,* or any other relevant professional or state regulatory code of professional conduct.

3.085 No Request for Hearing by Member. If the member does not request a hearing within thirty (30) days, the Ethics Committee recommendation shall become the final determination of the matter. The Ethics Committee Chair shall thereafter forward a determination of the matter to the Executive Director for execution.

3.086 Reopening a Case. If additional evidence of unethical conduct is brought to the attention of the Committee after a matter has been closed, the case may be reopened and acted upon under these *Procedures.*

3.087 Publication of Sanctions.

3.0871 Termination of Membership. Whenever an Ethics Committee recommendation for termination of membership becomes final, the Executive Director shall publicize this fact to the Association membership, including the relevant state or provincial division and committees and commissions of the Association. Publication will include notices both in *Family Therapy News* and with the annual membership dues statement, and will state the member's full name, any earned degree, his or her geographical location, and the violation of the section of the *Ethical Code* proven. Notification of a member's termination shall be provided to other relevant professional associations and state regulatory bodies.

3.0872 Publication of Other Sanctions. Publication of sanctions other than termination, including notifications of relevant professional associations and state regulatory bodies, may be directed by the Ethics Committee, within its sole discretion, in whatever manner and to whatever extent the Committee deems appropriate.

3.0873 Resignation from Membership. In situations in which a charged member resigned from AAMFT membership in the face of an Ethics Committee investigation, and a violation of the *Ethical Code* is subsequently proven, any publication of the findings and actions of the Ethics Committee shall include the fact of the member's resignation.

3.088 Membership Certificate. If a member is allowed to resign, or if his or her membership is suspended or terminated, he or she must at once surrender his or her membership certificate to the Executive Director.

4.00 Request for Hearing by Member.

4.01 Transmittal to the Judicial Council. If the member requests a hearing before the Judicial Council, then the Ethics Committee shall prepare and transmit to the Judicial Council the statement of the charges against the member and the action which the Ethics Committee recommends.

4.02 Presentation of the Case to the Judicial Council. In any hearing of the Judicial Council of the Association, the Ethics Committee, through its chair or his or her designee, assisted by legal counsel for the Association, shall present the case against the member pursuant to the rules established for the Judicial Council.

5.00 Records and Disclosure of Information.

5.01 Permanent Files. The permanent files of the Ethics Committee shall be maintained in the central office of the Association.

5.02 Confidentiality of Files. All information obtained by the Ethics Committee, including any investigating subcommittee, and all proceedings of the Ethics Committee, shall be confidential except as follows:

5.021 Disclosures by Investigating Subcommittee. Whenever the Ethics Committee appoints a subcommittee to investigate a case, the subcommittee may disclose such information as is necessary to pursue its investigation as described in #3.072 of the Ethics Committee *Procedures*. The subcommittee shall not consult with anyone not specified in the Ethics Committee instructions without receiving additional instructions from the Ethics Committee Chair and legal counsel for the Association.

5.022 Publication of Sanctions. Whenever the Ethics Committee orders publication of sanctions pursuant to #3.086 of the Ethics Committee Procedures, such publication shall be an exception to the rule of confidentiality stated in #5.02, above.

5.023 Disclosure to the Complainant. The Ethics Committee shall disclose to the complainant the disposition of a particular case.

5.024 State Regulatory Agencies and Professional Organizations. The Ethics Committee may inform state regulatory agencies, other professional organizations, or any other institution or organization which has disciplinary control over the member, of any disciplinary action taken against a member for violating the *Ethical Code.*

 5.0241 Inquiries from State Regulatory Agencies and Professional Associations. It is the policy of the AAMFT Ethics Committee to cooperate with state regulatory agencies other professional organizations, or any other institution or organization which has disciplinary control over the member or former member, when they inquire about any disciplinary action taken against a member or former member for violating the *AAMFT Code of Ethical Principles for Marriage and Family Therapists.* If the member or former member has never been found to have violated the *Ethical Code,* the State regulatory agency or professional association will be so informed. In cases where the member or former member has been found to have violated the *Ethical Code,* and when such a inquiry is received, the following procedures will be followed:

  5.02411 Notification of the Member. The member or former member will be notified in writing that such a request has been received and that AAMFT intends to comply by a specific date.

  5.02412 Content of Response to the Inquiry. The inquiry will be answered with a report from the Ethics Committee Chair. The report will include the following: (i) the principle(s)/subprinciple(s) of the *Ethical Code* that were violated; (ii) a brief statement regarding the nature of the offense; (iii) the disciplinary action taken, if any; and (iv) the date of the event and/or finding. A copy of the report will be sent to the member or former member.

5.025 Disclosures to AAMFT Governance Units.

 5.0251 Reports to the Membership Committee and the Commission on Supervision Regarding Applicants for AAMFT Membership or the Approved Supervisor designation. If an applicant for AAMFT membership or the AAMFT Approved Supervisor designation is currently the subject of a complaint filed with the Ethics Committee or has been found in violation of the *Ethical Code,* the Ethics Committee will make a report to the Membership Committee (in the case of an applicant for Membership) or to the Commission on Supervision (in the case of an applicant for the Approved Supervisor designation. The report of the Ethics Committee will state the principle(s)/subprinciple(s) of the *Ethical Code* violated or alleged to have been violated, a brief statement regarding the nature of the offense, the disciplinary action taken, if any, and the date of the event and/or finding.

 5.0252 Reports to the Commission on Supervision Regarding Approved Supervisors. When an Approved Supervisor has been found to be in violation of the *Ethical Code,* and after action, if any, by the Judicial Council, the Ethics Committee will submit a brief report on this violation to the Commission on Supervision. The report will state the section of the *Ethical Code* violated, a brief statement regarding the nature of the offense, the disciplinary action taken, and the date of the Committee's finding.

 5.0253 Reports to the Board Awards Subcommittee and the Elections Committee. If a person is currently the subject of a complaint filed with the Ethics Committee or has been found in violation of the *Ethical Code,* the Ethics Committee will make a report to the Board Awards Subcommittee when the member is a nominee for an honor, or to the Elections Committee when the member is a nominee for office, provided that the person has signed an appropriate waiver at the request of one of the Board Awards Subcommittee or the Elections Committee. The report of the Ethics Committee will state the principle(s)/subprinciple(s) of the *Ethical Code* violated or alleged to have been violated, a brief statement regarding the nature of the offense, the disciplinary action taken, if any, and the date of the event and/or finding.

5.026 Disclosures Required by Law. AAMFT may disclose such information when compelled by a validly issued subpoena, or when otherwise required by law.

5.03 Disposition of Files. Files for those members who are terminated or permitted to resign are maintained indefinitely. Files of cases in which the member is found not to have violated the *Ethical Code* are screened for identifiable (statistical) information and then destroyed alter one year. Files of cases closed for insufficient evidence are maintained for five years. Files of cases where the Committee has found a violation but where the sanction is less than termination of membership are maintained for five years. All case files containing identifiable information are destroyed one year after the Association is notified of death. The Committee may use its case files for archival, educative, or other legitimate purposes so long as identification of the parties is protected.

6.00 Advisory Opinions. The Ethics Committee, at its discretion, may choose to give an advisory opinion about an ethical issue raised by a member of the Association, but it is not required to do so. An advisory opinion will be given only when actual and not hypothetical question(s) have been asked. Such opinions will be rendered only in writing and in response to a written request.

III. The AAMFT Judicial Council.

1.00 Basis and Scope of Authority of the Judicial Council.

The *Bylaws* (Article VII, Section 1) provide for the function of the Judicial Council as follows:

The function of the Judicial Council shall be to hear impeachment charges against a member of the Board, an Officer of the Association, or a member of the Judicial Council; hear charges of violations of the *AAMFT Code of Ethical Principles for Marriage and Family Therapists* which are submitted for review pursuant to the Ethics Committee procedures; review Membership Committee decisions which deny applications for membership; review Commission on Supervision decisions which deny applications for approved supervisor; and hear other grievances brought by or against the Association pursuant to the rules and regulations adopted by the Board.

2.00 Membership of the Judicial Council.

Article VII, Section 1 of the *Bylaws* specifies the membership of the Judicial Council:

2.01 Membership and Term of Office. The Judicial Council shall consist of at least seven (7) Clinical Members of the Association, all of whom shall be appointed by the President with the approval of the Board. Each member of the Judicial Council shall serve for a five-year term. No member shall serve more than two consecutive terms.

2.02 Appointment of the Chair. The President shall appoint one member as Chairperson.

3.00 Procedures for Handling Complaints.

3.01 Role of the Council. One role of the Council is to hear charges of violations of the *Ethical Code* which are submitted for review pursuant to the Ethics Committee Procedures.

3.02 Council Constraints. Article VII, Section 1 of the *Bylaws* states that the Judicial Council shall operate pursuant to Judicial Council Rules which may be adopted by the Board from time to time. AAMFT adjudication proceedings are not formal legal proceedings.

3.03 Receipt of Charges from the Ethics Committee. If the Ethics Committee makes a formal recommendation that action be taken against a member and if, thereafter, the member requests a hearing before the Judicial Council, the Ethics Committee shall transmit to the Chair of the Judicial Council a statement of the charges against the member and the action recommended.

3.04 Initial Action by Chair of Judicial Council. Upon receipt of the statement of charges and recommended action from the Ethics Committee, the Chair of the Judicial Council or his or her designee (hereafter, Chair) shall:

3.041 Inform Member. The Chair will inform the charged member by certified mail, return receipt requested (or when necessary and appropriate. other written, secure, and confidential means), marked "personal and confidential" that his or her request for a hearing has been received and enclose a copy of the charges and recommended action; and

3.042 Appoint Hearing Panel. The Chair will appoint at least three members of the Judicial Council to serve as a Hearing Panel, and will designate one member of the Hearing Panel as Chair. A member of the Judicial Council shall not serve on a Hearing Panel in any case if, in the opinion of the Chair, he or she has a clear conflict of interests or personal bias.

3.05 Hearing Date and Location.

3.051 Location. Hearings will normally be held in Washington, DC. The Chair of the Judicial Council can schedule meetings outside of Washington, DC, only when the total meeting costs (members and staff travel, hotel, meals, etc.), would not exceed the total costs if the hearing were held in Washington. To plan a non-Washington hearing, the Chair of the Judicial Council must develop the comparable cost data and submit it to the Treasurer prior to scheduling or announcing such a meeting. If an out of town hearing would exceed the cost of a Washington based hearing, the Council may make a special request to the Treasurer for an exception to this policy. This request must include the comparable cost data and reasons why an exception should be considered.

3.052 Hearing Schedule. The Hearing shall be scheduled within 90 days after the case was submitted to the Judicial Council, on a date chosen by the Chair of the Hearing Panel. An extension of this 90 day deadline may be granted by the Chair of the Hearing Panel, at his or her sole discretion, when a request for such an extension has been made by the Chair of the Ethics Committee or by the member.

3.053 Notification of Participants. The Chair of the Hearing Panel shall notify the Chair of the Ethics Committee, legal counsel for the Association, and the member of the date and location of the hearing by certified mail, return receipt requested (or when necessary and appropriate, other written, secure, and confidential means), marked "personal and confidential."

3.06 Pre-Hearing Disclosure by the Member. At least 30 days before the hearing, the member must submit to the Chair of the Hearing Panel and the Chair or the Ethics Committee the following documentation:

>**3.061 A Statement of the Grounds for the Request for the Hearing:** The member must submit in writing which of the following grounds are the basis for his or her request of a review, and his arguments for these contentions, that is:

>>**3.0611 Findings.** The request is based on the contention that the findings of the Committee were not consonant with the facts, or that the member disputes the facts, and if so, which facts, and the member's argument for this contention.

>>**3.0612 Procedures.** The request is based on the contention that the Ethics Committee did not follow the Procedures for handling complaints, and the member's argument for these contentions.

>>**3.0613 Actions.** The request is based on the contention that the recommended actions of the Ethics Committee are inappropriate or too harsh, and the member's argument for this contention.

>>**3.0614 Other Grounds.** The request is based on other contentions, and the members argument for these contentions.

>**3.062 List of Witnesses and Summary of Testimony.** The member must submit in writing a list of any witnesses he or she intends to present, and a summary of the testimony they would present, so substantial portions of such testimony can be stipulated and not repeated during the actual hearing.

>**3.063 Statements by the Member and/or the Member's Attorney, and Additional Materials.** The member and/or his or her attorney may submit any additional written statements they may wish to make, as well as any additional materials they believe are relevant to the case.

3.07 Pre-Hearing Disclosure by Ethics Committee. At least 30 days before the hearing, the Ethics Committee shall furnish the charged member and Hearing Panel with copies of all relevant documents and the names of witnesses who will appear in support of the charges, if any. The Chair of the Ethics Committee will also submit a summary of the testimony the witnesses would present so substantial portions of such testimony can be stipulated and not repeated during the actual hearing.

3.08 Conduct of the Hearing.

>**3.081 Chairing the Hearing.** The Chair of the Hearing Panel shall preside over the hearing and assure that these Procedures are followed. The Chair will have access to legal counsel for advice on procedural matters.

>**3.082 Role of Ethics Committee.** The Ethics Committee shall present the charges against the member and shall have the right to:

>>**3.0821** be assisted by counsel for the Association;
>>**3.0822** present witnesses and evidence to support the charge;
>>**3.0823** cross-be witnesses who appear for the charged member;
>>**3.0824** offer rebuttal evidence;
>>**3.0825** make brief opening and closing statements.

>**3.083 Rights of the Member.** The charged member shall have the right to:

>>**3.0831** be assisted by counsel;
>>**3.0832** present witnesses or evidence;
>>**3.0833** cross-be witnesses against him or her;
>>**3.0834** appear on his or her own behalf;
>>**3.0835** make brief opening and closing statements.

3.084 Evidence. All evidence which is relevant and reliable, as determined by the Chair of the Hearing Panel, shall be admissible. The formal rules of evidence shall not apply.

3.085 Recording of the Hearing. A tape recording of the hearing shall be made at the charged member's expense.

3.086 Burden of Proof. The Ethics Committee shall have the burden of proof the charges by a preponderance of the evidence.

3.09 Decision of the Hearing Panel.

3.091 Deadline. The Hearing Panel shall issue its decision within 30 days after the hearing.

3.092 Content of the Decision. The decision shall state:

   3.0921 the Hearing Panel's findings of fact;

   3.0922 whether a violation of the Ethical Code was found and, if so, the section of the *Ethical Code* violated; and

   3.0923 the Hearing Panel's decision (that is, action ordered).

3.093 No Violation Found. If no violation of the *Ethical Code* is found, the Hearing Panel shall order that the member be cleared of all charges.

3.094 Violation Found. If a violation or violations of the *Ethical Code* are found, the Hearing Panel shall order action to be taken, including an order to cease and desist; censure, probation and/or rehabilitation, supervision, or education; performing community service; suspension (holding membership in abeyance for a specific purpose, for example, rehabilitation) or termination of membership (a permanent bar to readmission); suspension or termination of the Approved Supervisor designation; or any other action which the Hearing Panel deems appropriate. The decision shall also recommend the manner in which the action is to be instituted and/or supervised. If a member is allowed to resign, or his or her membership is suspended or terminated, he or she must at once surrender his or her membership certificate to the Executive Director.

3.095 Transmission to the Judicial Council Chair. The decision, shall he transmitted to the Chair of the Judicial Council.

3.096 Informing the Participants. The Chair of the Judicial Council shall inform, in writing, the following persons of the decision, after a review of the written decision by legal counsel for the Association: the member, the Chair of the Ethics Committee, and legal counsel for the Association. Notice of the decision to the member shall be by certified mail, return receipt requested (or when necessary and appropriate, other written, secure, and confidental means), marked "personal and confidential."

3.10 Appeal.

3.101 Member's Deadline. The member shall have 15 days from receipt of the Hearing Panel's decision to appeal to the Board of Directors.

3.102 Grounds. The only ground for appeal is that there were violations of these procedural rules of the Judicial Council which substantially impaired the member's ability to defend against the charges.

3.103 Council Transmittal to the Board. If an appeal is made to the Board of Directors, the Judicial Council shall transmit to the Board of Directors the statement of the charges, the recording, and the Hearing Panel's decision.

3.104 Member's Written Statement. In order to effectuate an appeal, the member shall state, in writing, to the Board of Directors the specific violations of these procedural rules by the Judicial Council and how they impaired the member's ability to defend against the charges.

3.11 Enforcement of Recommendation.

 3.111 Finalization of Decision. If no appeal is made within 15 days after the member has been notified of the decision of the Hearing Panel, the decision of the Hearing Panel shall become final.

 3.112 Transmittal of Decision. As soon as the decision becomes final, the Chair of the Judicial Council shall transmit the decision to the Executive Director. the Chair of the Ethics Committee, legal counsel of the Association, and to the person or persons who are responsible for instituting and/or supervising the decision.

 3.113 Publication of Sanctions.

  3.1131 Publication of Termination. Whenever the Judicial Council upholds an Ethics Committee recommendation for termination of membership, and whenever a Judicial Council order for termination of membership becomes final, then the provisions concerning publication found in Section II, #3.0871 of these *Procedures* apply.

  3.1132 Publication of Other Sanctions. Publication of sanctions other than termination, including notifications of relevant professional associations and state regulatory bodies, may be directed by the Judicial Council, within its sole discretion, in whatever manner and to whatever extent the Council deems appropriate.

  3.1133 Resignation from Membership. In situations in which a charged member resigned from AAMFT membership in the face of an Ethics Committee investigation, and a violation of the Ethical Code is subsequently proven, any publication of a finding of the Judicial Council shall include the fact of the member's resignation.

4.00 Records and Disclosure of Information.

 4.01 Records. All records of the Judicial Council proceedings, including the decisions, recordings of hearings. and supporting documents, shall be maintained in the central office of the Association.

 4.02 Confidentiality of Fines. All records of the Judicial Council proceedings shall be confidential except as follows:

  4.021 Publication of Sanctions. Whenever the Judicial Council orders publication of sanctions pursuant to #3.113 of the *Judicial Council Procedures,* such publication shall be an exception to the rule of confidentiality stated in #4.02, above.

  4.022 Disclosure to the Complainant. The Chair of the Ethics Committee shall disclose to the complainant the disposition of a particular case;

  4.023 State Regulatory Agencies and Professional Organizations. The Judicial Council may inform state regulatory agencies, other professional organizations. or any other institution or organization which has disciplinary control over the member, of any disciplinary action taken against a member for violating the *Ethical Code.*

  4.024 Disclosures Required by Law. AAMFT may disclose such information when compelled by a validly issued subpoena, or when otherwise required by law.

  4.025 Disclosure to Governance Units. The Judicial Council may inform AAMFT governance units of any disciplinary action taken against a member for violating the *AAMFT Code of Ethical Principles for Marriage and Family Therapists,* pursuant to these *Procedures,* Section II, #5.025 ff.

 4.03 Disposition of Fines. Files for those members who are terminated or permitted to resign are maintained indefinitely. Files of cases in which the member is found not to have violated the *Ethical Code* are screened for identifiable (statistical) information and then destroyed after one year. Files of cases closed for insufficient evidence are maintained for five years. Fines of cases where the Council has found a violation but where the sanction is less than termination of membership are maintained for five years. All case files containing identifiable Information are destroyed one year after the Association is notified of death of the member or the former member. The Council may use its case files for archival, educative, or other legitimate purposes so long as identification of the parties is protected.

IV. The AAMFT Board of Directors.

1.00 Appeals to the Board of Directors.

1.01 Grounds. The only basis for appeal to the AAMFT Board of Directors by a member regarding the decision of the Judicial Council is that there was a violation of the procedural rules of the Judicial Council, and that this violation substantially impaired the member's ability to defend against the charges.

1.02 Written Statement of the Member. In order to effectuate an appeal. the member shall state, in writing, to the Board of Directors the specific violation of the Judicial Council's procedural rules and how this violation substantially impaired the member's ability to defend against the charges. The Board of Directors shall consider the appeal solely on the basis of the member's written statement and the response of the Judicial Council or the Association's legal counsel (which may or may not be in writing), and there shall be no right to a personal appearance before the Board by the member or his or her personal representative. This letter must be sent to the AAMFT President at AAMFT headquarters within fifteen (15) days from the member's receipt of the Hearing Panel's decision.

1.03 Scheduling the Appeal. The Board of Directors shall consider the appeal at its next meeting her receiving the notice of the appeal. However, the President, at his or her sole discretion, may schedule the appeal to be heard at a subsequent board meeting.

1.04 Vote on the Appeal. A majority vote by the Board of Directors shall determine the appeal.

1.05 Board Decision. The Board of Directors shall issue a written decision on the appeal and shall inform the member and the Judicial Council of the decision in writing within thirty (30) days of the meeting. The Board must either affirm the Judicial Council's decision or order a new hearing before a hearing panel of the Judicial Council. The only basis for ordering a new hearing is the Board's decision that the member demonstrated there was a violation of the Judicial Council's procedures which did substantially impair the member's ability to defend against the charges.

BIBLIOGRAPHY

American Association for Counseling and Development. (1988). *Ethical standards*. Alexandria, VA: Author.

American Association for Marriage and Family Therapy. (1985). *Code of ethical principles for marriage and family therapists*. Washington, DC: Author.

American Association for Marriage and Family Therapy. (1988). *Code of ethical principles for marriage and family therapists*. Washington, DC: Author.

American Association for Marriage and Family Therapy. (1988). *Procedures for handling ethical matters*. Washington, DC: Author.

American Psychological Association. (1981). *Ethical principles of psychologists* (Rev. Ed.). Washington, DC: Author.

Appelbaum, P. S., & Rosenbaum, A. (1989). *Tarasoff* and the researcher: Does the duty to protect apply in the research setting? *American Psychologist, 44*(6), 885–894.

Aradi, N., & Piercy, F. (1985). Ethical and legal guidelines related to adherence to treatment protocols in family therapy outcome research. *American Journal of Family Therapy, 13*(3), 60–66.

Arcus, M. E. (1980). Value reasoning: An approach to value education. *Family Relations, 29,* 163–171.

Barton, W., & Barton, G. M. (1984). *Ethics and law in mental health administration*. New York: International Universities Press.

Barton, W., & Sanborn, C. J. (Eds.). (1978). *Law and the mental health professions: Frictions at the interface*. New York: International Universities Press.

Battin, M. P. (1983). Suicide and ethics. *Suicide and Life Threatening Behavior, 13*(4), 231–239.

Beier, E. (Ed.) (1987). Research update. Reprinted from *Clinician's Research Digest. The Psychotherapy Bulletin, 22*(2), 25–26.

Bernstein, B. E. (1979). Lawyer and therapist as an interdisciplinary team: Trial preparation. *Journal of Marital and Family Therapy, 5,* 93–100.

Bernstein, B. E. (1981). Malpractice: Future shock of the 80's. *Social Casework, 62,* 175–181.

Bersoff, D. N. (1976). Therapists as protectors and policemen: New roles as a result of *Tarasoff? Professional Psychology, 7,* 267–273.

Besharov, D. & Besharov, S. (1987). Teaching about liability. *Social Work, 32*(6), 517–521.

Birk, J. (1972). Effects of counseling supervision method and preference on empathic understanding. *Journal of Marital and Family Therapy, 2,* 215–226.

Bloom, B. (1973). *Community mental health: A historical and critical analysis*. Morristown, NJ: General Learning Press.

Borenzweig, H. (1981). Agency vs. private practice: Similarities and differences. *Social Work*, *5*, 239–244.

Brock, G. W., & Barnard, C. P. (1988). *Procedures in family therapy*. Boston: Allyn & Bacon.

Brock, G. W. & Coufal, J. C. (1989). Ethical behavior of marriage and family therapists. *Family Therapy Networker*, *13*, 27.

Brock, G. W., & Joanning, H. (1983). A comparison of the relationship enhancement program and the Minnesota couple communication program. *Journal of Marriage and Family Therapy*, *9*(4), 413–421.

Brock, G. W., & Sibbald, S. (1988). Supervision in AAMFT accredited programs: Supervisee perceptions and preferences. *American Journal of Family Therapy*, *16*, 256–261.

Brodsky, S. L., & Poythress, N. (1985). Expert on the witness stand: A practitioner's guide. In C. P. Ewing (Ed.), *Psychology, psychiatry and the law: A clinical and forensic handbook* (pp. 389–411). Sarasota, FL: Professional Resource Exchange.

Cohen, B. Z. (1987). The ethics of social work supervision revisited. *Social Work*, *32*(3), 194–196.

Cohen, R. J. (1979). *Malpractice: A guide for mental health professionals*. New York: The Free Press.

Cohen, R. J., & Mariano, W. E. (1982). *Legal guidebook in mental health*. New York: The Free Press.

Committee for the Protection of Human Participants in Research. (1982). *Ethical principles in the conduct of research with human participants*. Washington, DC: American Psychological Association.

Committee on the Family of the Group for the Advancement of Psychiatry. (1980). *New trends in child custody determinations*. United States: Law & Business/Harcourt Brace Jovanovich..

Corey, G. (1977). *Theory and practice of counseling and psychotherapy*. Monterey, CA: Brooks/Cole.

Corey, G., Corey, M. S., & Callahan, P. (1984). *Issues and ethics for the helping professions*. Monterey, CA: Brooks/Cole.

DeVries, R. G. (1986). The contest for control: Regulating new and expanding health occupations. *American Journal of Public Health*, *76*(9), 47–50.

Edwards, R. B. (Ed.) (1982). *Psychiatry and ethics*. Buffalo, NY: Prometheus Books.

Erikson, G. D. (1988). Against the grain: Decentering family therapy. *Journal of Marital and Family Therapy*, *14*(3), 225–236.

Everett, C. (1980). An analysis of AAMFT supervisors: Their identities, roles and resources. *Journal of Marital and Family Therapy*, *6*, 215–226.

Everett, C. & Volgy, S. (1983). Family assessment in child custody disputes. *Journal of Marital and Family Therapy*, *9*(4), 343–353.

Everstine, L. & Everstine, D. (1986). *Psychotherapy and the law*. Orlando, FL: Grune & Stratton.

Everstine, L., Everstine, D. S., Heyman, G. M., True, R. H., Frey, D.H., Johnson, H.G., & Seiden, R. H. (1980). Privacy and confidentiality in psychotherapy. *American Psychologist*, *35*, 828–840.

Ewing, C. P. (1985). Mental health clinicians and the law: An overview of current law governing professional practice. In C. P. Ewing (Ed.), *Psychology, psychiatry and the law: A clinical and forensic handbook* (pp. 509–523). Sarasota, FL: Professional Resource Exchange.

Ford, R. C., & McLaughlin, F. S. (1981). EAP's: A descriptive survey of ASPA members. *The Personnel Administrator*, *26*.

Fretz, B. & Mills, J. (1980). *Licensing and certification of psychologists and counselors*. San Francisco, CA: Jossey-Bass.

Furrow, B. R. (1980). *Malpractice in psychotherapy*. Lexington, MA: D. C. Heath.

Gardner, R. A. (1982). *Family evaluation in child custody litigation*. Creeskill, NJ: Creative Therapeutics.

Gardner, R. A. (1986). *Child custody litigation: A guide for parents and mental health professionals*. Creeskill, NJ: Creative Therapeutics.

Goldstein, J., Freud, A., & Solnit, A. (1973). *Beyond the best interests of the child*. New York: The Free Press.

Goldstein, J. Freud, A., & Solnit, A. (1979). *Before the best interests of the child*. New York: The Free Press.

Gomez-Mejia, L. R., & Balkin, D. B. (1980). Classifying work related and personal problems of troubled employees. *The Personnel Administrator, 25*.

Gross, S. (1978). The myth of professional licensing. *American Psychologist, 33*, 1009–1016.

Guerney, B. G., Stollak, G., & Guerney, L. (1971). The practicing psychologist as educator—An alternative to the medical practitioner model. *Professional Psychology, 2*, 276–282.

Gutsch, K. U. (1968). Counseling: The impact of ethics. *Counselor Education and Supervision, 7*, 239–243.

Gutsch, K. U., & Rosenblatt, H. S. (1973). Counselor education: A touch of Martin Buber's philosophy. *Counselor Education and Supervision, 13*, 8–13.

Guyer, M., & Ash, P. (1985). Law and clinical practice in child abuse and neglect cases. In C. P. Ewing (Ed.), *Psychology, psychiatry and the law : A clinical and forensic handbook* (pp. 305–330). Sarasota, FL: Professional Resource Exchange.

Haas, L. J., & Malouf, J. L. (1989). *Keeping up the good work: A practitioner's guide to mental health ethics*. Sarasota, FL: Professional Resource Exchange.

Haley, J. (1987). *Problem solving therapy* (2nd ed.). San Francisco, CA: Jossey-Bass.

Haley, J., & Hoffman, L. (1967). *Techniques of family therapy*. New York: Basic Books.

Hall, J. E. (1987). Records for psychologists. *Register Report, 14*(3), 3–4.

Hansen, J. C., & L'Abate, L. (Eds.) (1982). *Values, ethics, legalities and the family therapist*. Rockville, MD: Aspen.

Hines, P. M., & Hare-Mustin, R. (1978). Ethical concerns in family therapy. *Professional Psychology, 9*, 165–171.

Hofling, C. (Ed.). (1981). *Law and ethics in the practice of psychiatry*. New York: Bruner/Mazel.

Hogan, D. (1979). *The regulation of psychotherapists* (Vol. 1). Cambridge, MA: Ballinger.

Horsley, J. E., & Carlova, J. (1983). *Testifying in court* (2nd ed.). Oradell, NJ: Medical Economics.

Howard, G. (1985). The role of values in the science of psychology. *American Psychologist, 40*(3), 255–265.

Huber, C., & Baruth, L. G. (1987). *Ethical, legal and professional issues in the practice of marriage and family therapy*. Columbus, OH: Merrill.

Hunter, E. J., & Hunter, D. B. (Eds.). (1984). *Professional ethics and law in the health sciences*. Malabar, FL: Krieger.

Kelish, R. A., & Collier, K. W. (1981). *Exploring human values: Psychological and philosophical considerations*. Monterey, CA: Brooks/Cole.

Kentsmith, D. K., Salladay, S., & Meya, P. (Eds.). (1986). *Ethics in mental health practice*. Orlando, FL: Grune and Stratton.

Kitchner, K. S. (1986). Teaching applied ethics in counselor education: An integration of psychological process and philosophical analysis. Journal of *Counseling and Development, 64*, 306–310.

Knapp, S., & VandeCreek, L. (1987). Liability for contents in judicial disclosures. *The Psychotherapy Bulletin,* 21(3), 14–15.

Kosinski, F. A. (1982). Standards, accreditation and licensure in marital and family therapy. *Personnel and Guidance Journal, 60,* 350–352.

Kottler, J. (1983). *Pragmatic group leadership.* Monterey, CA: Brooks/Cole.

Larson, J. H., & Baugh, C. W. (1982). Needs and expectations of doctoral students in marriage and family therapy programs: An exploratory study. *Family Therapy, 9,* 231–238.

Liddle, H., Breunlin, D., Schwartz, R., & Constantine, J. (1984). Training family therapy supervisors: Issues of content, form and context. *Journal of Marital and Family Therapy, 2,* 139–150.

Lidz, C.,Meisel, A., Zerubavel, E., Carter, M., Sestak, R., & Roth, L. (1984). *Informed consent.* New York: Guilford Press.

Ludewig, K. (1986). To be direct or indirect . . . that is a question. In S. deShazer & R. Kral (Eds.), *Indirect approaches in therapy* (pp. 77–81). Rockville, MD: Aspen.

Mabe, A. R., & Rollin, S. A. (1986). The role of a code of ethical standards in counseling. *Journal of Counseling and Development, 64,* 294–297.

Manuso, J. (1979). Stress management in a large corporation. In Lorenz (Ed.), *Health promotion: New trends and perspectives.* New York: Van Nostrand Reinholt.

Margolin, G. (1982). Ethical and legal considerations in marital and family therapy. *American Psychologist, 37*(7), 788–801.

McKenzie, P., Atkinson, B., Quinn, W., & Heath, A. (1986). Training and supervision in marriage and family therapy: A national survey. *American Journal of Family Therapy, 14,* 293–303.

Melton, G. , Petrila, J., Poythress, N., & Slobogin, C. (1987). *Psychological evaluations for the courts.* New York: Guilford Press.

Meyerstein, I., & Todd, J. C. (1980). On the witness stand: the family therapist and expert testimony. *American Journal of Family Therapy, 8*(4), 43–51.

Miller, M. O. & Sales, B. D. (1986). *Law and mental health professionals.* Washington, DC: American Psychological Association.

Musetto, A. P. (1985). Evaluation and mediation in child custody disputes. In C. P. Ewing (Ed.), *Psychology, psychiatry and the law: A clinical and forensic handbook* (pp. 281–303). Sarasota, FL: Professional Resource Exchange.

National Association of Social Workers. (1980). *Code of ethics.* Silver Springs, MD: Author.

Nichols, J. F. (1980). The marital and family therapist as an expert witness: some thoughts and suggestions. *Journal of Marital and Family Therapy, 6*(3), 293–299.

Nietzel, M. T., & Dillehay, R. C. (1986). *Psychological consultation in the courtroom.* New York: Pergamon Press.

O'Connell, S. D. (1984). Promise of treatment as an opening strategy for psychotherapy. *Psychotherapy, 21*(4), 473–478.

Omer, H., & London, P. (1988). Metamorphosis in psychotherapy: End of the systems era. *Psychotherapy, 25*(2), 171–178.

Parenting Plus. (1984). *Parenting skills inventory.* La Canada, Canada: Author.

Phillips, A. (1961) A study of prolonged absenteeism in industry. *Journal of Occupational Medicine,* December.

Piercy, F. P., & Sprenkle, D. H. (1983). Ethical, legal, and professional issues in family therapy: A graduate level course. *Journal of Marital and Family Therapy, 9*(4), 393–401.

Reamer, F. G. (1987). Ethics committees in social work. *Social Work, 32*(3), 188–192.

Roederer, D. & Shimberg, B. (1980). *Occupational licensing: Centralizing state licensure functions.* Lexington, KY: The Council of State Governments.

Rosenbaum, M. (Ed.). (1982). *Ethics and values in psychotherapy: A guidebook.* New York: The Free Press.

Sales, B. D. (Ed.). (1977). *Psychology in the legal process.* New York: Spectrum.

Saposnek, D. T. (1983). *Mediating child custody disputes.* San Francisco, CA: Jossey-Bass.

Scheirer C. J., & Hammonds, B. L. (Eds.). (1982). *Psychology and the law.* Washington, DC: American Psychological Association.

Schutz, B. M. (1982). *Legal liability in psychotherapy.* San Francisco, CA: Jossey-Bass.

Schwitzgebel, R. L., & Schwitzgebel, R. K. (1980). *Law and psychological practice.* New York: John Wiley and Sons.

Seldes, G. (1985). *The great thoughts.* New York: Ballantine.

Sell, J., Gottlieb, M., & Schoenfeld, L. (1986). Ethical considerations of social/romantic relationships with present and former clients. *Professional Psychology: Research and Practice, 17*(6), 504–508.

Seymour, W. R. (1982). Counselor/therapist values and therapeutic style. In J. C. Hansen and L. L'Abate (Eds.), *Values, ethics, legalities and the family therapist* (pp. 41–60). Rockville, MD: Aspen.

Shapiro, D. L. (1984). *Psychological evaluation and expert testimony.* New York: Van Nostrand Reinhold.

Shimberg, B. (1980). *Occupational licensing: A public perspective.* Princeton, NJ: Employment and Training Administration, U.S. Department of Labor.

Shuman, D. (1986). *Psychiatric and psychological evidence.* Colorado Springs, CO: McGraw-Hill.

Simon, C. (1988, June). Boundaries of confidence. *Psychology Today,* pp. 23–26.

Skafte, D. (1985). *Child custody evaluations: A practical guide.* Beverly Hills, CA: Sage.

Slaughter, C. (1986). Sunset and occupational regulation: A case study. *Public Administration Review, 46*(3), 241–245.

Smith, J., & Bisbing, S. B. (1987). Sexual exploitation of patients: The civil, criminal and professional consequences. *Trial, 23,* 65–70.

Sporakowski, M. J. & Staniszewki, W. P. (1980). The regulation of marriage and family therapy: An update. *Journal of Marital and Family Therapy, 6*(3), 335–348.

Staff. (1986). Civil liability for disclosure of confidential information—California. *The AAMFT Legal Consultation Plan Newsletter,* December, pp. 2–4.

Staff. (1987). *The AAMFT Legal Consultation Plan Newsletter,* Spring.

Staff. (1989a). Managed care: The growing standardization of mental health care. *Psychotherapy Finances, 16*(5), 1–2.

Staff. (1989b). Legislation: The slowdown in mandated mental health coverage. *Psychotherapy Finances, 16*(5), 5.

Staff. (1989c). Managed care: Marketing your practice to preferred provider organizations. *Psychotherapy Finances, 16*(6), 1–4.

Steere, J. (1984). *Ethics in clinical psychology.* Capetown, South Africa: Oxford University Press.

Stromberg, C. D. (1987). Managing the risks of practice. *Register Report, 13*(4), 3.

Stromberg, C. D., Haggarty, D., Leibenluft, R. F., McMillian, M. H., Mishkin, B., Rubin, B. L., & Trilling, H. R. (1988). *The psychologist's legal handbook.* Washington, DC: The Council for the National Register of Health Service Providers in Psychology.

Strupp, H. (1988). *Commentary. Psychotherapy, 25*(2), 182–184.

Thiers, N. (1987, November 12). Counselors keep wary eye on liability developments. *Guidepost,* pp. 1, 16.

Thompson, A. (1983). *Ethical concerns in psychotherapy and their legal implications.* Lanham, MD: University Press of America.

Thoreson, R. W., & Hosokawa, E. P. (Eds.). (1984). *Employee assistance programs in higher education*. Springfield, IL: Charles C. Thomas.

Tremper, C. R. (1987). Organized psychology's efforts to influence judicial policy-making. *American Psychologist, 42*, 496–501.

VandeCreek, L. (1986). Patient records as evidence in malpractice litigation. *The Psychotherapy Bulletin, 21*(2), 6–8.

Van Hoose, W. H., & Paradise, L. V. (1979). *Ethics in counseling and psychotherapy*. Cranston, RI: Carroll Press.

Van Hoose, W. H., & Kottler, J. A. (1985). *Ethical and legal issues in counseling and psychotherapy* (2nd ed.). San Francisco, CA: Jossey-Bass.

Wellner, A. M. (Ed.). (1978). *Education and credentialing in psychology: Proposal for a national commission in education and credentialing in psychology*. Washington, DC: American Psychological Association.

Wendorf, D., & Wendorf, R. J. (1985). A systemic view of family therapy ethics. *Family Process, 24*, 443–460.

Woody, J. D., & Woody, R. H. (1988). Public policy in life threatening situations: A response to Bobele. *Journal of Marital and Family Therapy, 14*(2), 133–137.

Woody, R. H., & Associates. (1984). *The law and practice of human services*. San Francisco, CA: Jossey-Bass.

Woody, R. H. (1985). Public policy, malpractice law and the mental health professional: Some legal and clinical guidelines. In C. P. Ewing (Ed.), *Psychology, psychiatry and the law: A clinical and forensic handbook* (pp. 509–523). Sarasota, FL: Professional Resource Exchange.

Woody, R. H. (1987). 50 ways to avoid malpractice (cassette recording). Chicago, IL: American Association for Marriage and Family Therapy.

Zimet, C. (1989). The mental health care revolution: Will psychology survive? *American Psychologist, 44*(4), 703–708.

LEGAL REFERENCES

Arizona Revised Statute for Privileged Communication, §32-2085 (1965).
Bates v. *State Bar of Arizona,* 433 U.S. 350 (1977).
Buwa v. *Smith,* 84-1905 NMB (1986).
Canterbury v. *Spense,* 464 F. 2d. 772 (D.C. Cir. 1972), *cert. den.* 93 S.Ct. 560 (1972).
Connecticut Public Act No. 85-507, §20-195b (1985).
Cotton v. *Kambly,* 300 N.W. 2d. 627 (Mich. App. 1980).
Currie v. *United States,* 644 F. Supp. 1074, 1083 (M.D. N.C. 1986).
Cutter v. *Brownbridge,* Cal. Ct. App., 1st Dist. (1986).
Fischer v. *Metcalf,* No. 86-1366, Fla. Ct. App., 3d. (1987).
Gaspar v. *Lighthouse,* 73 Md. App. 367, 583 A. 2d. 1358 (1987).
Georgia Statutes, §43-7A-6(a), Chapter 7A (1985).
Hales v. *Pittman,* 118 Ariz. 305, 576 P. 2d. 493 (1978).
Hall v. *Stitch, Ph.D., and the Schulte Institute for Psychotherapy and Human Sexuality, Inc., Schulte, M.D., and Schulte;* Maricopa County, Ariz. Supr. Ct. Case No. 87-07895 (1987).
In Re Carrafa, 77 Cal. App. 3d. 788, 143 Cal. Reptr. 848 (1978).
In Re Perez, 14 Ill. App. 3d. 1019, 304 N.E. 2d. (1973).
Jordan v. *Kelly,* 728 F.2d.1 (1st Cir. 1984).
Kahn v. *Burman,* 673 F. Supp. 210 (E.D. Mich. 1987).
Kansas v. *Munyon,* 726 P. 2d. 1333 (1986).
Kiser v. *Commonwealth of Virginia* (1984).
Loving v. *Virginia,* 87 S. Ct. 1817 (1967).
McDonald v. *Clinger,* 446 N.Y.S. 2d. 801 (1982).
McIntosh v. *Milano,* 403 A. 2d. 500 (N.J. S. Ct. 1979).
Michigan Child Custody Act (1970).
Michigan Comprehensive Laws, Ann. §722.22-722-27 (Supp. 1971).
Nebraska Statutes, §43-292-4 (1981).
Nevada Statutes, §17, Chapter 374 (1973).
New Jersey Revised Statutes, New Jersey Marriage Counseling Act, Annotated §45: 8B-29 (1969).
Olson v. *Flinn,* Miss., 484, So. 2d. 1015 (1986).
Omer v. *Edgren,* 685 P. 2d. 635 (Wash. App. 1984).
People v. *District Court, City and County of Denver,* 719 P. 2d. 722 (Colo. 1986).
People v. *John B.,* No. 87 Daily Journal D.A.R. 3538, Calif. Court of Appeal (2d. App. Div., 1987).
Posner v. *Posner,* 233 SO. 2d. 381 (FL. 1970).
Richard F. H. v. *Larry H. D.,* No. AO 37782, Cal. Ct. App., 1st Dist. Div. 5 (1988).

Rodriguez v. Jackson, 118 Ariz. 13, 574 P. 2d. 481 (App. 1978).
Roy v. Hartogs, 381 N.Y.S. 2d. 587 (App. Term. 1976).
Sard v. Hardy, 291 Md. 432, 379 A. 2d. 1014 (1977).
State v. Loebach, 310 N.W. 2d. 58 (Minn., 1988).
Tarasoff v. Regents of California, 131 Cal. Rptr. 14, 551 P. 2d. 334 (1976).
Uniform Adoption Act (U.L.A.) (1969).
Uniform Marriage and Divorce Act (U.L.A.), §402-409 (1970).
Whitree v. State of New York, 56 Misc. 2d. 693, 290 N.Y.S. 2s. 486 (1968).
Zipkin v. Freeman, 436 S.W. 2d. 753 (Mo. 1968).

INDEX

Permissions Credits

This constitutes a continuation of the copyright page.

pp. 4–5, 12, 13, 16, 17, 21–22, 25, 27, 29, 31, 44—Excerpts from the *AAMFT Code of Ethical Principles for Marriage and Family Therapists* (1988) and the *AAMFT Procedures for Handling Ethical Matters* (1988) are reprinted by permission of the American Association for Marriage and Family Therapy.

pp. 16–17, 19, 22, 28, 31—Excerpts from *Ethical Principles of Psychologists, American Psychologist* (June 1981), Vol. 36, No. 36, 633–638. Copyright 1981 by the American Psychological Association. Reprinted by permission of the publisher.

pp. 16, 18–19—Excerpts from the *Code of Ethics of the National Association of Social Workers* (1980). Reprinted with permission from National Association of Social Workers, Inc., Silver Spring, MD.

p. 48—Based on *Malpractice: A Guide for Mental Health Professionals* by Ronald Jay Cohen. Copyright © 1979 by The Free Press, a Division of Macmillan, Inc. Reprinted by permission of publisher.

pp. 68–69—Based on C. D. Stromberg (1987) and J. E. Hall (1987). Reprinted with permission from the *Register Report* (13:4 and 14:3, respectively), published by the Council for the National Register of Health Service Providers in Psychology.

p. 69—Based on L. Vandecreek (1986), Patient records as evidence in malpractice litigation, *Psychotherapy, 21* (2). Used by permission of the Editor, *Psychotherapy.*

pp. 73–74—Reproduced with permission from *Testifying in Court,* 2nd ed., by J. E. Horsley with J. Carlova. Copyright © 1983 by Medical Economics Company, Inc., Oradell, NJ 07649. All rights reserved.

p. 73—Reprinted with permission from M. T. Nietzel and R. Dillehay, *Psychological consultation in the courtroom* , Copyright 1986, Pergamon Press PLC.

p. 92—Adapted from *Psychiatric and Psychological Evidence,* by Daniel W. Shuman, copyright 1986 by McGraw-Hill, Inc. Adapted by permission of Shepard's/McGraw-Hill, Inc. Further use is strictly prohibited.

pp. 101–102, 108—Based on personal communication with Robert E. Lee, Ph.D.

p. 107—Based on personal communication with Thomas Clark, Ph.D.

Appendix A—Excerpted from "Ethics and Practice," an article that first appeared in the *Family Therapy Networker.* It is reprinted here with permission. To order back copies or a subscription ($20), call (301) 589-6536.

Appendixes C and D—The *AAMFT Code of Ethical Principles for Marriage and Family Therapists* (1988) and the *AAMFT Procedures for Handling Ethical Matters* (1988) are reprinted by permission of the American Association for Marriage and Family Therapy.